The Language of Self

THE LANGUAGE OF SELF

Strategies of Subjectivity in the
Novels of Don DeLillo

Phill Pass

PETER LANG
Oxford · Bern · Berlin · Bruxelles · Frankfurt am Main · New York · Wien

Bibliographic information published by Die Deutsche Nationalbibliothek
Die Deutsche Nationalbibliothek lists this publication in the Deutsche Nationalbibliografie;
detailed bibliographic data is available on the Internet at http://dnb.d-nb.de.

A catalogue record for this book is available from the British Library.

Library of Congress Cataloging-in-Publication Data:

Pass, Phill, 1981-
 The language of self : strategies of subjectivity in the novels of Don DeLillo / Phill Pass.
    pages cm
 Includes bibliographical references and index.
 ISBN 978-3-0343-1711-5 (alk. paper)
 1. DeLillo, Don--Criticism and interpretation. I. Title.
 PS3554.E4425Z78 2013
 813'.54--dc23
                    2013027767

ISBN 978-3-0343-1711-5

Peter Lang AG, International Academic Publishers, Bern 2014
Hochfeldstrasse 32, CH-3012 Bern, Switzerland
info@peterlang.com, www.peterlang.com, www.peterlang.net

All rights reserved.
All parts of this publication are protected by copyright.
Any utilisation outside the strict limits of the copyright law, without the
permission of the publisher, is forbidden and liable to prosecution.
This applies in particular to reproductions, translations, microfilming,
and storage and processing in electronic retrieval systems.

This publication has been peer reviewed.

Printed in Germany

If we take literary works seriously, the perspective must be inverted: it is literature which encompasses and explains language, literature is a theory of language [...]

— TZVETAN TODOROV, *The Poetics of Prose*, p. 190

Contents

Acknowledgements ix

Introduction 1

SECTION 1 Dasein 23

CHAPTER 1
'[L]ife narrowed down to unfinished rooms':
Isolation and the Language of Self 25

CHAPTER 2
'[Y]our link to the fate of mankind':
Connection and the Language of Self 41

SECTION 2 Phenomenology 69

CHAPTER 3
'With a word they could begin to grid the world':
Denotation and the Language of Self 71

CHAPTER 4
'[T]o smash my likeness, prism of all my images':
Hyperreality, ἀλήθεια (truth) and the Language of Self 101

SECTION 3   Das Man — 121

CHAPTER 5
'Capital burns off the nuance in a culture':
Consumption, Capital, *Chrimatistikós* and the
Middle American Enunciation of Self — 123

CHAPTER 6
'[T]he banned materials of civilization':
Waste, *Sinthomo*sexuality and Middle America — 145

CHAPTER 7
'[T]o maintain a force in the world that comes into people's sleep':
Power, Alterity and the Formation of Hegemony — 163

CHAPTER 8
'[T]he balance of power and the balance of terror':
Terrorism and the *uneigentlich* Publicness of *das Man* — 183

CONCLUSION
To '[e]xplore America in the screaming night':
The Language of Self as the Foundation of Future
DeLillo Criticism — 205

Selected Bibliography — 213

Index — 219

Acknowledgements

Without the help, support and generosity of the following people this monograph would not have been possible:

My first such acknowledgement is of my parents and the care and tolerance which they showed towards me and my work. More times than I care to remember my days with them alternated between reading, writing and exercising. Little room was left for anything else, including conversation, and for the most part they tolerated such behaviour with a level of forbearance and grace which I can never repay.

I would like to extend my thanks to Dr Tom Jones and Dr Chris Gair. Their comments were invaluable and the discourse which we shared helped me feel that the work mattered, and was cared about, beyond a relatively narrow circle which sustained me for four years.

A deep gratitude goes to Ms Sandra Wallace. More times than I can count she showed near infinite patience and goodwill in saving me from myself during the various administrative calamities that my obsession with my research brought about. Without her kindness and willingness to help, I would never have completed my doctoral work.

Of my context in St Andrews I would like to acknowledge, in particular, the Martin Heidegger reading group – Jake Andrews, Christina Andrews, Ben Davies, Hannah Swithinbank, Nora Bartlett and Dr Sarah Dillon. If nothing else they showed me that my interests were not too bizarre to share, and the good discussions, and good wine, were a highlight of those years. My students in St Andrews also helped shape this monograph, in particular my literary theory class. A special thank you also goes to Julie Macdonald, Luke Hindmarsh, Victoria Fairclough, Anna Stewart and Caroline Walters.

For conversations, insights and patient copy editing a further thank you is owed to Natalie Riley.

Fiona Hanley has shared my interest in the philosophy of language and subjectivity, and has helped shape my development as a thinker and writer, leading me to question and reflect upon what had once seemed certain.

For the current monograph, and its very existence as a published text, I would like to thank the team at Peter Lang, and in particular Christabel Scaife, Alessandra Anzani and Hannah Godfrey.

My final two acknowledgements are the hardest to write, perhaps because there is the sense that they are interwoven into every page of the monograph, and a thank you in a preamble such as this feels, if anything, to obscure the depth of that debt, rather than to form an adequate act of acknowledgement.

The first of these acknowledgements is addressed to Don DeLillo. The complexity, delicacy and nuance of his fiction is the reason that this monograph exists. If not for him, and his writing, the last few years of my life would have lacked such richness. As presumptuous as it is to state, his work has given me a chance to think and to write, to reassess what it means to be, and that is a debt which cannot be repaid.

And for Professor John Burnside, the most far-reaching of acknowledgements is required. For nearly a decade, our connection and friendship has sustained me and helped me grow as a thinker and a writer. The opportunity to collaborate and work together with John has changed the way in which I view the possibilities of literature and criticism. Without his tolerance, generosity, insight and intelligence this project would not exist.

Introduction

In Don DeLillo's 1997 novel, *Underworld*, Nick Shay narrates the experience of looking out over a darkened New York City during the Northeast blackout of 9 November 1965. Nick's narration forms the final note of the novel's fifth section, 'Better Things for Better Living Through Chemistry', one of a series of 'selected fragments Public and Private in the 1950s and 1960s'.[1] Of particular significance is the concluding paragraph of Nick's vignette:

> I didn't call Marian. I felt a loneliness, for lack of a better word, but that's the word in fact, a thing I tried never to admit to and knew how to step outside of, but sometimes even this was not means enough, and I didn't call her because I would not give in, watching the night come down. (DeLillo, 1997, p. 637)

While the above quotation will receive detailed analysis later in the monograph, for the moment I will focus on a series of questions which it suggests: why does Nick not wish to call Marian? Why would such a call be considered giving in, and a giving in to what? What is so dangerous in the act of naming loneliness? How can Nick usually 'step outside' of such a feeling? What does it mean to be outside of what the Self feels and experiences? And what are the mechanisms by which this state is achieved and maintained?

What underlies these differing questions is that they are concerned with the manner in which the individual negotiates connection with the Other, and the strategies and techniques used to shape the form which such interactions can take. In this respect, Nick is not exceptional in DeLillo's work, but is rather emblematic of the manner in which the majority of the novelist's characters struggle to balance isolation and connection, independence

---

[1] Don DeLillo, *Underworld* (New York: Scribner, 1997), p. 499. Further references are given after quotations in the text.

and dependency, exile and belonging. What distinguishes Nick's reflection upon loneliness is how explicitly these concerns are rendered.

In the wealth of literary criticism that has accompanied DeLillo's writing a concern with subjectivity has predominated. Yet, rather than addressing the questions outlined above – the mechanisms, motivations and strategies undertaken by DeLillo's characters in shaping their subjectivity – such critical production has too often focused upon classifying the novelist's work within competing modernist/postmodernist paradigms. In his essay 'The Romantic Metaphysics of Don DeLillo', Paul Maltby addresses this issue, arguing that rather than embracing 'postmodern conceptions of the self as, typically, the tenuous construct of intersecting cultural codes', DeLillo instead utilizes an earlier concept of a 'deep-rooted, plenitudinous I-centered subject'[2]: conforming to the Romantic metaphysics of the essay's title. For Maltby, DeLillo's 'fiction [thus] betrays a conservative tendency' in its 'response to the adverse cultural effects of late capitalism' which 'obscures, if not undervalues, the need for radical change at the level of the material infrastructure.'[3]

Conversely, for those such as the Jerusalem Prize committee – and the authors of the various DeLillo monographs[4] – the tendencies which Maltby criticizes as conservative, and reactionary, are exactly those which underpinned DeLillo's selection for an award whose purpose is to honour a 'writer whose work best expresses the freedom of the individual in society'.[5] As the committee observed, the supposedly reactionary trends in DeLillo's

2 Paul Maltby, 'The Romantic Metaphysics of Don DeLillo', *Contemporary Literature*, 37:2 (1996), pp. 258–77, p. 271.
3 Ibid., p. 275. Philip Nel offers a comparable treatment of DeLillo's supposedly Romanticist/Modernist/conservative tendencies, stating 'that the kind of modernism to which DeLillo has moved appears to be the modernism canonized by academics in the 1950s – a modernism of form' [Philip Nel, 'Don DeLillo's Return to Form: The Modernist Poetics of *The Body Artist*', *Contemporary Literature*, 43:4 (2002), pp. 736–59, p. 736].
4 To be discussed below.
5 'Jerusalem Prize for Don DeLillo', *Publishers Weekly*, http://www.publishersweekly.com/pw/print/19990503/31660-jerusalem-prize-for-don-delillo-.html [accessed 28 July 2007].

Introduction 3

fiction are instead seen as indicative of an 'unrelenting struggle against even the most sophisticated forms of repression of individual and public freedom in modern culture during the last half-century', demonstrating 'the power of language and literature to unveil niches of intimacy even in the midst of a crowd.'[6]

In recent DeLillo scholarship it is this latter perspective which has predominated[7] – perhaps in part a reaction against accusations of DeLillo's perceived conservatism – and this has coincided with the proliferation in critical discourse focusing upon DeLillo's work that has characterized the previous decade. Of the monograph-length, single-author studies undertaken to date, seven have been published since 2000,[8] despite the author's publishing career having begun in the 1960s.[9] Prior to this increase, DeLillo studies were predominantly undertaken in journal articles, which, due to the nature of the form, resulted in a generally narrow focus upon specific texts, typically viewed in isolation.[10]

---

6   'Jerusalem Prize for Don DeLillo', *Publishers Weekly*, http://www.publishersweekly.com/pw/print/19990503/31660-jerusalem-prize-for-don-delillo-.html [accessed 28 July 2007].
7   Seven of the nine single-author, book-length studies on DeLillo's work have been published since the awarding of the Jerusalem Prize. While I do not argue for a causal link – the publication of *Underworld* (1997) seeming far more likely – the prize is still indicative of a perceived sense of DeLillo's fiction as a form of literary activism which dominates much of the critical response e.g. the view advanced in the monographs of Osteen, Kavadlo, Cowart, Schuster and Boxall.
8   Correct as of the time of writing. The 1980s and 1990s saw only one work respectively, namely Tom LeClair, *In the Loop* (Champaign; IL: University of Illinois Press, 1987) and Douglas Keesey, *Don DeLillo* (New York; NY: Twayne, 1993).
9   Don DeLillo's first published short story was 'The River Jordan', *Epoch*, 10:2 (1960), pp. 105–20.
10 Notable exceptions include: Steffen Hantke, '"God save us from bourgeois adventure": The figure of the terrorist in contemporary American conspiracy fiction', *Studies in the Novel*, 28:2 (1996), pp. 219–44; Thomas Carmichael, 'Lee Harvey Oswald and the Postmodern Subject: History and Intertextuality in Don DeLillo's *Libra*, *The Names*, and *Mao II*', *Contemporary Literature*, 34:2 (1993), pp. 204–18; and Paul Maltby, 'The Romantic Metaphysics of Don DeLillo'.

Such a phenomenon was observed by Joseph Dewey in the introduction to his monograph *Beyond Grief and Nothing*, in which he stated that there is 'an impressive accumulation' of 'takes' on 'several designated DeLillo novels'.[11] For Dewey, however, 'such targeted analysis' lacks 'a satisfying arc, a helpful trajectory that reads DeLillo from his earliest stories to his most recent work' (Dewey, p. 4). While *Beyond Grief and Nothing* was published in the midst of this proliferation of book-length discourse, Dewey argued that the majority of this production engages with the author's work 'at a rarefied level of theoretical argument that can intimidate a reader' who is 'first approaching' the novels (Dewey, p. 5). The principal aim of Dewey's project is thus to overcome this perceived deficiency and to provide an accessible update to 'Douglas Keesey's invaluable introduction', facilitating study at an intermediate level (Dewey, p. 5).[12]

Beyond providing such an engaging overview of the texts, Dewey's analysis proposes that 'across five decades of fiction' DeLillo has charted 'the loss of the authentic self after a half-century assault of images from film, television, tabloids, and advertising'. Such a context has combined to produce 'a shallow culture' which is so 'enamored of simulations' that it is now 'unable to respond to authentic emotional moments without recourse to media models'. Dewey proposes that '[w]hatever poignancy DeLillo's characters manage comes when they demand the privilege of a self

---

11 Joseph Dewey, *Beyond Grief and Nothing: A Reading of Don DeLillo* (Columbia: University of South Carolina Press, 2006), p. 4. Further references are given after quotations in the text.

12 Dewey's work is thus in the tradition of the *Continuum Contemporaries* series whose purpose 'is to provide accessible and informative introductions to the most popular, most acclaimed and most influential novels of recent years' [Stated on the back covers of both John Duvall, *Don DeLillo's Underworld: A Reader's Guide* (London: Continuum, 2002) and Leonard Orr, *Don DeLillo's White Noise: A Reader's Guide* (London: Continuum, 2003)]. Such an endeavour can also be observed in the Harold Bloom edited *Bloom's Modern Critical Views: Don DeLillo* (London: Chelsea House, 2003) which provides a set of short (generally two page) perspectives of DeLillo's work focusing on *The Names, Mao II, Libra, White Noise* and *Underworld*. Thus, as Dewey observed, prior to his monograph there was no single accessible overview of the entirety DeLillo's work suitable for an introductory or intermediate reader.

Introduction 5

to explore', even if, in their 'clearer moments', they believe 'that it simply is not there.' To conceptualize this change, Dewey argues that DeLillo's fiction 'has centered on three specific cultural pressures': that of 'the intoxicating (melo)drama of the cold war', the 'shooting of John F. Kennedy' and the 'irresistible pressures of electronic media.' In eschewing an overly theoretical tone, however, his work does not provide a comprehensive analysis of how subjectivity forms in a context dominated by these three phenomena, an aporia further accentuation by Dewey's striving for accessibility over complexity (Dewey, pp. 6–7).

By contrast, other DeLillo monographs – whilst still aiming to provide a 'satisfying trajectory' – adopt a more theoretical tone. Working in the tradition of LeClair, such criticism generally follows a similar argumental pattern, striving to produce texts that undo 'some of the artificial dualism of current academic criticism', which, as the former notes, includes reductive binary classifications such as 'traditional and experimental, realistic and self-referential, modern and postmodern.'[13] While arguing that such dualism is 'artificial', LeClair still considers dualistic oppositions to be a defining characteristic of DeLillo's novels. *In the Loop* argues that DeLillo's work 'consistently creates polarized structures', part of 'a double-binding aesthetic' of 'communication loops ranging from the biological to the technological, environmental to personal, linguistic, prelinguistic, and postlinguistic' (LeClair, pp. x–xi). It is this which, for LeClair, gives DeLillo's work its complexity and ambiguity, since such duality is 'both saving and destroying' for the characters, writer and readers, allowing the possibility of viewing DeLillo's work as in some way regenerative or redemptive, even as it depicts an ontical diminishing of Self (LeClair, p. xi).

Working in a similar vein, Mark Osteen's monograph *American Magic and Dread: Don DeLillo's Dialogue with Culture* – the harbinger of the millennial proliferation in critical production – proposes that DeLillo 'undertakes a dialogue with American cultural institutions and their discourses', dramatizing the 'dialectical relationship between, as well as

---

13 Tom LeClair, *In the Loop*, p. xii. Further references are given after quotations in the text.

the myriad shapes, meanings, and consequences of, American magic and dread.'[14] Positing, like the majority of DeLillo criticism, that the novelist's characters suffer 'the bombardment of consciousness by cinematic and consumer images; the fetishization of secrecy, violence, and celebrity' and by the 'fragmentation of the grand narratives of history, heroism, and high culture', Osteen argues that all of these factors 'combine to induce a paralysing dread' (Osteen, p. 1). Assailed by such forces, Osteen argues that DeLillo's characters seek solace in 'forms of magic – quasi-religious rituals, pseudodivine authorities, miraculous transformations – that they hope will help them rediscover sacredness and community', overcoming the dread which they feel (Osteen, p. 1).

As such a thesis would suggest, Osteen's work explores 'the tension between American individualism and the pull of public life'. Rather than this forming the central, dominant focus of his analysis, however, it is instead one of 'a set of related themes' which 'DeLillo's work repeatedly addresses', including 'the prevalence of spectacle', the 'decay of historical consciousness' and 'the complicity of late capitalist society with antisocial phenomena such as murder, war, pornography', all of which, he argues, result in an 'unfulfilled yearning for transcendence'. In order to capture this range of phenomena Osteen focuses on DeLillo's 'manifold generic and intertextual sources', rather than theorizing the specific textual details of how individual subjectivity is formed and shaped within the novels. Such analysis consequently risks descending into a litany of possible sources which seem far removed from the specifics of the characters under discussion, as form, structure and in particular intertextuality, is preferenced over a close analysis of the mechanisms by which subjectivity is formed (Osteen, p. 2).

This tendency is further problematized by Osteen's assertion that even 'if the characters' magical remedies fail, their quests still provide glimpses of a potentially redemptive realm', echoing LeClair's work and the opinion of the Jerusalem prize committee. This need to see DeLillo's prose

---

14 Mark Osteen, *American Magic and Dread: Don DeLillo's Dialogue with Culture* (Philadelphia; PA: University of Pennsylvania Press, 2000), p. 1. Further references are given after quotations in the text.

Introduction 7

as redemptive – and consequently in opposition to dominant postmodern paradigms – while providing an invaluable account of how his 'work catalogues the varieties of American religious experience' can also result in much of the ambiguity and ambivalence of DeLillo's depictions being lost. It is precisely this refusal of easy forms of classification, closure and co-option, which, I would argue, is one of the novelist's defining qualities (Osteen, p. 2).

As with the monographs discussed above, Cowart's work reflects a similar desire to overcome the modernist/postmodernist polarity. Considering this polarization, in its postmodern strand, to overly stress 'the affinity between DeLillo and Baudrillard' and to thereby risk 'overstating DeLillo's involvement with – as opposed to criticism of – the image',[15] Cowart's thesis instead proposes that 'DeLillo embraces an "eros" of the word, a libidinal principle of artistic creation' (Cowart, 2002, p. 182). While linguistic resistance proves ineffectual for DeLillo's characters who are unable to bring about 'any reversal of the postmodern condition', Cowart's monograph proposes that '[i]f there is a resister, it is DeLillo himself' and that '[i]f there is a site of resistance, it is language, the very medium that supposedly exemplifies the hopelessness of laying a foundation' and of 'making a stand' (Cowart, 2002, pp. 4–5). Cowart's work thus argues for a far broader understanding of the term language than that advanced 'in the otherwise admirable book-length studies of DeLillo by LeClair, Keesey, and Osteen' (Cowart, 2002, pp. 1–2). As Cowart notes, while 'DeLillo has contributed to the substantial, growing body of literature that explores the essential circularity of signification in all its forms' (Cowart, 2002, p. 2), the focus of his depiction, and Cowart's analysis, remains upon how 'DeLillo's interrogations of language' and his 'fictive strategies' were used 'to make language yield up its secrets' (Cowart, 2002, p. 6), revealing 'the extra dimensions of DeLillo's thinking about language' beyond those commonly addressed by postmodernist criticism (Cowart, 2002, p. 2). As Cowart observes, echoing Martin Heidegger, the ostensible aim of his project, unlike such

---

15 David Cowart, *Don DeLillo: The Physics of Language* (Athens; GA: University of Georgia Press, 2002), p. 4. Further references are given after quotations in the text.

postmodern work, is to focus upon 'DeLillo's career-long exploration of language as cultural index, as "deepest being," as *numinosum*', thereby both analysing the language DeLillo uses and attempting to posit what lies beyond conventional linguistic understanding (Cowart, 2002, pp. 1–2).

This trend to conceive of DeLillo's fiction as a search for transcendence – a genealogy of 'American religious experience' (Osteen, p. 2) and as *numinosum* – reaches its apogee in Kavadlo's monograph *Don DeLillo: Balance at the Edge of Belief*. As with the works discussed above, Jesse Kavadlo also strives to transcend the categorization of DeLillo's fiction within a modernist/postmodernist paradigm, viewing the novels as more than 'a mere map of the postmodern landscape' populated with lingering modernist legacies.[16] Kavadlo instead aims to demonstrate that DeLillo's work 'transcends' such a focus 'by revealing what it means to be human, not just at the end of the twentieth century, but for all of modernity' (Kavadlo, 2004, p. 5). In pursuit of such a reading, Kavadlo proposes that *White Noise*, *Libra*, *Mao II*, *Underworld* and *The Body Artist*, explore 'a world of solipsism and desiccated spirituality, a place rife with rejection of belief in favor of confused cerebral pursuits and false idols, of casually rampant faithlessness and unexamined pessimism' (Kavadlo, 2004, p. 4). Kavadlo's work therefore attempts to place DeLillo's oeuvre within a spiritual context by avoiding the predominant, critical preoccupation 'with the ways in which these novels do or don't describe or prescribe aspects of the contemporary world', and which result in such analysis 'remain[ing] within the worlds the novels deride' (Kavadlo, 2004, p. 4).

In order to fulfil this aim, Kavadlo utilizes an alternate critical lexicon since he considers that 'DeLillo does nothing less than locate and expose fear, love, and evil in the world', terms, which, as Kavadlo notes, 'postmodernists typically dismiss' (Kavadlo, 2004, p. 7). Building upon this mention of evil, the spiritual dimension which Kavadlo posits is shown to have a particularly Christian quality through the language used, far exceeding that of Osteen's analysis and his exploration of American religious experience.

---

16 Jesse Kavadlo, *Don DeLillo: Balance at the Edge of Belief* (Frankfurt: Peter Lang, 2004), p. 5. Further references are given after quotations in the text.

Introduction

Kavadlo's work accordingly utilizes terms such as 'redemption', 'evil', 'belief', 'morality', 'souls' and most revealingly, 'transubstantiation',[17] all of which serve to place Kavadlo's analysis within a specifically Catholic context. This religious dimension allows Kavadlo to claim that DeLillo's 'acts of narration are attempts to redeem his characters', and, in so doing, he 'redeems our own character, and our own world' (Kavaldo, 2004, p. 7). While Kavadlo's exploration of 'DeLillo's use of balance – as a trope within the novels, and as a self-conscious expression of the author's place in the world' (Kavaldo, 2004, p. 10) provides a useful perspective, his need to continually stress the spiritual and Catholic dimension of DeLillo's work results, oftentimes, in a tenuousness to his analysis, an attempt to frequently support his thesis with reference to what is absent in the texts, rather than what is present, thereby focusing upon the novels' extra-textuality – a tendency Kavadlo shares, to a lesser extent, with Osteen.

Such a focus upon extra- and intertextuality can also be observed in Peter Boxall's monograph *Don DeLillo: The Possibility of Fiction*, which proposes that DeLillo's work is concerned 'with the ways in which the progression towards an ultimate, apocalyptic communicability is shadowed and undermined by an opposite movement towards erasure, silence and darkness.'[18] Building upon, and diverging from, Osteen's analysis, Boxall argues for 'an approach to this delicate relation in DeLillo between what can be said, preserved, "saved", and what cannot be brought to the surface', thereby remaining 'shrouded in the past, and secreted in an unforeseeable future' (Boxall, p. xi). Such supposed striving 'towards an ethics of globalisation' on DeLillo's part, is perceived, by Boxall, as an attempt at understanding 'how the possibilities of global communication relate to the violence of global capital and global terror', correlating to Fukuyama's theory of a millennial end of history (Boxall, p. xi).

---

17 Transubstantiation is used twice in Kavadlo's analysis as a metaphor for a character's actions or desires, rather than as a direct reference to the Catholic sacrament of the Eucharist. n.b. pp. 44 and 58.
18 Peter Boxall, *Don DeLillo: The Possibility of Fiction* (London: Routledge, 2006), p. xi. Further references are given after quotations in the text.

As a form of ethics, DeLillo's fiction is characterized by Boxall as an act of 'imaginative resistance to or dissent from the tyranny of globalisation', a means of finding an 'ethical and poetical expression' that 'does not simply reduce itself to regressive forms of terror' (Boxall, p. xi). DeLillo's work is instead viewed as 'animated by the spirit of a future in which anything is possible' and his writing is seen as an affirmation of the 'possibility of fiction, as it is thought and performed': namely 'the possibility that we might find, in the poetry of nobody home', a 'trace of what Marx called the poetry of the future' (Boxall, p. xi). For Boxall, the striving for such poetry does not produce a form of fiction which 'find[s] itself redeemed or guaranteed by Osteen's "art", or by Cowart's "language"', but is instead focused upon futurity (Boxall, p. 15). Exploring this millennial conception, Boxall, as with the other monographs discussed above, 'seeks to move beyond the assumptions that are at work in the theorisation and the deployment of the terminology of postmodernism', drawing instead upon a range of theoretical perspectives to characterize DeLillo's work as 'neither a postmodern abandonment of the political nor an aesthetic or political resistance to theory' (Boxall, p. 15).

While Osteen's, Cowart's, Kavadlo's and Boxall's analysis can arguably be placed within a common tradition which attempts to posit and analyse a numinous quality within DeLillo's texts, the remaining single-author monographs still to be discussed do not accord with such a model. While all three attempt to supersede the modernist/postmodernist dialectic – an approach common to all the monographs discussed – they do so in a manner which allows for the exploration of alternative critical perspectives, ranging from ecocriticism to the cyborg theories of Donna Harraway. What is of particular interest in terms of this project is that they all attempt to explore the interaction between subjectivity and environmental impacts particular to postmodernity.

For Elise Martucci, working within the tradition of essays such as Louisa Mackenzie's 'An Ecocritical Approach to Teaching *White Noise*',[19]

---

19 Louisa Mackenzie, 'An Ecocritical Approach to Teaching *White Noise*', in Tim Engles and John Duvall (eds) *Approaches to Teaching DeLillo's White Noise* (New York; NY: The Modern Language Association of America, 2006), pp. 50–62.

Introduction

Michael Moses' 'Lust Removed from Nature',[20] and Cynthia Deitering's 'The Postnatural Novel: Toxic Consciousness in Fiction of the 1980s',[21] it is the ecocritical dimension of DeLillo's writing which is the primary focus. Using a framework derived primarily from Lawrence Buell's theory of the environmental unconscious advanced in *Writing for an Endangered World*,[22] Martucci argues that while 'DeLillo explores the way in which new technologies create a world of simulacra and simulation', his fiction still 'keeps the material world at the forefront of his novels, thereby illuminating the environmental implications of these technologies and emphasizing the lasting significance of place to our consciousness.'[23] It is through 'DeLillo's representation of children, and his presentation of language and art', Martucci argues, that his novels show 'the damaging effects of our consumer culture' whilst also demonstrating 'the human ability to adapt' and 'survive' by 'transcending the materialism and irresponsibility that are inherent dangers' (Martucci, p. 3).

For Randy Laist, author of *Technology and Postmodern Subjectivity in Don DeLillo's Novels*, the interaction between self and environment is likewise the object of critical analysis. Rather than concentrating upon the environmental unconscious, it is instead technology which is his primary focus, working in the tradition of essays such as Basu Birman's 'Reading the Techno-Ethnic Other in Don DeLillo's White Noise'.[24] Using a critical

20   Michael Moses, 'Lust Removed from Nature' in Frank Lentricchia (ed.) *New Essays on White Noise* (Cambridge: Cambridge University Press, 1991), pp. 63–86.
21   Cynthia Deitering, 'The Postnatural Novel: Toxic Consciousness in Fiction of the 1980s' in Cheryll Glotfelty and Harold Fromm (eds) *The Ecocriticism Reader: Landmarks in Literary Ecology* (Athens; GA: University of Georgia Press, 1996), pp. 196–203.
22   Lawrence Buell, *Writing for an Endangered World: Literature, Culture and Environment in the U.S. and Beyond* (Cambridge, Mass.: Harvard University Press, 2001).
23   Elise A. Martucci, *The Environmental Unconscious in the Fiction of Don DeLillo* (London: Routledge, 2007), p. 2. Further references are given after quotations in the text.
24   Basu Birman, 'Reading the Techno-Ethnic Other in Don DeLillo's White Noise' in *The Arizona Quarterly*. 61:2 (2005), pp. 87–103.

framework which combines phenomenology and the cyborg theories of Donna Haraway, Laist's work proposes that 'DeLillo is a phenomenologist of the contemporary technoscape and an ecologist of a new kind of natural habitat'.[25] Arguing that DeLillo's characters are portrayed as 'cyborgs manqué, devotees of a technological transcendence that is tantalizingly immanent in the glistening precision of consumer technologies', Laist's work explores 'the encounter of a DeLillian subject with an environment that has been shaped and saturated by technology' (Laist, p. 3). Positing 'the manner in which contemporary technologies reconfigure the relationship between ego and environment, between nature and nurture, and between the soul and the world', Laist echoes Osteen's work with an increased technological awareness, proposing that the 'typical DeLillian character is suspended between dread and awe, between randomness and conspiracy, between science and religion', 'symptoms of the fundamental, viral interfusion of self and circuitry, of a character's phenomenological experience and the American environment he inhabits' (Laist, pp. 3–4).

In a similar manner, Marc Schuster's invaluable monograph *Don DeLillo, Jean Baudrillard, and the Consumer Conundrum* also explores a seemingly 'viral interfusion' of self and environment. Rather than technology per se, however, it is instead consumer culture which is the environmental factor Schuster focuses upon. Principally taking the form of an exploration of the 'affinities'[26] between DeLillo's novels and the theories of Jean Baudrillard, Schuster's monograph strives to 'unpick and develop' the '[i]nstinctive connections' which 'are easily, indeed instantly' formed between DeLillo and Baudrillard (Schuster, p. ix). Bringing 'the works of DeLillo and Baudrillard into dialogue with each other', Schuster hopes 'to determine the potential for reversing the trends described by the French theorist' that are depicted in DeLillo's novels (Schuster, p. 2).

---

25   Randy Laist, *Technology and Postmodern Subjectivity in Don DeLillo's Novels* (Frankfurt: Peter Lang, 2010), p. 3. Further references are given after quotations in the text.
26   Marc Schuster, *Don DeLillo, Jean Baudrillard, and the Consumer Conundrum* (Youngstown; NY: Cambria Press, 2008), p. ix. Further references are given after quotations in the text.

Introduction

Schuster's 'volume [consequently] examines the ways in which DeLillo's novels interrogate the notion of ambivalence' as advanced by Baudrillard (Schuster, p. 2). Denoting 'the incessant potential for the destruction of the illusion of value that is at the heart of consumer ideology', Schuster argues that it is the concept of ambivalence advanced by Baudrillard which forms the basis of commodification and of sign value (Schuster, p. 2). It is within such a context that Schuster argues that 'DeLillo's novels present consumer culture not just as a backdrop but as a matrix of contemporary values' (Schuster, p. 4). Unlike Baudrillard, who 'sees hyperreality as a state that can only stifle humanity', DeLillo views the 'hyperreal landscape' 'as a proving ground *for* humanity' (Schuster, p. 6), a medium against which the 'characters struggle to define and redefine themselves' (Schuster, p. 4). For Schuster, DeLillo's fiction reveals 'the author's own ambivalence towards consumer culture' as he 'recognizes' its 'potential for degrading and dehumanizing the masses', yet, conversely, of also providing 'an arena in which the smallest acts of intimacy have the potential to take on the greatest significance' (Schuster, p. 7).

As the above survey has demonstrated, the existing monograph-length works on DeLillo's texts share a number of methodological tendencies in common, the most prominent of which is to focus upon intertextuality – as evidenced, in particular, by Boxall's, Osteen's and Cowart's work – as well as a concern with the externality of DeLillo's texts (a tendency particularly noticeable in the attempts to trace the numinous quality of DeLillo's fiction). What unites both of these approaches is a shared attempt to posit DeLillo's intentions and purpose. I would argue that this has become a new form of critical saturation in regards to DeLillo criticism, mirroring the modernist/postmodern paradigm from which such textual analysis endeavoured to escape.

Against this emerging critical consensus, the methodology of this monograph is to focus upon the texts themselves, rather than dwelling upon concerns of intertextuality and externality which has already been addressed so extensively. Similarly, the subsequent literary analysis will refrain from positing authorial intention or motivation, such as on one hand any theorized libidinal gains which DeLillo may derive from his texts, or, on the other, any forms of political activism which their creation may represent. For a writer such as DeLillo, whose work is praised for the complexity of its characters and their resistance to easy forms of categorization or closure – a fact which has encouraged such a breadth and range of criticism – the application of deterministic conceptions to his writing practice would seem inconsistent and symptomatic of the very oversimplification which the texts avoid. In keeping with such a methodology, DeLillo's sporadic interviews and journalistic works will not be used, nor will journalistic receptions of DeLillo's work be addressed, as both have been extensively, if not exhaustively, used in the existing criticism which focuses upon the novels' externality and intertextuality. The texts themselves will instead form the focus of inquiry from which a comprehensive theory of subjectivity in DeLillo's novels will be proposed, one that concentrates upon the depictions of characters within an environmental context.

From this starting point, I will propose that a highly complex bi-partite structure can be observed in the formation of subjectivity within DeLillo's novels. In order to conceptualize this, a specific lexicon will be needed and this will be derived from the opening section of *Mao II* (1991) entitled 'At Yankee Stadium'. Since the action centres around the massed marriage of 17,000 members of the Unification Church and the scattering of disparate individuals who view the event, issues of collectivism versus individuality are highlighted within the section, providing the terminology with which this monograph can address the structure of subjectivity in DeLillo's novels.

Through the depiction of Rodge and Maureen, who scan the crowd as they attempt to locate their daughter, Karen, the novel dramatizes the tension between connection and isolation. Striving to separate her – at least cognitively – from a seemingly impersonal crowd, her parents wish to re-impose a conception of subjectivity which accords with their own. It is precisely this individuation, however, which Karen desires to avoid and which has led her to participate within a mass marriage, permanently endeavouring to evade the individuation which her parents strive to reinscribe. The metaphor which DeLillo utilizes to explore this fundamental conflict between collectivity and individuality is that of the 'language of self'.[27] It is this quotation which will provide the first, and primary, terminology used in this book, an umbrella term for subjectivity within DeLillo's novels. To compliment this nomenclature, the term enunciation will be used to designate a specific ontical form of the language of Self. Etymologically, the strength of such usage arises from the sense of an enunciation as something which the Self articulates at a specific moment, the product of that context, yet also, simultaneously, part of a wider discourse and project of subjectivity. While a particular enunciation may become part of a larger narrative of Self, the chosen term, as a verb with connotations of ephemeral action, connotes subjectivity in DeLillo's novels as an ongoing process which the Self must strive to maintain and that evolves over time.

As the passage demonstrates, while Karen perceives such a language to be constituted of a single possible enunciation from which she strives to be 'immunised' (DeLillo, *Mao II*, p. 8) – the Middle American articulation of the suburban 'land of lawns' whose discrete houses and signifying walls, fences and hedges, both separate and connect the subjects which they contain – the nuance and complexity of DeLillo's treatment demonstrates such a belief to be erroneous. Karen is instead seeking freedom from a particular balance between individuation and collectivism, between connection and isolation, which forms the syntax for the Middle American language of Self.[28] Rather than such a nuanced enunciation of Self, a finely-tuned balance of partial-publicness and moderate-isolation, Karen instead strived for 'the crowd shout' and 'democratic clamor' provided by the immolating 'blast of Master's being'; a far more extreme form of collectivism and a marginalizing of individuation (DeLillo, *Mao II*, pp. 9–10). Viewed from Rodge's perspective such a quest appears to have been successful and he considers her to be lost amongst the 'undifferentiated mass' who have surrendered their individuality and become 'one body' (DeLillo, *Mao II*, p. 3), 'a toy with thirteen thousand parts', an 'innocent and menacing thing'

---

27 Don DeLillo, *Mao II* (London: Penguin, 1992), p. 8. Further references are given after quotations in the text.
28 Within this book both Self and Other will be routinely capitalized in order to highlight the provisional, constructed nature of each concept, and to stress the manner in which they are sites of contestation in DeLillo's texts.

(DeLillo, *Mao II*, p. 7). Reflecting upon the massed crowd containing his daughter, Rodge understands the attraction of the Master and is forced to admit to himself 'how happy they look', concluding that 'they follow the man because he gives them what they need', a chance to escape the delicate balance of the Middle American Self and the pressure which its maintenance creates (DeLillo, *Mao II*, p. 7).

Through the language of Self, the opening section shows that even in the midst of her mass marriage, in the presence of the Master's being, she still retains a sense of Self, highlighted by the repeated mentions of what 'she' saw and felt. However hard she may try, 'Karen's mindstream' always remains just that, her own consciousness, singular and indivisible (DeLillo, *Mao II*, p. 8). Such is the strength and nuance of the metaphor of the language of Self that even Karen's attempt to join the immolating crowd and democratic clamour of the Unification Church can be seen as merely another enunciation, rather than a wholly divergent subjectivity. She still remains an individual, possessed of a grid 'of pinpoint singularities' – it is merely the particular form in which they are arranged which has altered (DeLillo, *Mao II*, p. 7). This is further emphasized later in the novel when the narrator describes *her* struggle to embrace the collectivist 'truth of the body common' and that the wearing of communal underwear still gave *her* 'a strange feeling', making *her* 'want to walk along a little shrivelled inward', a 'guilty and dangerous thought' (DeLillo, *Mao II*, p. 77). Karen is inevitably unable to obtain an enunciation of Self free of individuality which is necessary to be wholly enmeshed within the shelter of the collective Other, as her instinctive turn 'inward' demonstrates. Even within the Unification Church and the experience of a mass marriage, Karen's existence still remains a form of the enunciation of Self, albeit one which stresses connection at the expense of isolation.

It is in this respect that the strength of DeLillo's metaphor of the language of Self becomes apparent. As with any language it does not consist of a single possible enunciation but is instead inherently a flexible, multipositional continuum. *Mao II* consequently demonstrates that while the Middle American enunciation may be one such linguistic position, the Unification Church represents another form of that same language, rather than its antithesis: a reshaping of the enunciations of its participants into a particularly extreme and monolithic form. Just as with the Middle American enunciation of Self, it takes an effort of will to sustain a stable language in the face of both 'internal' and 'external' pressures; the 'grid of pinpoint singularities' to which the novel refers and which constitute a particular enunciation (DeLillo, *Mao II*, p. 80). Unable to maintain the discipline necessary for life in the Unification Church and its monolithic enunciation of Self, Karen is also unable to re-establish the significations required for Middle America. The novel subsequently explores her attempt at shaping a new enunciation, an authentic balance of connectivity and individuation inextricably contained within the continuum of the language of Self.

While it is only in *Mao II* that this particular metaphor is used, this monograph argues that the basic paradigm which it depicts is present throughout DeLillo's work. Rather than particular novels positing divergent theories of subjectivity, each instead represents an attempt to understand an ontical instance of the same paradigmatic negotiation of isolation and connection. What differs in each case is the particular balance of those two omnipresent polarities, and accordingly an analysis of DeLillo's other characters reveals how each is an attempt at understanding and exploring a differing attempt to reconcile these two impulses. It is in this respect that the language of Self has its etymological strength as it underlines the sense in which each manifestation, as a linguistic form, is the product of a process of largely self-conscious, though not necessarily volitional, signification which is subject to intelligibility, and, like any other text, shaped by issues of access, author(ity) and control.

Through the use of this lexicon derived from *Mao II*, subjectivity will be proposed as a form of signification – a language[29] – which posits, and

---

29   The linguistic nature of subjectivity in DeLillo's fiction has also been observed by Cowart who noted that rather than conforming to the insistence of 'post-Freudian psychoanalysis' that 'the Symbolic Order estranges the subject from itself, DeLillo plays, like Rilke, with conceits of self-definition through some kind of cosmic verbal exchange' which, echoing Heidegger, DeLillo 'imagines' as 'a symbiosis, a defining mutualism, of speaker and spoken', thereby 'foster[ing] subjectivity' [David Cowart, Op. Cit, pp. 5–6]. Due to the divergent focus of Cowart's monograph this observation

mediates, the tension between connection and isolation. As the above analysis of *Mao II* has demonstrated, a language purely of isolation or of connection is shown to be unachievable and instead each individual, consciously or not, enunciates a particular point within this continuum.

To explore this language, this monograph is divided into three sections. The first section, entitled 'Dasein', will attempt to view the language of Self in isolation, or at least as much as is possible with a writer whose work is as complex and nuanced as that of DeLillo. While any such exclusion is by nature artificial, such an approach will allow a theorization of the foundational mechanisms by which subjectivity is constructed in DeLillo's texts, providing the basis for the subsequent analysis of the interaction between Dasein and its environment. The first section is divided into two chapters which explore the parallel, omnipresent strands of the language of Self: that of isolation and connection.

The first chapter, '"[L]ife narrowed down to unfinished rooms":[30] Isolation and the Language of Self', addresses the desire for a subjectivity formed through isolation, and purely the product of individual agency. '"[Y]our link to the fate of mankind"[31]: Connection and the Language of Self', the second chapter, explores the alternative fascia of the language of Self and charts the opposing desire for a Self formed through connection and alterity. Using a predominantly Heideggerian theoretical matrix,[32] this

---

has not been transformed into a comprehensive account of the linguistic nature of subjectivity in DeLillo's fiction.

30 Don DeLillo, *Running Dog* (London: Picador, 1992), p. 54. Further references are given after quotations in the text.
31 Don DeLillo, *Mao II*, p. 78.
32 DeLillo's connection with Heidegger has been noted by such critics as Cowart and most prominently by Cornel Bonca in his essays 'Being, Time, and Death in DeLillo's *The Body Artist*', *Pacific Coast Philology*, 37 (2002), pp. 58–68 and Cornel Bonca, 'Don DeLillo's *White Noise*: The natural language of the species', *College Literature*, 23:2 (1996), pp. 25–45. As Bonca observes, 'DeLillo's tightest philosophical connections are not with Baudrillard or Lyotard, but with Heidegger' and accordingly the philosopher is a 'ghost' who 'exerts a powerful presence in DeLillo's work; he hovers over it all, or under it all – a fitfully locatable roar' [Cornel Bonca, 'Don DeLillo's *White Noise*: The natural language of the species', endnote 5].

Introduction

chapter argues for alterity and wounding as central to any such endeavour. In both chapters the same sections of DeLillo's novels will be analysed, showing how a particular enunciation is in fact produced through a negotiation between the omnipresent spectres of isolation and connection. While the subject may have a particular desire for one extreme, such exclusivity is not possible and each enunciation represents a particular amalgam of the language of Self.

Entitled 'Phenomenology', the second section attempts to build upon this foundational framework of subjectivity, striving to overcome the artificial exclusion necessary for the initial positing of such a schema. Building upon the bipartite model of 'Dasein', 'Phenomenology' proposes that any enunciation of Self, whether striving for an exclusively isolated, connected, or balanced composition, is observable in DeLillo's fiction through the media of λόγος[33] (logos) and image. Entitled '"With a word they could begin to grid the world"[34]: Denotation and the Language of Self', the third chapter explores the interaction of λόγος and subjectivity, focusing upon the relationship between enunciations of Self and the linguistic theories of Wittgenstein, Benjamin and Heidegger. The fourth chapter, '"[T]o smash my likeness, prism of all my images"[35]: Hyperreality, ἀλήθεια (truth)[36] and the Language of Self', explores the often competing, yet always coexistent medium of the image and its role in the formation of subjectivity and art. Addressing Baudrillard's concept of hyperreality which has often

---

[33] The Greek literation has been retained to emphasize continuity with Heidegger's *Sein und Zeit*, highlighting the specific context in which the term is used in this project. n.b. Martin, Heidegger, *Being and Time*, John Macquarrie and Edward Robinson (trans.) (London: Blackwell, 2000), pp. 55–8. Further references are given after quotations in the text.

[34] Don DeLillo, *Libra* (London: Penguin, 1989), p. 414. Further references are given after quotations in the text.

[35] Don DeLillo, *Americana* (London: Penguin, 2006), p. 236. Further references are given after quotations in the text.

[36] c.f. Martin Heidegger, 'The Origin of the Work of Art', in *Poetry, Language, Thought*, Albert Hofstadter (trans.) (London: Harper Perennial, 2001), pp. 15–86, p. 35. Further references are given after quotations in the text.

been correlated with DeLillo's work, the chapter utilizes the language of Self to provide an alternate perspective upon the relationship between Baudrillard and DeLillo, using Heidegger's later theories of the image and of the clearing of truth.

Building upon this analysis, the third section, entitled 'Das Man', explores the manner in which the individual – Dasein – interacts with, shapes, and is shaped by, their social context. Just as Dasein enunciates a particular articulation of the language of Self, so too do particular groups of individuals shape collective enunciations. As DeLillo's fiction demonstrates, such groupings can vary in size from a handful of individuals to an entire class, but in each instance a complex, nuanced interaction occurs between the enunciating individual and their collective, social context, mediated through λόγος and image. In DeLillo's fiction these interactions are particularly noticeable in regards to consumption and power, which are the predominant media through which public, collective enunciations are signified and solidified.

The fifth chapter, '"Capital burns off the nuance in a culture"[37]: Consumption, Capital, *Chrimatistikós* and the Middle American Enunciation of Self', argues that commoditization is used in the formation of a stable, secure public enunciation of Self. '"[T]he banned materials of civilization"[38]: Waste, *Sinthomo*sexuality, and Middle America', the sixth chapter, will, contrastingly, present waste as the opposing fascia, always present and always interacting with the subject who consumes, disrupting public enunciations and providing access to a hidden *jouissance*, conceptualized, primarily, through the theoretical work of Lee Edelman.

The final binary explores issues of power and terror in the establishment and maintenance of public languages of Self. '"[T]o maintain a force in the world that comes into people's sleep": Power, Alterity and the Formation of Hegemony', the seventh chapter, addresses the role of control in the creation and maintenance of both collective and individual enunciations of Self, drawing upon Foucault's analysis of power. The eighth

---

37 Don DeLillo, *Underworld*, p. 776.
38 Ibid., p. 286.

Introduction

and final chapter, '"[T]he balance of power and the balance of terror"[39]: Terrorism and the *uneigentlich* publicness of *das Man*', examines the alternate fascia from both an individual and public level, proposing that such divergent individuals are marginalized by prevailing, public enunciations and embrace terror as a form of resistance to Middle American conformity.

39 Don DeLillo, *Underworld*, p. 76.

SECTION 1

Dasein

CHAPTER I

'[L]ife narrowed down to unfinished rooms'[1]: Isolation and the Language of Self

For the majority of DeLillo's male protagonists isolation is the predominant state to which they aspire. Rather than an opportunity for intersubjectivity, the Other is perceived as a source of dread. Such a tendency has been noted, at least in part, by other DeLillo scholars such as McGowan who observed, in reference to *Underworld*, that there has been a 'dramatic change in the structure of society', marked by a 'turning away from the Other and toward narcissistic self-absorption'.[2] This chapter argues that for DeLillo's male protagonists this self-absorption arises from the desire for isolation and autonomy, an attempt to create a self-actualized subjectivity which is as free as possible from need and dependency upon the Other. Exploring and conceptualizing this desire, the subsequent analysis focuses upon the enunciations of David Bell, Glen Selvy, Bill Gray and Nick Shay. In addition to providing relatively separable enunciations from the interaction of other signifying systems, the four characters chosen cover a wide chronological range, beginning with DeLillo's debut novel *Americana* (1971), *Running Dog* (1978), *Mao II* (1991) and finishing with *Underworld* (1997). By examining material from across DeLillo's oeuvre it will be demonstrated that in spite of variations in strategy and environment, the fundamental paradigm of the striving for a predominantly isolated enunciation of Self remains consistent, comprising three principal components: a space – either literal or cognitive – within which the individual can create a second, 'true' Self,

---

1   Don DeLillo, *Running Dog*, p. 54.
2   Todd McGowan, 'The Obsolescence of Mystery and the Accumulation of Waste in Don DeLillo's Underworld', *Critique: Studies in Contemporary Fiction*, 46:2 (2005): pp. 123–45, p. 124.

shaping their own enunciation; a self-disciplining structure which allows the subject to mediate physical or emotional interaction with the Other; and thirdly, an investment with, or fetishization of, objects which reinforce and maintain this isolated subjectivity.

In *Americana*, David Bell, the first person narrator of DeLillo's debut novel, articulates his subjectivity through a linguistic metaphor which provides cognitive space and allows for the construction of a second Self. While it would be another twenty years before DeLillo coined the phrase 'the language of self', *Americana* depicts a comparable means of achieving such space and autonomy. As David observes, he 'visualized' his 'mind as a dark room with many doors' inside of which a 'black machine ticked', a true Self protected from contact with the Other (DeLillo, *Americana*, p. 36). Such a metaphor captures Bell's sense of subjectivity as the product of conscious, individual signification. As with written and verbal language, an alteration in the number of doors which David allows to open results in a differing signification, altering meaning, shaping his enunciation of Self and controlling the balance of connection and isolation:

> I functioned best with several doors open. Sometimes I opened more doors, let in more light, risked the truth. If anyone seemed to perceive a distant threat in my remarks or actions, I closed all the doors but one. That was the safest position. But usually I kept three or four doors open. The image of this room was often with me. When I spoke at a meeting I could see the doors opening and closing in my mind and soon I arrived at the point where I could regulate the ebb and flow of light with absolute precision. I got a raise and then another. (DeLillo, *Americana*, pp. 36–7)

While David would prefer to open as many doors as possible, leaving 'the black machine' of his 'inner' Self unconstrained, he is aware that by so doing he will 'let in more light', revealing more of his secret, 'inner' Self, and allowing a greater possibility of connection. It is for this reason that Bell describes an existence where the majority of his doors are shut as 'the safest position' to adopt (DeLillo, *Americana*, pp. 36–7). Light, as a revealing force, betrays the fear which connection holds for the individual – of being seen and known in a way in which the Self cannot control. Rather than shaping his own enunciation, David would instead become decentred; a raw material to be moulded and formed by the radical alterity of the Other, rendered dependent upon them for the possibility of subjectivity. While the individual may wish to live a life without constraint, such openness leaves a vulnerability to the Other, to a light which would change the balance of power at the thetic point and leave the Self susceptible to external control. Fearing connection, David learns to control the arrangement of doors, to react to a situation and to control the amount of himself which he reveals, preferring isolation over connection and submerging the latter fascia of the language of Self.

The apogee of this fear of exposure arises, as it often does for DeLillo's protagonists, with the experience of desire. While the metaphor of eight doors and the black machine provides him with a means of achieving isolation and control in his everyday interactions – such as those with his co-workers – it alone proves an insufficient defence against the Other to whom he is most vulnerable. So extensive is this feeling of threat in the presence of a lover that he 'needed every ego-scrap' to remain within himself as a defence against alterity, since David 'feared [his] own disappearance' which could result from openness and connection (DeLillo, *Americana*, p. 41). Consequently, in his ex-wife's presence, David does not risk opening a single door, ensuring that 'he remained unrevealed' and maintaining a policy of total exclusion as he 'refused to give her any sense of [him]self', an act of self-discipline which thereby prevents any compromise of his desire for self-mediated isolation (DeLillo, *Americana*, p. 41). In place of such mediated openness, David told 'nothing but lies', creating a further linguistic barrier between his enunciation and the threat of the Other (DeLillo, *Americana*, pp. 57–8). David thus comes 'to understand the attraction of pathological lying' as it provides the ability to 'construct one's own reality', isolating the Self more fully from the threat of the Other (DeLillo, *Americana*, pp. 57–8).

Such is the extreme nature of David's fear of extinction that he reinforces the protective medium of his metaphor and self-discipline with a fetishistic investment in objects. Manifested most clearly following sex, David 'went naked down the stairs, carrying [his] shoes and clothing' rather than risk the vulnerability of sleep, or the moment after waking before his defences are adequately in place (DeLillo, *Americana*, p. 60). Rather than connection and companionship, David instead 'wanted to wake up alone', a 'characteristic' of his, which, as he notes, 'many women learned to despise down through the years', reflecting a consistent resistance to alterity (DeLillo, *Americana*, p. 60). Rather than waking to the threat and uncertainty of the Other, to a potential loss of control and enunciation, David instead immerses himself in the objects with which he has carefully constructed his surroundings:

> My apartment welcomed me, dim and silent, the red-wine flavor of paintings and rugs, the fireplace and oak panelling, the black leather upholstery, old and comfortably cracked, the dull copper mugs on the mantelpiece and the burnished ale tone of the desk lamp – all warm and familiar and needing no acknowledgment, all reminding me that solitude asks no pledges of anyone. (DeLillo, *Americana*, p. 60)

It is precisely this absence of a willingness to acknowledge the Other, a freedom from pledges and responsibility, which are the comfort and reward of solitude and isolation. As such it is divorce, emblematic of the denial of connection with the Other, which David terms as the 'most important step in arriving at a truly radiant form of self-donative love' (DeLillo, *Americana*, p. 285). For Bell, such a love for the Self is only possible with the denial of the Other, shielded from the threat of connection by the isolation of his enunciation and the objects which constitute his environment.

A similar strategy can be observed in Glen Selvy, the protagonist of *Running Dog*, who also shapes an enunciation of Self designed to limit the potential threat of connection. Like David, Glen supports such a deployment through a linguistic framework, self-discipline and a relationship with objects. Conceiving of himself as 'a reader', somebody who 'read his man,' Glen utilizes this metaphor to refer to both himself and his clandestine profession, conveying the sense in which he considers subjectivity to be a text which can be read (DeLillo, *Running Dog*, p. 54). Within this paradigm it is connection and isolation which governs access – shaping the texts intelligibility – and Glen's primary motivation in the construction of his enunciation is thus to ensure that he is a reader rather than read, isolated rather than connected. It is for this reason that Glen has gravitated to a profession which allowed him to 'creat[e] his own operational environment' with 'little outside direction' and 'no sense of policy', an apparently self-actualizing enunciation (DeLillo, *Running Dog*, p. 54).

'[L]ife narrowed down to unfinished rooms'

To maintain this status and position of authority – in both senses – Glen self-consciously shapes a 'calculated existence' consisting of the rigours of a routine whose self-discipline ensures a life 'narrowed down to unfinished rooms' (DeLillo, *Running Dog*, p. 54). As the use of the word 'calculated' indicates, while this conception of subjectivity may be volitional, to execute it effectively and remain in the position of reader rather than read requires competence, rigour, and most importantly control. Glen's routine is accordingly as much a mental process as a physical discipline or counter-espionage strategy:

> The routine in one sense was his physical movement between New York and Washington, and the set pieces of procedure, the subroutines, that were part of this travel. In a larger context the routine was a mind set […] (DeLillo, *Running Dog*, p. 81)

It is the strength of Selvey's 'routine' and the mindset which it creates that allows him to avoid connection when surrounded by people:

> The routine. Cab, terminal, plane, terminal, car. He moved through it apart from other people, sitting in aisle seats, standing at the edge of waiting lines, unobtrusively watchful, last on, first off. (DeLillo, *Running Dog*, p. 53)

Through the rigidity of his self-discipline, Glen, like David, shapes an enunciation which stresses isolation and resists the possibilities of connection. As with the metaphor of the doors in *Americana*, routine in *Running Dog* achieves its power as a result of the signifying space being unknowable outside of the self, remaining unread:

> No one he knew, or might talk to in the intervening period, would ever suspect the nature of his business. It was carried on beneath the level of ordinary life. This is why it made no difference where he lived. It was all the same, mere coloration for the true life, for the empty meditations, the routine, the tradecraft, the fine edge to be maintained in preparation […] (DeLillo, *Running Dog*, p. 54)

Stressing unobtrusiveness and secrecy, Glen's routine functions as his 'true life', the way in which his 'mind had come to work', the specific 'areas' which he 'avoided' and 'the person' which he'd 'become', parallel to, but unaffected by, conventional, public, enunciations of Self (DeLillo, *Running Dog*, p. 81):

> What it meant. The full-fledged secrecy. The reading. The routine. The double life. His private disciplines. His handguns. His regard for precautions. How your mind works. The narrowing of choices. What you are. (DeLillo, *Running Dog*, p. 183)

It precisely this narrowing which provides Glen's routine with its defensive strength and which, when viewed from the perspective of the fascia of isolation, can be seen, like David's enunciation, as an attempt to create a space free from the influence of the Other.

While routine provides a means of defending the Self against the perils of connection, allowing Glen 'to build almost a second self', '[s]omeone smarter and more detached', such a strategy requires augmentation and maintenance through a fetishization of objects (DeLillo, *Running Dog*, p. 83). For Selvy it is firearms and the '[p]roper maintenance of old combat gear' which provides such a defence for his constructed Self (DeLillo, *Running Dog*, p. 81). As the narrator observes, '[w]here the routine prevented Selvy from seeking human links, it [instead] prompted him to study the interactions within the mechanisms' (DeLillo, *Running Dog*, pp. 82–3). Looking at the parts of the gun 'laid out at his fingertips', Glen perceives an 'order' in their 'grouping', a 'distinct precision', which can be assembled and disassembled at will, irrespective of the subjectivity, desires and vagaries of a living Other. Unlike the shifting longings and hidden motivations of individuals, when Glen examines the parts of a gun '[h]e could see how each surface was designed to adapt to at least one other surface' in a manner which is stable and knowable (DeLillo, *Running Dog*, p. 82). A firearm is thus the ultimate text which can be interpreted by a reader such as Selvy, and which, if properly maintained and used, cannot change without the will or agency of the user:

> He controlled the weapon, his reflexes and judgement. Maintaining the parts and knowing the gun's special characteristics were ways of demonstrating involvement in his own well-being. (DeLillo, *Running Dog*, p. 82)

For 'Selvy, guns and their parts amounted to an inventory of personal worth', helping to maintain the language of Self he has constructed (DeLillo, *Running Dog*, p. 82).

Such a fear of the potential loss of agency through connection is also a central concern of Bill Gray, one of four protagonists in *Mao II*. As discussed above, it was in this novel that the term the language of Self was coined. Viewed within this context, each character can be seen as a different enunciation along the spectrum of the language of Self, reflecting a unique balance of connection and isolation (DeLillo, *Mao II*, p. 8). For Bill Gray it is the latter which is the predominant mode of his enunciation. Through his writing Bill has created a 'secret' and 'private language' which has allowed him to fabricate 'a second self', analogous to that produced by Glen Selvy's routine and referred to by the same term (DeLillo, *Mao II*, p. 37). As with Glen, this alternate subjectivity becomes the medium through which his enunciation is created:

> Every sentence has a truth waiting at the end of it and the writer learns how to know it when he finally gets there. On one level this truth is the swing of the sentence, the beat and poise, but down deeper it's the integrity of the writer as he matches with the language [...] (DeLillo, *Mao II*, p. 48)

It is this process of matching the undisciplined Self to an ideal, self-generated order, which is analogous to Selvy's routine and Bell's metaphor, allowing for the self-conscious shaping of an enunciation:

> [...] I've always seen myself in sentences. I begin to recognize myself, word by word, as I work through a sentence. The language of my books has shaped me as a man. There's a moral force in a sentence when it comes out right. It speaks the writer's will to live. The deeper I become entangled in the process of getting a sentence right in its syllables and rhythms, the more I learn about myself. (DeLillo, *Mao II*, p. 48)

Through its almost endless potential for re-writing, such literary creation represents the ultimate self-determining enunciation, further augmented by a fetishization of the material methods of such production, including the room Bill sets aside solely for that purpose, and objects such as his typewriter whose only function is the facilitation of this 'second self'. As with Bell and Selvy, such an enunciation is only possible through a separation from the Other maintained by a comparable utilization of routine. This principally consists of ensuring that everything which 'isn't directly centered on work revolves around concealment, seclusion, ways of evasion' (DeLillo, *Mao II*, p. 45). In order to prevent the destabilizing presence of the Other, his assistant, 'Scott[,] works out the routes of simple trips [Bill] occasionally make[s]', and establishes 'procedures for people coming to the house' (DeLillo, *Mao II*, p. 45), thereby limiting the potential effect upon the Self.

Unlike the previous two enunciations discussed, however, while Bill's prose-Self seemingly possesses an isolated, infinitely positional subjectivity, the act of publishing results in its entry into the public sphere. While Bill takes many of the same precautions as David and Glen to ensure the autonomous space for an isolated language of Self, the nature of the publicness of his enunciation poses problems which they do not have to face, the antipode of Glen's reader/read duality. For a novelist such as Bill the threat of the Other thus does not principally arise from a partner, or a co-worker, but instead from the actions of readers such as Scott. As the latter recalls:

> Somebody gave me Bill's first novel to read and I said, Whoa what's this? That book was about me somehow. I had to read slowly to keep from jumping out of my skin. I saw myself. It was my book. (DeLillo, *Mao II*, p. 51)

It is precisely this question of the ownership of the enunciation which Bill constructs that creates a particular problem for its status as an isolated language of Self. While a novel in progress, as a space free of mediation from the Other, provides an unconstrained opportunity to create a second, true Self – as with Selvy's routine, or Bell's metaphor – such freedom becomes compromised once the work is finished and released. Unlike the productions of David or Glen, whose subjective experience remains largely private, Bill's most personal and isolated enunciation of Self, by necessity, enters the public sphere. Agency and control thereafter becomes a subject of contestation, between writer and reader, threatening the very isolation that allowed its genesis:

> Maybe I don't want to feel the things other people feel. I have my own cosmology of pain. Leave me alone with it. Don't stare at me, don't ask me to sign copies of my books, don't point me out on the street, don't creep up on me with a tape recorder clipped to your belt. (DeLillo, *Mao II*, p. 45)

'[L]ife narrowed down to unfinished rooms'

The physical isolation, fetishization of objects and the extreme measures and 'procedures' which Bill undertakes are consequently ways of maintaining Bill's personal 'cosmology of pain', insulating him from having 'to feel the things other people feel' and jeopardizing the hermetic integrity of his enunciation.

It is in *Underworld*, however, that this desire to limit the potential effect of the Other is given its most complex and nuanced portrayal. For Nick Shay, a principal character and intermittent narrator, a metaphor is also used to posit this second Self, derived through a doctrine of negative theology which creates the requisite cognitive space for an isolated enunciation of a 'true' Self. The key apophasical text with which Nick engages is the anonymously authored *The Cloud of Unknowing*, a work of fourteenth-century mysticism written as a handbook for contemplatives – people who had largely abandoned any concern for earthly life in favour of an attempt to find a mystical union with God.

Perhaps surprisingly for a modern audience – who would typically associate such a project with austerity – the author of *The Cloud* suggests that an apophasic relationship is not best achieved through emotional denial and absence but instead by constant erotic absorption, internalized and directed towards an absent God. Ensuring that their 'whole life now must always consist of desire', the neophyte can attempt to 'make progress on the level of perfection', lifting up their 'heart towards God with a humble stirring of love', a 'desire [that] must always be shaped in your will by the hand of almighty God and with your own consent'.[3] It is this latter concern with the role of both 'will' and 'consent' which links such a project with the spaces created by David, Glen and Bill.

Rather than some form of mystical union imposed by a divine Other – rooted in connection – apophasic communion is instead a relationship initiated by the contemplative and shaped through their will and volition: the cognitive space of such a 'second self' is predicated upon the absence

---

3 Anon, 'The Cloud of Unknowing', in *The Cloud of Unknowing and Other Works*, A.C. Spearing (trans.) (London: Penguin, 2001), pp. 21–2. Further references are given after quotations in the text.

of a divine Other and accordingly remains rooted in isolation rather than connection. Following such a path, Nick creates a self-reflective space in which the Other is deliberately and justifiably excluded, allowing the freedom to shape, without interference, a second, truer Self, protected from connection by the conceit of a divine being who withholds itself.

As with David, Glen and Bill, self-discipline is needed to reinforce and defend this cognitive space, maintaining the integrity of such an enunciation. God, as the narrator of *The Cloud* observes, 'is a jealous lover and will put up with no rivalry, and he will not work in your will unless he is with you alone by himself' (Anon, 2001, p. 21). In order to preserve this solitary union with what *The Cloud* terms as the contemplative's 'spiritual bridegroom', the neophyte must do what they 'can to forget all of God's creations and all their actions', so that their 'thoughts and desires are not directed and do not reach out towards any of them' (Anon, 2001, pp. 21–2). The means of achieving this is 'to put a cloud of forgetting beneath you, between you and everything that was ever created', a reciprocal relationship between the second Self which apophasis creates and the self-discipline which is necessary for its maintenance (Anon, 2001, p. 26).

Unlike the contemplatives described by the anonymous author of *The Cloud*, Nick does not live a monastic life, and the issue of the self-discipline necessary for such an existence is accordingly more complex. For the majority of the events narrated Nick has a spouse and children, a career and a life of suburban domesticity. Such ties compel Nick to maintain human connections on a daily basis, and, unlike David and Bill, he is still married to, and living with, his wife. This proximity makes the strategies and routines deployed by the other three unfeasible for Nick to adopt, as any kind of physical separation is harder to achieve and a fully contemplative life is unobtainable. Distance instead has to be of a cognitive, rather than physical nature, and it is in this respect that the apophasic quality of *The Cloud* again proves a valuable resource.

Applying the barrier of the cloud of forgetting, Nick is able to maintain a constant distance from the people who surround him. As the narrator observes, Nick's wife, Marian:

[...] had a demon husband if demon means a force of some kind, an attendant spirit of discipline and self-command, the little flick of distance he'd perfected, like turning off a radio. (DeLillo, *Underworld*, p. 261)

It is in this sense that, as Nick observes, he had 'always been a country of one', maintaining 'a certain distance' in his 'makeup, a measured separation like my old man's' (DeLillo, *Underworld*, p. 275). The word which he chooses to describe this existence is '*lontananza*', '[d]istance or remoteness', interpreted as 'hard-edged and fine-grained', 'the perfected distance of the gangster, the syndicate mobster' (DeLillo, *Underworld*, p. 275):

Once you're a made man, you don't need the constant living influence of sources outside yourself. You're all there. You're made. You're handmade. You're a sturdy Roman wall. (DeLillo, *Underworld*, p. 275)

It is through the apophasic nature of Nick's second Self that he can remake himself into 'a sturdy Roman wall', a 'made man'.

Such is the temporal range of *Underworld*'s portrayal, however, that in addition to the alterity of the Other, Nick is also assailed by what Heidegger termed as historicity (*Historizität*)[4] – the enduring legacy of his past – which pre-dates apophasic longing and the cloud of forgetting. As Leonard Wilcox notes in his essay 'Don DeLillo's *Underworld* and the Return of the Real', Nick's 'life contains a traumatic residue, an unrationalized remainder' of the 'aftereffects of two events of his youth' – his abandonment by his father and his shooting of the waiter, George Manza.[5] Due to the scope of

---

4   c.f. Martin Heidegger, *Being and Time*, p. 41.
5   Leonard Wilcox, 'Don DeLillo's *Underworld* and the Return of the Real', *Contemporary Literature*, 43:1 (2002), pp. 120–37, p. 125. Advancing a psychoanalytic reading of Nick's inability to connect with the Other, Wilcox concentrates upon the circular, repetitious nature of the narration of Nick's trauma, arguing that it represents an inability to adequately reconcile the events described. This book instead proposes that within the context of the language of Self, Nick's actions can be seen as an example of a ubiquitous trend in DeLillo's fiction in which male protagonists seek a form of enunciation which is predominantly one of isolation, thereby attempting to resist the mediation of the Other and to exclude memories and emotions which threaten this denial of connection.

Underworld, which, uniquely amongst DeLillo's works, chronicles nearly a half-century, the novel is able to depict the changing effect which Nick's past has upon his enunciation. As Heidegger states:

> [...] Dasein 'is' its past in the way of *its* own Being, which, to put it roughly, 'historizes' out of its future on each occasion. Whatever the way of being it may have at the time, and thus with whatever understanding of Being it may possess, Dasein has grown up both into and in a traditional way of interpreting itself: in terms of this it understands itself proximally and, within a certain range, constantly. By this understanding, the possibilities of its Being are disclosed and regulated. Its own past – and this always means the past of its 'generation' – is not something which *follows along after* Dasein, but something which already goes ahead of it. (Heidegger, 2000, p. 41)

Viewed within such a perspective, the 'unrationalized remainder' of this traumatic event which Nick endures thus continues to exert a shaping influence, not only on his present, but also upon his future potentiality of Being. The repression of his past is thus not only of crucial importance in making his present more emotionally bearable, but also in resisting the future shaping influence of the Other. Nick accordingly struggles against the alterity of his past, striving to defend the independence of his enunciation through the deployment of a second, apophasic Self, and its cloud of forgetting.

As with David, Glen and Bill, Nick Shay reinforces this defensive potential of his enunciation – in its defence of both past and present – with an accompanying investment in objects. For Nick this takes the form of the displacement of emotion and alterity onto the material commodity of the winning homerun baseball from the 1951 Giants versus Dodgers pennant game. Part of the very fabric which constitutes New York's communities, the baseball has come to embody this rivalry, a tribalizing force which Nick embraces, counter-intuitively, in order to resist alterity. As he observes, he 'was the only Dodger fan in the [Bronx] neighbourhood' who chooses to support the Brooklyn team (DeLillo, *Underworld*, p. 93). Rather than the secular prayer of baseball, a communal experience of mediated connection and alterity in which people gather together in a baseball stadium, or listen collectively to the radio broadcast, Nick instead transforms the sport into a nascent form of his subsequent apophasic longing. As he observes, he 'liked to be alone', 'listen[ing] to Dodger games on the roof' so that when he 'died inside when they lost' he could 'die alone', an experience with which '[o]ther people interfered' (DeLillo, *Underworld*, p. 93).

Despite Nick's rejection of baseball as community, his investment is such that, as a matter of life and death, he is still exposed to the alterity of wounding. Baseball accordingly does not represent a safe space devoid of consequence into which Nick can pour his longing and need when compared to his later apophasic relationship with the divine, who, as perpetually absent, cannot pose the possibility of connection. It was thus not the teams moving West which took 'Nick's heart and soul' as by that point '[t]here was nothing left to take'. Worn down by alterity, he was already 'a nonfan by that time', '[b]urnt out.' Nick's fetishizing of the homerun baseball is instead due to its potential to act as a permanent reminder of the perils of connection and alterity, a symbol of the need to bury and resist a traumatic past which he cannot face, repressing its historicity (DeLillo, *Underworld*, p. 93).

Rather than symbolizing the collective experience of the shot heard around the world, the baseball instead becomes a more idiosyncratic memorial, emblematic of Nick's desire for a predominantly isolated language of Self. As he observes:

> 'The next day [after the game] I think it was I began to see all sorts of signs pointing to the number thirteen. Bad luck everywhere. I became a budding numerologist. I got pencil and paper and wrote down all the occult connections that seemed to lead to thirteen [The Number assigned to the Pitcher, Branca]. I wish I could remember them. I remember one. It was the date of the game. October third or ten-three. Add the month and day and you get thirteen.' (DeLillo, *Underworld*, p. 95)

Rather than rushing out onto the street as his colleague Sims did in St Louis in the aftermath of the game, Nick instead turns inward, to the occult, to hidden signs and systems, to a secret knowledge known only to the cognoscenti and consequently, a progenitor of his apophasic immersion. For Nick, as for Marvin, the memorabilia dealer, the baseball becomes a 'pathological obsession' (DeLillo, *Underworld*, p. 96), a personal, private means of displacing emotional pain and anxiety at the prospect of any form of alterity:

> '[...] I didn't buy the object for the glory and drama attached to it. It's not about Thomson hitting the homer. It's about Branca making the pitch. It's all about losing. [...] It's about the mystery of bad luck, the mystery of loss. I don't know. I keep saying I don't know and I don't. But it's the only thing in my life that I absolutely had to own.' (DeLillo, *Underworld*, p. 97)

The baseball comes to represent the uncontainable nature of alterity, yet, also, the accompanying need for the subject to attempt to repress it. Consequently, rather than the baseball being publicly displayed as a symbol of connection, of people being drawn together – 'the last time people spontaneously went out of their houses for something', gathering together in celebration or commiseration – it instead becomes an emblem of private pain and loss, hidden away to be examined alone and in secret (DeLillo, *Underworld*, p. 94). As Brian observes:

> 'He [Nick] thinks about what it means,' Glassic said. 'It's an object with a history. He thinks about losing. He wonders what it is that brings bad luck to one person and sweetest of good fortune to another. [...]' (DeLillo, *Underworld*, p. 99)

Rather than confronting the alterity of his past directly, or the perils of connection, Nick instead displaces his emotions onto the fetishized object when they become too much to contain within his apophasic longing. Mediating upon loss and contingency within a displaced form, as a mystery to be picked up on occasion, then set aside, Nick can use the object to remain safe beneath the cloud of forgetting and the self-discipline of his demonic self.[6]

---

[6] Jesse Kavadlo also argues for a religious fetishizing of the homerun baseball. As he observes: 'Nick Shay's relentless pursuit of the baseball – a kind of American Holy Grail – is the primary expression of the restless religious impulse evident in *Mao II*. His search for innocence lost becomes a transpersonal symbol that embodies the capacity for faith itself' [Jesse Kavadlo, *Don DeLillo: Balance at the Edge of Belief*, p. 102]. Such a perspective, however, does not incorporate any account of the centrality of the baseball in Nick's formation of subjectivity and, strangely, for a monograph which has such a pronounced religious dimension, the interaction of baseball, the occult and *The Cloud of Unknowing* is also not discussed.

While the nomenclature used to describe the language of Self thus varies in DeLillo's fiction, all of its manifestations have been shown to conform to the same basic paradigm and can be viewed as arising from a similar conception of subjectivity. Creating a language whose dominant fascia is one of isolation, each enunciation consists of a construct within which the individual generates the conceptual space and freedom to create and shape its desired form; a unique manifestation of the same basic paradigm. For David this is achieved through the metaphor of eight doors bordering a black machine. Glen utilizes a metaphor of reader and read to construct a 'second self'. While less elaborate than David's construction, it is far more pervasive in its interweaving within every facet of Glen's life. For Bill, it is the novels which he authors that provide this space, transforming his enunciation through the language which he shapes. Nick Shay, unlike David, Glen and Bill, utilizes a religious text to form a second Self. In spite of this theistic dimension, however, its function is essentially the same. Through apophasis, he constructs a separate space in which to signify his enunciation.

Each of these spaces are subsequently augmented by a rigid code of self-discipline which provides structure and form, helping maintain the isolated enunciation, conferring stability and preventing atrophy and degradation. For David, this manifests as a self-conscious control of the eight doors which govern access to his Self, defended through pathological lying which provides resistance to the alterity of those who are closest. In Glen's case, it is a routine which is embraced, governing and proscribing every aspect of his daily life. In a similar vein, Bill's self-discipline revolves around keeping his location secret which consumes every aspect of his waking life. Nick's self-discipline, unlike that of the others, consists of a demonic Self which allows him to be emotionally absent through 'the little flick of distance' he maintains.

This absorption in routine is reinforced with an investment in objects which underpin and support the second Self and its accompanying structure. For David this consists of a conventional delight in the colours and textures which constitute his apartment, providing a haven from the possibility of connection. The nature of Glen's routine prevents such stability, and instead his investment takes the form of the predictability and power of weaponry. For Bill, fetishization is of the materials which make his writing possible, providing a sense of grandeur and purpose to his evasion of the Other and culminating in his fascination with the materiality of his unfinished final novel. Contrastingly, Nick's fetishization of the material commodity of the homerun baseball is both simpler yet further reaching, balancing a public symbol with a personal idiosyncratic investment.

As the subsequent chapter entitled '"[Y]our link to the fate of mankind"[7]: Connection and the Language of Self' will demonstrate, however, the tendency towards isolation is only one aspect of the enunciations constructed by David, Glen, Bill and Nick, and in preferencing isolation over connection they are not necessarily stable in nature. By exploring their languages of Self discussed above from the alternate perspective of connection, a more complete understanding of both subjectivity and interpersonal interaction will be achieved.

---

[7] Don DeLillo, *Mao II*, p. 78.

CHAPTER 2

'[Y]our link to the fate of mankind'[1]: Connection and the Language of Self

As every enunciation of Self is formed in the negotiation between isolation and connection, the significations of David Bell, Glen Selvy, Bill Gray and Nick Shay fail to achieve a purely isolated language. Whereas the previous chapter explored their desire for separation and the mechanisms deployed in its pursuit, the following analysis discusses how connection proves to be unavoidable. Through the critical lens of Martin Heidegger's phenomenal ontology it will be argued that the above pursuit of isolation is in fact the product of conventional, unfulfilling forms of connection. Whilst appearing to individuate, such problematic connections instead eliminate the possibility of sustainable, individual subjectivity. This argument forms the basis of a subsequent highlighting of the importance of a negotiation between Self and Other, necessary for the formation of an intersubjectivity which is both fulfilling and individuating. While David, Glen, Bill and Nick obtain the possibility of such intersubjective enunciations, in each case their failure to abandon their previous, unsuccessful significations and to engage with the Other in a nuanced, mediated form, results in an ultimate inviability of Self. The novels instead present the only sustainable form of subjectivity as the product of a mediated form of connection, one which creates rather than dissolves the Self.

Conceptualizing his subjectivity through the metaphor of 'a dark room with many doors', David protects his enunciation by self-disciplined isolation, reinforced through the fetishization of objects. When such a strategy is examined in light of the fascia of connection, however, it becomes

1   Don DeLillo, *Mao II*, p. 78.

apparent that David has achieved neither a stable nor fulfilling enunciation. This is most clearly portrayed through the centrality of the λόγος within the fascia of connection:

> Jane was always trying to discuss these things with me. In her confusion she was comforted by the sound of voices. It was an article of her faith that tragedy could be averted, or at least detained in the sweep of its tidal and incomprehensible darkness, by two reasoning people sitting in a familiar room and discussing the matter. (DeLillo, *Americana*, p. 167)

Though Jane wishes for a relationship based upon connection with the Other, it is an alterity limited to that between 'two reasoning people' who are 'sitting in a familiar room', mediated through the λόγος. Rather than the desire for total surrender sought by Karen Janey, it is instead a partial publicness similar to that of Rodge and the Middle American 'land of lawns' to which Jane aspires. It is in this attempt at creating a delicate, nuanced enunciation, that the importance of the phenomenological ontology of Martin Heidegger can be observed as a means of conceptualizing both connection and isolation within the language of Self.

For Heidegger, as for Jane, it is the λόγος which is crucial in the formation and shaping of subjectivity. As he observes, '*[o]nly as phenomenology, is ontology possible*' (Heidegger, 2000, p. 60), drawing upon the etymology[2] of the former term – phenomenon (Φαινόμενον)[3] and λόγος – to convey his belief that there is an inextricable connection between image, perception, language and subjectivity. Dasein's Being, for Heidegger, is thus '"defined" as the ζῶον λόγος ἔχον – as that living thing whose Being is essentially determined by the potentiality for discourse,' through which a process of 'synthesis' can occur (Heidegger, 2000, p. 47):

---

2   For negative perspectives upon Heidegger's etymological method see Frederic Jameson *Postmodernism, or, The Cultural Logic of Late Capitalism* (London: Verso, 1991) and Theodor Adorno, *The Jargon of Authenticity* Knut Tarnowski and Frederic Will (trans.) (London: Routledge, 2003).
3   c.f. Martin Heidegger, *Being and Time*, pp. 49–55.

> [...] 'synthesis' does not mean a binding and linking together of representations, a manipulation of psychical occurrences where the 'problem' arise of how these bindings, as something inside, agree with something physical outside. Here the συν has a purely apophantical signification and means letting something be seen in its *togetherness* [*Beisammen*] with something – letting it be seen *as* something. (Heidegger, 2000, p. 56)

Rather than ordering something already perceived, it is instead only through language as discourse, as λόγος, that an object can be apprehended.

It is this inextricability of language and perception which underpins Heidegger's theory of being-in-the-world (*In-der-Welt-sein*),[4] his central concept of the nature of subjectivity:

> When Dasein directs itself towards something and grasps it, it does not somehow first get out of an inner sphere in which it has been proximally encapsulated, but its primary kind of Being is such that it is always 'outside' alongside entities which it encounters and which belong to a world already discovered. Nor is any inner sphere abandoned when Dasein dwells alongside the entity to be known, and determines its character; but even in this 'Being-outside' alongside the object, Dasein is still 'inside', if we understand this in the correct sense; that is to say, it is itself 'inside' as a Being-in-the-world which knows. (Heidegger, 2000, p. 89)

Rather than some 'inner' world of a disembodied Cartesian ego, Heidegger's concept of being-in-the-world proposes that subjectivity arises from an interaction of Self and 'external' environment, which is in turn perceived and synthesized through the ordering force of the λόγος.

Such Being-in-the-world, alongside a range of phenomena, is not solely limited to inanimate objects, but also encompasses Dasein's encounter with the Other. For Heidegger, being-in-the-world is thus always being-with-others (*Mitsein Andere*)[5] and as such, rather than leaving an 'inner' mental life to connect with the Other, Dasein instead lives permanently alongside other subjects in a perpetual state of possible connection. What governs this interaction and shapes Dasein's treatment of the Other is Heidegger's

---

[4] c.f. Martin Heidegger, *Being and Time*, p. 78.
[5] c.f. Martin Heidegger, *Being and Time*, p. 155.

concept of care (*Sorge*),[6] the means by which Dasein comes to perceive and treat those it encounters as more than an object to be manipulated. Again it is language which mediates this care, transforming the subject's perception of the Other into an awareness that they are a volitional entity possessed of their own subjectivity, providing the foundation for connection and intersubjectivity or isolation and monadism:

> The λόγος lets something be seen (Φαίνεσθαι), namely, what the discourse is about; and it does so either *for* the one who is doing the talking (the *medium*) or for persons who are talking with one another, as the case may be. (Heidegger, 2000, p. 56)

It is through language that perception and subjectivity is shared, raising the monadic into the intersubjective: a mediated form of connection.

Jane's enunciation correlates with such a Heideggerian conception of subjectivity, and while she wishes to construct a Self which emphasizes connection, she does not wish to experience the full undifferentiated force of alterity. Instead, it is the 'article of her faith' in the power of the λόγος to mediate connection, promote care and ensure that 'tragedy could be averted' or 'detained' which underpins her enunciation: it is thus the heteronormative union of two people 'discussing the matter' (DeLillo, *Americana*, p. 167) which is sought, correlating to a particular mode of Heideggerian subjectivity. Whether such an enunciation could be fulfilling or stable – authentic (*eigentlich*)[7] in Heidegger's Lexicon – is never explored in *Americana*. Rather than alterity, Jane is instead confronted with the syntax of David's own language of Self which stresses isolation and denies the power of the λόγος.

Refusing himself meaningful access to language, David renders a Heideggerian conception of subjectivity unobtainable. Rather than embracing *Angst*[8] and its authentically individuating potential, David instead chooses evasion and denial:

---

6   c.f. Martin Heidegger, *Being and Time*, p. 157.
7   c.f. Martin Heidegger, *Being and Time*, p. 68. As opposed to inauthentic (*uneigentlich*).
8   'Anxiety'. n.b. Martin Heidegger, *Being and Time*, p. 227.

[I] feared silence less than the involvement of words. Distance, silence, darkness. In the vastness of these things I hoped to evade all need to understand and to cancel all possibility of explaining. (DeLillo, *Americana*, p. 167)

While speech may provide a means for the Other to elicit connection, it also, as λόγος, is key to the possibility of perception. In fleeing to his 'silent' (DeLillo, *Americana*, p. 60) apartment, David is avoiding the 'possibility of explaining' the 'vastness' of the 'silence' and 'darkness', of all 'these things' which he 'hoped to evade all need to understand' (DeLillo, *Americana*, p. 167). Without λόγος facilitating an encounter with this void – what Heidegger termed as being-towards-the-end (*Sein zum Ende*)[9] and being-towards-death (*Sein sum Tode*),[10] the ultimate horizon of Being – authentic subjectivity is impossible. David's signification of Self is consequently unstable and he succumbs to the very perils of connection which he strove to avoid.

As Heidegger observed, what differentiates authentic and inauthentic being-towards-death is the attitude evidenced towards the prospect of mortality and the emotion felt at its possibility:

Dasein does not, proximally and for the most part, have any explicit or even any theoretical knowledge of the fact that it has been delivered over to its death, and that death thus belongs to Being-in-the-world. (Heidegger, 2000, p. 295)

It is only when such a realization arrives that the '[t]hrownness into death reveals itself to Dasein in a more primordial and impressive manner through *Angst*, a crushing burden for the Self and the reason that 'proximally and for the most part Dasein covers up its ownmost Being-towards-death, fleeing *in the face* of it' (Heidegger, 2000, p. 295). What Dasein instead embraces is a 'falling, everyday Being-towards-death', defined by 'a constant *fleeing in the face of death*' (Heidegger, 2000, p. 298), or at least in the face of its authentic individuation. Such an evasion shifts '[d]ying, which is essentially mine in such a way that no one can be my representative' into

---

9   c.f. Martin Heidegger, *Being and Time*, p. 289.
10 c.f. Martin Heidegger, *Being and Time*, p. 277.

a 'perverted' event of a 'public occurrence which the "they" encounters' (Heidegger, 2000, pp. 296–7).

This concept of *das Man*[11] is crucial to the possibility of a fulfilling, stable enunciation because, as Heidegger argues:

> The 'who' is not this one, not that one, not oneself [man selbst], not some people [einige], and not the sum of them all. The 'who' is the neuter, *the 'they'* [*das Man*]. (Heidegger, 2000, p. 164)

As the neuter, immersion within *das Man* 'dissolves one's own Dasein completely into the kind of Being of "the Others", in such a way, indeed, that the Others, as distinguishable and explicit, vanish more and more' (Heidegger, 2000, p. 164). This dissolving of both the Self and the individuality of the Other is how 'the real dictatorship of the "they" is unfolded' (Heidegger, 2000, p. 164) as:

> [w]e take pleasure and enjoy ourselves as *they* [*man*] take pleasure; we read, see and judge about literature and art as *they* see and judge, likewise we shrink back from the 'great mass' as *they* shrink back; we find 'shocking' what *they* find shocking. The 'they', which is nothing definite, and which we all are, though not as the sum, prescribes the kind of Being of everydayness (Heidegger, 2000, p. 164)

By fleeing from this truth, *Angst* can seemingly be displaced and accordingly 'Dasein puts itself in the position of losing itself in the "they" as regards a distinctive potentiality-for-Being which belongs to Dasein's ownmost Self' (Heidegger, 2000, p. 296). So pervasive is this tendency that Heidegger argues that:

> [...] factical existing is not only generally and without further differentiation a thrown potentiality-for-being-in-the-world, but it has always likewise been absorbed in the 'world' of its concern. In this falling Being-alongside, fleeing from uncanniness announces itself; and this means now, a fleeing in the face of one's ownmost Being-towards-death. (Heidegger, 2000, pp. 295–6)

---

11   'The "they"'. n.b. Martin Heidegger, *Being and Time*, p. 150.

The prospect of death accordingly provides the clearest locus of the role of the Other in Heidegger's theory. Authentic being-towards-death is the ultimate individuating experience and provided it is not fled from, it results in forms of care which in their idiosyncrasy resist publicness. Confronted with *Angst*, however, a 'fleeing in the face of one's ownmost Being-towards-death' typically results, causing a falling into the neutering embrace of *das Man*. While intersubjectivity may provide the possibility of authenticity, inauthentic connection with the Other also evokes the prospect of the total extinction of Self and all that is individuating.

In his denial of linguistic connection Bell ironically succumbs to the empty publicness of *das Man*, dissolving his 'own Dasein completely into the kind of Being of "the Others"' (Heidegger, 2000, p. 164). The failure of David's enunciation does not arise from the threat of a specific Other, or from connection, as he believes, but it instead seemingly unravels as a result of its own inauthenticity:

> I could see the doors opening in the dark room in my mind, three, four, five doors opening, and fresh light planking down across the floor. In the past I had always been able to control the doors but now they seemed to swing open freely, wind-driven, banging the walls. Control was still possible but I did not try to attain it. Light began to fill the room and I thought I might reach eight doors, a new record. (DeLillo, *Americana*, pp. 78–9)

As Bell notes, while '[c]ontrol was still possible' the failure of his enunciation is one of will and desire, the result of its unfulfilling nature.

Rather than having fashioned an authentic, idiosyncratic subjectivity, David has instead adopted an inauthentic, given way of living. As he observes, within the United States 'there is a universal third person, the man we all want to be' and which '[a]dvertising has discovered', a form of the publicness of *das Man* which seemingly is not rooted in either connection or language. For David, the effect of a commercial should be to make the individual 'want to change the way he lives', to move 'from first person consciousness to third person'. The correlation between such an endeavour and Heidegger's theory can be observed in the fact that the German pronoun used for the third person singular is *man* – used in the English sense of 'one does', 'one goes' etc – connecting the dream 'third person singular' to the publicness of *das Man*. This is further compounded by an additional grammatical feature of the German language in which '*man*' is always the subject of any sentence in which it appears, taking the nominative case and displacing the particularity of the first person within the generality of an undifferentiated third. 'Advertising is [thus] the suggestion that the dream of entering the third person singular might possibly be fulfilled', a nominative case free of the pressure of maintaining an idiosyncratic enunciation such as that of David's metaphor (DeLillo, *Americana*, p. 270).[12]

It is through cinema, another intensely marketed form, that the most vivid depiction of entry into the third person singular occurs. As with advertising, the Hollywood film industry sells a similar dream, providing David with an opportunity for incorporation in both senses. Recounting the experience of seeing Burt Lancaster's enlarged image in *From Here to Eternity*, David describes how it evokes a profound longing to be safe within its 'conflux of shadow and time [where] there was room for all of us' (DeLillo, *Americana*, p. 13). Lancaster's image literally becomes an embodiment of the third person singular, of one individual form containing a multitude of Others. David accordingly tries to 'extend' himself 'until the molecules parted' and he 'was spliced into the image', escaping his sterile and unfulfilling first person singular for the seemingly intransient perfection of third person publicness, achieved without specific alterity or connection (DeLillo, *Americana*, p. 58).[13] In a novel bereft of transcendence, however, such a dream cannot be realized and neither his molecules, nor those of Lancaster's image, are able to achieve a stable and lasting union. Unable to transcend, the closest David can get to the third person singular is the advertisers' consumerist dream: an attempt to live and to feel as others do. Consequently, what is inauthentic in the American form of *das Man* is that it demands a withholding of Self and a longing for the image, preventing

---

12   The consumerist dimension of this statement will receive further analysis in chapter 5 '"Capital burns off the nuance in a culture": Consumption Commodity, Capital, *Chrimatistikós* and the language of Self'.

13   The role of the image in these quotations will be the subject of further exploration in chapter 4 '"[T]o smash my likeness, prism of all my images": Hyperreality, ἀλήθεια and the language of Self.'

both the authentic connection of being-with-others and the individuation of being-towards-death. As a result, David's 'whole life' seems like 'a lesson in the effect of echoes': that he 'was living in the third person', though one deprived of Lancaster's stability and fulfilment (DeLillo, *Americana*, p. 58).

Like David, Glen Selvy uses similar strategies to maintain his isolation and remain 'apart from other people' (DeLillo, *Running Dog*, p. 53). Creating the language of Self of a reader whose 'routine' structures and disciplines both his 'mind set' and his interaction with his environment, Glen 'build[s] almost a second self', someone 'smarter and more detached' (DeLillo, *Running Dog*, pp. 81–3). Unlike Bell, however, Glen's language of Self is also part of an intersubjective context beyond the monadic individual, which, while providing his enunciation with external support, creates contradictions in terms of its classification into either a predominantly connected or isolated mode of signification. While Glen may have 'created his own operational environment' with 'little outside direction' and 'no sense of policy', the decision to instigate a particular action is not his own. His autonomy is one of devolution and while he may be able to determine how to act upon mission priorities, he is not free to set them or to question the orders which he receives. 'Periodically' Glen 'reported' for 'a technical interview, or polygraph, or lie detector test', signifying the extent to which he is merely a cog within a larger machine, with its own aims and priorities, reducing him to a phenomenon to be assessed, measured and categorized by the Other, contained within its taxonomy (DeLillo, *Running Dog*, p. 54). While he may be 'a reader' of others within the parameters of a particular mission, he, in turn, is a subject to be read by his superiors, to be ordered and disposed (DeLillo, *Running Dog*, p. 54). Though on the level of the mission Glen's enunciation may be one of isolation, when viewed from a wider perspective it can be seen as a narrow space of seeming autonomy within a larger context of connection. Even such intersubjectivity is seemingly paradoxical, as, while existence within the organization may be a form of intersubjectivity, such an enunciation is dependent upon secrecy and isolation.

Just as David's desire for silence denies a genuine confrontation with Being-towards-death, Glen's routine also results in a 'narrowing of choices', a shaping of '[h]ow your mind works' and of '[w]hat you are', preventing authentic being-towards-the-end (DeLillo, *Running Dog*, p. 183):

> In a larger context the routine was a mind set, all those mechanically performed operations of the intellect that accompanied this line of work. You made connection-A but allowed connection-B to elude you. You felt free to question phase-1 of a given operation but deadened yourself to the implications of phase-2. (DeLillo, *Running Dog*, p. 81)

It is precisely this conception of 'mind set' shaping and limiting what the Self chooses to perceive, curtailing the questions which are asked, that prevents Glen from being resolute (*entschlossen*)[14] at the prospect of his own end. Instead, it signifies a fleeing into the publicness of *das Man*, into thinking as *they* think, doing as *they* do, observing the limits which *they* observe, ultimately resulting in inauthentic *Sein sum Tode*. While Glen may periodically be monitored – his enunciation examined, explored, catalogued and contained – the hierarchical nature of the organization means that the layers above Glen are shielded from the unconstrained force of his own alterity, and he in turn is wholly denied potential intersubjectivity.

Such a carefully balanced enunciation, however, is destabilized once Glen encounters Moll Robbins, a journalist working for the publication *Running Dog*. Her alterity impacts him in such a way that the scission damages the unity of Self to which Glen clings. Moll's presence causes Glen to break the sexual dictates of his routine that limits his encounters to '[s]ex with married women only,' who, in the entanglements and structures of their other relationships, would be denied the capacity to influence Glen's life, make demands and intertwine themselves with his existence, destroying the isolation necessary for his profession. With Moll, however, Glen has 'broken the sex rule' and with its demise a number of other strictures also collapse (DeLillo, *Running Dog*, p. 81). Her alterity shatters the hermetic seal of Glen's enunciation, opening his language to the effect of the Other, causing it to lose its structural integrity.

---

14   c.f. Martin Heidegger, *Being and Time*, p. 314.

This shattering of Glen's enunciation leaves him vulnerable to the destabilizing force of the 'unexpected' presence of an operational 'connection' which 'didn't fit the known world as recently constructed', becoming 'a peculiar element in a series of events otherwise joined in explainable ways' (DeLillo, *Running Dog*, p. 82). As the narrator observes:

> This was where the routine was important. He stuck to the routine. The routine enabled him mentally to bury this queer bit of intelligence. [...] It wasn't within Selvy's purview to meditate on additional links, even when they might pertain to his own ultimate sustenance. Especially then. That was why the routine existed. (DeLillo, *Running Dog*, p. 82)

Once Glen's enunciation is destabilized, the structured denial of authentic being-towards-death crumbles under the pressure of inconsistency. Faced with the choice between persevering with a failed enunciation or attempting to construct a new form, Glen instead chooses to remain in a liminal state. Rejecting the wounding of Moll's alterity, Glen heads out towards the desert and replaces her presence with that of a woman who does not pose the same threat, whom he can dismiss as merely 'the girl' (DeLillo, *Running Dog*, p. 182).

Such evasion is insufficient, however, and the disruption of Glen's routine continues to allow the wounding of alterity, forcing him to explore and question the connections which were previously off-limits:

> It was becoming clear. He was starting to understand what it meant. All that testing. The polygraphs. The rigorous physicals. The semisecrecy. All those weeks at the Mines. Electronics. Code-breaking. Currencies. Weapons. Survival. [...] All the paramilitary sessions. The small doses of geopolitics. The psychology of terrorism. The essentials of counter-insurgency. [...] What it meant. The full-fledged secrecy. The reading. The routine. The double life. His private disciplines. His handguns. His regard for precautions. How your mind works. The narrowing of choices. What you are. It was clear, finally. The whole point. Everything. (DeLillo, *Running Dog*, p. 183)

As Glen comes to realize '[a]ll this time he'd been preparing to die' (DeLillo, *Running Dog*, p. 183) and crucially he concludes that this form of being-towards-death is a product of *das Man*'s inauthentic publicness:

> It was a course in dying. In how to die violently. In how to be killed by your own side, in secret, no hard feelings. They'd been grooming him. They'd spotted his potential his capacity for favourable development. All this time. [...] We are teaching you how to die violently. This is the only death that matters, steel or lead or tungsten alloy, death by hard metal, taking place in secret. (DeLillo, *Running Dog*, p. 183)

Rather than using this realization to occasion a genuine confrontation with *Angst* and being-towards-the-end, Glen instead attempts to retreat to the mediated form of publicness which defined his training as a 'falling Being-alongside', a 'fleeing from uncanniness' in 'the face of one's ownmost Being-towards-death' (Heidegger, 2000, pp. 295–6). Glen's choice to return to where he was trained and to wait for a squad sent to kill him – to die 'violently', a result of the machinations of his 'own side, in secret' with 'no hard feelings' – is accordingly a decision to remain within the publicness of *das Man*, in spite of the realization of its inauthentic nature:

> 'The thing about Selvy. Selvy's more serious than any of us. He believes. You ought to see where he lives. Where he used to live. Buried in some rat-shit part of the city. Isolated from contact. He'd do it for nothing, Selvy. The son of a bitch believes.' (DeLillo, *Running Dog*, p. 141)

Failing to be resolute in the face of Being-towards-the-end, Glen clings to the monolithic nature of his faith, its singular truth, unmatched by that of his contemporaries. It is only through the exigencies of the mission that Selvy justifies his enunciation, obtaining a purpose and a point to his existence. Without such support, Glen 'didn't know what' it was that he was living '[i]n preparation for' and what it was that he was striving towards (DeLillo, *Running Dog*, p. 54). Without a purpose, his faith in 'the life' pertains to nothing beyond the Self, becoming merely solipsistic and unfulfilling (DeLillo, *Running Dog*, p. 141). Glen's death and rejection of the Other can consequently be viewed as a means of escaping the final, total collapse of the purpose of his life, of being forced to confront the *Angst* of authentic being-towards-the-end.

For Bill Gray, as for Glen Selvy, an analysis of his language of Self from the perspective of connection reveals that while his enunciation may appear to be predominantly one of isolation, it is instead the product of an inauthentic publicness. As with David and Glen, Bill uses three methods to attempt to ensure his isolation and autonomy: the creation of a second, linguistic self; physical isolation; and an investment with objects. Through such a language of Self, Bill possesses the ability to 'recognize' himself, 'word by word', in the utterances which he creates. Having a space free from the effect of the Other allows Bill the appearance of total autonomy as he 'work[s] through a sentence', simultaneously altering the shape of the Self which it reveals. Since the 'language' of Bill's books has 'shaped' him 'as a man', and he alone has governed the form which that language has taken, he has seemingly achieved a means of creating a self-contained, isolated enunciation (DeLillo, *Mao II*, p. 48).

Such an appearance of freedom, however, as discussed in the previous chapter, only remains as long as the novel stays within the private sphere. Once published, Bill's enunciation – his 'second self' – has the potential to impact its reader with his alterity (DeLillo, *Mao II*, p. 37). The routine which reinforces this enunciation thus takes a two-fold purpose, firstly to maintain the space from which to shape such a language, and secondly, to defend Bill against the effects which it has upon the Other. Transforming a private language of Self into a commodity which enters the public sphere, Bill unwillingly creates the potential for an enunciation based upon connection and the intersubjectivity of the λόγος. As he observes:

> Maybe I don't want to feel the things other people feel. I have my own cosmology of pain. Leave me alone with it. (DeLillo, *Mao II*, p. 45)

The excessive lengths to which Scott is driven in his desire for connection with Bill – obtaining a job in the publisher's mail room, tracking down post marks, and then 'five weekends of vain surveillance' – show how deep the latter's resistance was to wounding by and for the Other, yet also how powerful a need for connection which is created (DeLillo, *Mao II*, pp. 60–1):

> I went back to school for a year but then I dropped out again and fell into another spiral of drugs and nonbeing. [...] Somebody gave me Bill's first novel to read and I said, Whoa what's this? That book was about me somehow. I had to read slowly to keep from jumping out of my skin. I saw myself. It was my book. Something about the way I think and feel. He caught the back-and-forthness. The way things fit almost anywhere and nothing gets completely forgotten. (DeLillo, *Mao II*, p. 51)

Rather than Bill using the λόγος to foster an isolated enunciation, or authentic intersubjectivity, his resistance to genuine connection transforms his enunciation into a hierarchical asymmetry, an inversion of the relationship which characterized Glen and his superiors. While Scott initially attempts to connect with Bill through the medium of the written word, mirroring the author's own literary production, such an endeavour fails to breach Gray's containment:

> He wrote nine or ten letters, ambitious and self-searching, filled with things a luckless boy wants to say to a writer whose work has moved him. He hadn't known he could summon these deep feelings or express them with reckless style and delight, certain cosmic words typed in caps and others spelled oddly to reveal second and third meanings. The letters released something, maybe a sense that he was not alone, that the world was a place where travellers in language could know the same things. (DeLillo, *Mao II*, p. 58)

It is precisely this idea of a shared journey to which Bill is so resistant, as evidenced in the disparity of his response of 'one letter back, two lines, handwritten in a hurry' (DeLillo, *Mao II*, p. 58). In spite of the terseness of such a reply, the impact of Bill's language of Self in the social sphere is so extreme that a reader such as Scott can still feel that the 'book was about me', a privileged communication between writer and reader which seemingly constitutes a direct form of address. It is this supposed intimacy which gives Scott the sensation of 'jumping out' of his skin, shedding his previous inadequate enunciation for an ostensible intersubjective communion. The asymmetry of such connection, however, does not allow the λόγος to bring either Bill or Scott into a confrontation with authentic being-towards-death, resulting instead in the publicness of *das Man* and its 'nonbeing'.

While Scott is able to force himself within Bill's private sphere, once he has entered that sanctum he does not attempt to forge this access into intersubjectivity. All that Scott wishes is to be within 'Bill's material mesh, drawing the same air, seeing things Bill saw', just as David wished his molecules to splice into those of Lancaster's cinematic image (DeLillo, *Mao II*, pp. 60–1). Rather than radically contesting the grounds of Bill's enunciation, and in so doing, shaping his own, Scot's ultimate role becomes one of facilitation rather than challenge.

Denied access to alterity through his self-imposed isolation, Bill is contained within a sterile bubble whose inauthentic nature is revealed in his dependence upon substances – whether illicit, prescription or alcoholic – required to anaesthetize the *Angst* arising from the experience of being guilty (*Sein schuldig*)[15] felt at living an inauthentic life. This inauthenticity is reflected in the text of his current novel, since it is the words he has used to shape himself as a man, to posit his enunciation, which have resulted in an inadequate, inauthentic signification:

> [he] saw the entire book as it took occasional shape in his mind, a neutered near-human dragging through the house, humpbacked, hydrocephalic, with puckered lips and soft skin, dribbling brain fluid from its mouth. (DeLillo, *Mao II*, p. 55)

Rather than shaping himself towards an authentic subjectivity, which in turn creates better work, allowing the potential for a better Self, inauthenticity instead creates a negative feedback loop in which worse prose results in increasingly inadequate subjectivity, in turn lessening Bill's creative potential:

> I keep seeing my book wandering through the halls. There the thing is, creeping feebly, if you can imagine a naked humped creature with filed-down genitals, only worse, because its head bulges at the top and there's a gargoylish tongue jutting at a corner of the mouth and truly terrible feet. It tries to cling to me, to touch and fasten. A cretin, a distort. (DeLillo, *Mao II*, p. 92)

Such deformity contrasts with Bill's 'great early work' (DeLillo, *Mao II*, p. 73) which was the product of a writer living in New York with meaningful interpersonal connections, confronting the inauthenticity of *das Man* and attempting to be authentic in the face of such publicness: a tension which generated prose that meaningfully addressed such fallen Being.

Despite being so strongly impacted by this early work, it is precisely the inauthentic form of Bill's later enunciation which Scott seeks to maintain. Through promoting the stagnation and stability of the monolithic, stable image of Bill the author, Scott can continue to take shelter within Bill's

---

15 c.f. Martin Heidegger, *Being and Time*, p. 327.

enunciation, safe in the knowledge that it will not evolve beyond the necessity of his presence. As Scott observes, Bill 'can't let the [current] book be seen' because if he chooses to publish '[i]t's all over' (DeLillo, *Mao II*, p. 73):

> The book is a grossity. We have to invent words to describe the corpulence, the top-heaviness, the lack of discernment, pace and energy. [...] People will look at the great early work in a new way, searching for signs of weakness and muddle.' (DeLillo, *Mao II*, p. 73)

Rather than allowing the disaster of publication which would force Bill to confront the inauthentic nature into which his language of Self has devolved, Scott instead wishes that they remain within the elaborate structures which they have built. Such a desire is one of self-preservation, since, as with David's attempt at immersion within Burt Lancaster's image, it is Bill's enunciation which is protecting Scott from the harrowing 'spiral of drugs and nonbeing'. As Bill observes, the '"[k]id thinks he owns my soul"', the very thing which has become Scott's own enunciation of Self, the shelter within which he hides (DeLillo, *Mao II*, p. 73). Without Scott's mediation, Bill's edifice would collapse and Scott's life would cease to have meaning. In their inauthentic co-dependence both Bill and Scott deny themselves genuine intersubjectivity rooted in confrontation with being-towards-the-end.

While Bill's decision to be photographed by Brita represents an attempt to escape from the pressure of being hunted, it is also indicative of a deeper longing to shatter the monolith of his inauthentic subjectivity. Unlike the autonomous space of his writing, Bill's decision to invite '[g]uests who bring ideas from outside', provides an opportunity for both alterity and *Angst* to effect his enunciation (DeLillo, *Mao II*, p. 67). As Bill observes, 'I've become someone's material', vulnerable to their alterity and control and as a result '[a]lready I see myself differently', '[t]wice over or once removed' (DeLillo, *Mao II*, p. 44). It is for this reason that Bill 'need[s] these pictures', '[t]o break down the monolith I've built', 'an angry grudging force' which is 'totally independent of my conscious choices' (DeLillo, *Mao II*, p. 45): just as it is precisely this self-realization to which Scott is so resistant.

That Bill is aware of the exposure to alterity inherent in this process of artistic creation is demonstrated by his musings upon the topic:

> 'We're alone in a room involved in this mysterious exchange. What am I giving up to you? And what are you investing me with, or stealing from me? How are you changing me? I can feel the change like some current just under the skin. Are you making me up as you go along? Am I mimicking myself? And when did women start photographing men in the first place?' (DeLillo, *Mao II*, p. 43)

By allowing space for this impact of alterity, Bill's enunciation can be freed from its negative feedback loop, breaking a cycle from which Bill is not capable of extricating himself. Destroying the hermetic seal of his previous, failed enunciation, Bill has the possibility of constructing a new intersubjectivity. For the Others who depend upon his language of Self, however, this shattering creates an accompanying disturbance in their own enunciation:

> We have a life here that's carefully balanced. There's a lot of planning and thinking behind the way Bill lives and now there's a crack all of a sudden. What's it called, a fissure. (DeLillo, *Mao II*, p. 57)

It is precisely that 'crack', that 'fissure', which Bill requires in order to escape from the inauthentic blend of connection and isolation which has perverted his language of Self. As with the enunciations of Glen and David, once a fracture appears, an inauthentic language of Self collapses due to its internal inconsistency.

Participation within Brita's project, however, does not lead to a new form of subjectivity: Bill chooses to ignore the opportunity presented and to remain within a liminal state rather than embracing the pain and uncertainty of an authentic enunciation. Rather than constructing a new subjectivity based upon alterity and intersubjective recognition, Bill instead strives to modify his authentic enunciation into a more sustainable form, rooted in a greater degree of isolation. After heading to London to give a reading, Bill ostensibly tries to exchange himself for a prisoner held by a terrorist cell, a plan so confused and poorly thought through as to be evidently a camouflage for a more complex motivation. Travelling into the Eastern Mediterranean in haphazard pursuit of his stated goal, Bill largely shuts himself off from the alterity of foreign cultures. Rather than an exchange, or an immersion within an alternate socio-political reality, it is instead isolation, and a desired rejuvenating of his 'second self' which provide the motivation for Bill's journey:

> It wasn't that no one spoke English. He forgot they did or preferred not to speak himself. Maybe he liked the idea of point. You could get to depend on pointing as a kind of self-enforced loneliness that helps you advance in moral rigor. (DeLillo, *Mao II*, p. 160)

In place of intersubjectivity is the 'loneliness' and 'rigour' of the written word, used by Bill to reconstruct his language of Self into an authentic form, the 'only way he knew to think deeply in a subject' (DeLillo, *Mao II*, p. 160).

Instead of a desire to free the prisoner or engage with the experience of terror, Bill wishes to co-opt the poet's historicity (*Historizität*) to free himself from his own prison of an inauthentic language of Self. Safe within the isolating confines of his hotel room Bill chooses to write 'through the long mornings, slowly building chains of thought, letting the words lead him into that basement room', an attempt to '[f]ind the places where' he 'converge[s] with' the imprisoned poet (DeLillo, *Mao II*, p. 160). While seemingly representative of a wish for connection, such a perspective is complicated by Bill's composition occurring through a 'self-enforced loneliness' whose isolation is ascribed a 'moral rigor'. Rather than connection and alterity, the key to Bill's new creative work is a desire, through the imagination of his 'second self', to experience authentic being-towards-death:

> In his room he thought about the hostage. He tried to put himself there, in the heat and pain, outside the nuance of civilized anxiety. He wanted to imagine what it was like to know extremes of isolation. (DeLillo, *Mao II*, p. 154)

In his writing, Bill tries to reconnect with the 'feeling [of] something familiar, something fallen into jeopardy', which he describes as 'the shattery tension, the thing he'd lost in the sand of his endless novel', an experience of being-towards-death free of fallen Being whose very 'endless[ness]' means

'[Y]our link to the fate of mankind' 59

that it can never evoke being-towards-the-end, only the publicness of *das Man* (DeLillo, *Mao II*, p. 168).

Bill's desire for a confrontation with mortality, correlating with a Heideggerian conception of subjectivity, is fatally flawed however:

> Dying is something that every Dasein itself must take upon itself at the time. By its very essence, death is in every case mine, in so far as it 'is' at all. (DeLillo, *Mao II*, p. 284)

Authentic subjectivity in a Heideggerian sense does not arise from using the prospective death of another as a proxy. Such an attempt merely provides entry into another form of inauthenticity, comparable to that of the endless novel. Lacking resolution in the face of his own end, Bill, like Glen, ultimately chooses a purposeless death over the final collapse of an inauthentic language of Self.

A similar lack of resoluteness can be observed in Scott's resistance to his own need to create a new enunciation following Bill's departure. Rather than the death which Bill chooses, Scott turns to a '[p]leasure in lists', an endless catalogue of Bill's literary estate and his aborted novel; a non-fatal though equally irresolute form of fallen Being which again denies the possibility of an end, embracing instead an infinite futurity (DeLillo, *Mao II*, p. 142):

> Of course the lists of things were also things. An item on a list might generate a whole new list. He knew if he wasn't careful he'd get mired in a theory of lists and lose sight of the things that needed doing. There was pleasure in lists, taut and clean. Making the list, crossing off the items as you complete the tasks. It was a small whole contentment, a way of working toward a new reality. (DeLillo, *Mao II*, p. 139)

This concept of a 'new reality', populated with the 'things' which Scott himself seemingly creates, replicates Bill's struggle in that it too is merely a reshaping of a former, problematic blend of inauthentic connection and isolation. Rather than forming a new enunciation, Scott instead comforts himself with the belief that 'Bill would make a return to the book', bringing the 'fresh energy' needed to 'cut it back, gut it, strip it six ways to Sunday', reinvigorating their shared enunciation (DeLillo, *Mao II*, p. 142). Stating that 'Bill's return would not be complete without Scott, of course', he clings to the belief that '[w]hen the time was right Bill would contact him' and then Scott would 'drive off in the long night to join Bill and make their new beginning' (DeLillo, *Mao II*, p. 143). The obsessive compilation of lists therefore provides a means of managing the intervening time, of protecting Scott from an authentic confrontation with being-towards-the-end, evoked by the prospect that Bill will never return:

> The point of these lists and tasks seemed to be that when you performed each task and crossed off the corresponding item on the list and when you crumpled and discarded all the lists and stood finally and self-reliantly in a list-free environment, sealed from worldly contact, you were proving to yourself that you could go on alone. (DeLillo, *Mao II*, p. 139)

Dwelling in the remains of Bill's literary estate, Scott continues to be sheltered from having to face the potential 'nonbeing' of his own existence.

As with David, Glen and Bill, Nick Shay also attempts to form a second Self, using the apophasic text of *The Cloud of Unknowing*. Striving for a predominantly isolated enunciation, Nick's apophasic longing seemingly provides a site free from the influence of the Other and from his own historicity: an existence insulated between the cloud of forgetting and the cloud of unknowing. While the previous novels portray isolation as largely a relief, an escape from the perils and pain of alterity, *Underworld* contains a far more nuanced conception of the consequence and experience of seclusion:

> I felt a loneliness, for lack of a better word, but that's the word in fact, a thing I tried never to admit to and knew how to step outside of, but sometimes even this was not means enough, and I didn't call her because I would not give in, watching the night come down. (DeLillo, *Underworld*, p. 637)

Unlike David, Glen or Bill, Nick's isolation is not just a struggle against the Other, but also a conflict with the weakness of the Self. Loneliness accordingly becomes a constant peril, a phenomenon to be resisted and suppressed: one to which Nick never 'admit[s]' and, for the most part, knew 'how to step outside of'.

'[Y]our link to the fate of mankind'

The unfulfilling nature of this strategy, however, is shown through his encounter with Donna whom he meets at a 'swingers' convention. Sharing an attraction rooted in the intensity with which their alterity impacts and wounds the other – as Donna observes, '"[a]ctually you sort of hate us, don't you?"' – it is this intensity which captivates her and her husband as they try and understand what motivates the extreme nature of Nick's reaction (DeLillo, *Underworld*, p. 292). The conclusion which she reaches is, fittingly, one of connection versus isolation:

> 'You hate the fact that it's public. You can't stand us coming out here and saying it and doing it and acting it out. We talked about this at dinner.' (DeLillo, *Underworld*, p. 293)

While she turns out to be correct – though not for the reasons she supposes – her own enunciation is actually closer to that of Nick Shay than they both seem to realize:

> 'I'm a person if you ask me questions. You want to know who I am? I'm a person if you're too inquisitive I tune you out completely.' (DeLillo, *Underworld*, p. 292)

As Nick observes, Donna is a '[p]rivate person who fucks strangers', possessing a comparable flick of distance (DeLillo, *Underworld*, p. 292). The nature of their connection, however, means that Nick is not simply another anonymous partner, essentially interchangeable with the procession of Others who have come before, and who, presumably, will follow.

Nick's own reaction to Donna's alterity is even more pronounced. As he observes, '[y]ou make me aggressive, a little reckless', causing Nick to 'relapse' to the previous Self shaped by his repressed past. As he states, he was 'backsliding a mile a minute' as he re-engages with his historicity and its accompanying *angst*. Such alterity, however, is insufficient to bridge the distance between their isolated enunciations and when Nick initially 'moved into a kiss' Donna 'did not lean away' but only 'returned a certain tepid sip, a hint of distances' which they had 'yet to cross.' To bridge that gap and prevent the consummation becoming 'a hate fuck', or degenerating into 'the malaise of bleak bargain sex', Nick chooses to reveal himself, parting the cloud of forgetting and allowing the Other a glimpse of his historicity and the care such connection can evoke (DeLillo, *Underworld*, pp. 293–5).

Such a temporary surrender of an isolated enunciation of Self also occurs for Donna during their encounter. While she states that she 'didn't come to this freaking outback to be analysed', or to allow the Other to reach her on an emotional level, she still remains in Nick's hotel room, listening to the story he tells of his past and its alterity. Her interaction with Nick is therefore an 'exception' to the 'indiscriminate fucking' which typifies her isolated enunciation (DeLillo, *Underworld*, p. 298). Once Nick has started to reveal himself, his actions transform the nature of their connection, causing her to show more than a tepid sexual interest:

> Oddly now she reached down and took my hand and moved it up along the inside of her thigh and placed it sort of cuppingly snug in her crotch, adjusting her posture to get completely comfy, like a child at story time. (DeLillo, *Underworld*, p. 296)

Just as Donna is Nick's 'unsafe' 'relapse', '[n]ot the first but the first in a very long time', equally he is also her transgression, a breaking of the rules which govern the impersonal, anonymous, extramarital sex in which she engages (DeLillo, *Underworld*, p. 298). What occurs between Donna and Nick is therefore an equally transgressive act for both parties, breaching their isolated, heteronormative enunciations.

While Nick chooses to temporarily escape the confines of his enunciation, embracing the impact of Donna's alterity, the latter's willingness is open to question. Their consummation consequently contains an element of coercion as Nick forces her to go beyond the boundaries of sex as recreation, compelling her to recognize him intersubjectively and creating an undertone of sexual and emotional domination:

> She fell into pretend sleep, leave-me-alone sleep, but I eased onto the blanket and pressed myself upon her, breathing the soft heat of her brow and tasting at the end of my tongue the smallest beadlets of fever. I heard room maids talking in the hall and knew we were gone from each other's life, already and forever. But some afterthing remained and kept us still, made us lie this way a while, Donna and I, in the all-and-nothing of our love. (DeLillo, *Underworld*, pp. 300–1)

Even in its wake he still 'pressed' himself onto her, wanting to suck in every drop expelled from her body, even though they 'were hollowed out like scooped guava when it was over' (DeLillo, *Underworld*, p. 300), emblematic of a desire to maintain for as long as possible the 'afterthing' which remained.

Once Nick returns to Phoenix he attempts to fall back into his previous, predominantly isolated enunciation of Self, yet the wounding of Donna's alterity still remains. As he notes, he 'withhold[s] the deepest things from those who are closest and then talk[s] to a stranger in a numbered room', the very crux of the contradiction in his language of Self: the coexistence of the need for connection – 'the all-and-nothing' of meaningful love – and the apophasic isolation of the cloud of forgetting. While he rhetorically questions '[w]hat's the point of asking why?', the ineffectiveness of such an evasion is demonstrated by the fact that he needs 'the daily wheel of work' in order to 'evade' the 'vexing questions' which his union with Donna has raised (DeLillo, *Underworld*, p. 300).

Since the predominantly religious enunciation he developed with the Jesuits in Minnesota proves insufficient as a defence against the wounding of alterity, Nick reinforces it with an investment in the hierarchical, plutocratic structure of The Waste Management Corporation. As he notes, while he 'was the juniormost fellow with the fixed smile' he 'wanted to be bound to the company'. Through such an investment he once again attempts to reshape himself, 'correct[ing] my foot-drag step', 'hear[ing] my voice' and seeing 'my smile' as if from the third person. Like David, Nick 'earned an office at the end of the hall' where he 'wore a crisp gray suit and grew stronger by the day' (DeLillo, *Underworld*, p. 301). The self-conscious manner in which he strives for such a union, however, shows that he is displacing the same longing he invested within an apophasic conception of God onto an alternate, corporate focus. Its similar inauthenticity is revealed through his reference to viewing himself in the third person, the publicness of *das Man* which replicates his previous contradictions and those of David in *Americana*.

In the denouement of the novel, however, such conflict seems to have been overcome. Upon discovering his wife's affair with his colleague, Brian, Nick is forced to confront Marian through the lens of authentic care, viewing her as more than merely a component in the construction of his own isolated enunciation. For critics who view the novel in largely Freudian terms – Peter Boxall and Jesse Kavadlo respectively consider the novel to be the unfulfilled promise of Oedipal desire finally granted in *Underworld*[16] and 'the creation story of the Fall, recast through the lens of the Oedipal struggle' (Kavadlo, 2004, p. 125) – such an occurrence is seen in a largely positive light.

For Boxall, DeLillo's previous novels had been defined by a 'desire to enter into an unboundaried freedom', balanced 'against the forces that hem desire in, that control and position the desiring spirit' (Boxall, 2006, p. 167). From its 'very beginning', however, Boxall argues that *Underworld* portrays such 'constraints against which DeLillo's narrators have struggled' to seemingly 'have been lifted' (Boxall, 2006, p. 167):

> [...] as if *Underworld* enters into a kind of reconciliation, as if there is no longer a struggle or a contradiction between the desiring self, and the patriarchal order. (Boxall, 2006, p. 167)

The final breakdown of Nick's enunciation is therefore seen as a kind of 'unknotting' achieved 'in homeliness, in the discovery of his own paternal, American voice', linked to a larger millennial moment – its 'political echo' – conceptualized through Fukuyama's end of history (Boxall, 2006, p. 179).

For Kavadlo, as for Boxall, the reconciliation of Nick with his wife – following paternal abandonment and forbidden desire[17] – represents an 'Oedipal conclusion' to events on both a personal and political level (Kavadlo, 2004, p. 125). Unlike Fukuyama's end of history, however, the resolution posited in Kavadlo analysis – in keeping with the religious dimension of his monograph – is a conflation of the Oedipal and the biblical in the promise of a new Eden, free from forbidden desire. The development of nuclear weapons is thus perceived as 'the acquisition of forbidden knowledge' which created the 'un-Edenic qualities inherent in and associated with the period' (Kavadlo, 2004, p. 125). Relegated to 'uneasy and

---

16   n.b. Peter Boxall, *Don DeLillo: The Possibility of Fiction*, p. 177.
17   Both Boxall and Kavadlo focus upon Klara as a Jocasta figure.

'[Y]our link to the fate of mankind' 65

uncomfortable shades of gray' in the post-war, such binaries and their supporting conventional and nuclear armaments are transformed 'to the status of waste products', the legacy of the fall, mirroring the individuals who are 'left over after the easy balances, the comforting dichotomies and dialectics' have also been transformed into 'waste' (Kavadlo, 2004, p. 134). Reflecting this sense of both physical and psychological phenomena acquired through the fall being transmuted into a by-product, Kavadlo proposes that 'Nick's unconscious' is a microcosm of this larger social dimension, 'a bomb needing to be defused, as dangerous as the nuclear waste at the end of the novel' and a subject for recycling (Kavadlo, 2004, p. 135).[18] Nick's reconciliation with his wife is thus seen as a defusive act, allowing Kavadlo to perceive the novel's ending as at least half-way hopeful, mirroring its opening line and evoking both the moment of the fall and the promise of a new Eden (Kavadlo, 2004, p. 135).

What both readings of Nick's 'reconciliation' (Boxall, 2006, p. 192) fail to adequately conceptualize, however, is the nuance of his subjective experience of this phenomenon. While in the surrender of his historicity to Marian 'all the things she spied' seem to have 'come to some completion', the next two sentences are revealing of Nick's own dissatisfaction with the extent to which such revelation has helped form a new, authentic enunciation of his own (Don DeLillo, *Underworld*, p. 807):

---

18   This interlinking of the personal and the social is explored through a discussion of the role of the homerun baseball, which rather than functioning as part of an anchoring point of an enunciation of Self, is instead conceived of as an object which both 'distinguish[es]' Nick 'as an individual' and also 'connect[s]' him in the most romantic sense of the word to the aura associated with the ball and the collective experience of the game and the pitch' [Jesse Kavadlo, *Don DeLillo: Balance at the Edge of Belief*, p. 135]. Rather than this combination of isolation and connection forming a constant tension and negotiation, the foundation of the language of Self, for Kavadlo it is instead perceived as evoking an unproblematized 'comfort' of 'collective experience', a potential for collective recycling into a new Eden [Jesse Kavadlo, *Don DeLillo: Balance at the Edge of Belief*, p. 135]. Comfort is thus perceived as the redemptive force, a form of recycling which is 'ultimately, the shared goal of the waste manager and the author' [Jesse Kavadlo, *Don DeLillo: Balance at the Edge of Belief*, p. 135].

If not for me, then for her. Because I don't know what happened, do I? (Don DeLillo, *Underworld*, p. 807)

Marian has gained what she wished, the shattering of Nick's daemonic enunciation through her adulterous relationship, achieving the heteronormative union which Jane was unable to acquire. Her actions and Shay's reaction, however, do not seem to be equally fulfilling. While she has gained the intersubjectivity which she desires, Nick himself is still unable to adequately cope with his historicity. Such is the extent of this doubt that even in his supposed reconciliation Nick ends the second sentence with a question that's never answered, indicative of a historicity which remains inauthentic and a being-towards-the-end which can never be realized in an authentic manner.

While Boxall accepts that a tension remains, that as 'joyfully' as Nick 'accepts his familial role' he still 'longs for the ecstasy of self-alienation', such a conflict is perceived as distinctly secondary. In keeping with his thesis of the millennial moment and the end of history, the tension Nick experiences is described as an 'erotic pleasure' arising from 'abandoning himself to that in history which is unrecoverable', dissolved within a larger narrative which 'wheels forward toward American completion' (Boxall, 2006, p. 192). This contrapuntal 'movement towards the distant, alienated third person' is seen as merely 'a kind of transgressive, insurgent undercurrent that leads back towards the forbidden and the taboo, towards Oedipal transgression and a wilful refusal of the interpellating power of the patriarchal American voice', rather than as indicative of an ultimate failure of authentic intersubjectivity (Boxall, 2006, p. 192).[19]

Viewed within the context of the language of Self, this transgressive urge is not simply that of the *jouissance* of Oedipal transgression derived from an unrecoverable history, a sporadic Lacanian undercurrent of the

---

19   Though not explicitly stated as such, this is analogous to Lacan's death drive, the enduring urges of the *chora* which are generally contained by the symbolic *Nom du père*.

Real[20] to a dominant, Symbolic reconciliation. Equally, it does not take the form of a partially recovered Eden and its promise of a world without end, rooted in futurity and the absence of being-towards-the-end. Rather, it functions as a mark of systemic failure, the collapse of an enunciation and an indication of its inauthentic publicness which cannot authentically engage with historicity and being-towards-the-end. While provisionally accepting Boxall and Kavadlo's arguments that the Cold War binaries have collapsed and entered a post-war condition[21] – though not an adoption of Fukuyama's end of history or of messianic promise – the denouement of *Underworld* indicates that on a personal level the same crises and tensions remain which define the language of Self, the vacillation between the desire for connection and isolation.

Nick is accordingly faced with the same dilemma that has confronted all of DeLillo's characters from his debut novel *Americana* (1971), through *Running Dog* (1978), *Mao II* (1991) and *Underworld* (1997). What has altered in the intervening period is the social context within which each enunciation is deployed, and the interaction which occurs through the language of Self. The second section of this monograph, 'Phenomenology', will explore how this language of Self manifests through the interrelation of λόγος and image.

---

20 Symbolic, Imaginary and Real will routinely be capitalized when used within a Lacanian context, stressing their specialized usage and differentiating such signification from the shared terminology, and divergent understandings, of other theorists such as Jean Baudrillard.
21 As I will argue in chapters 5, 6, 7 and 8, such a post-war state does not equate with either completion, millennial fulfilment or the potential for a new Eden. The tensions between the two fascias of the language of Self remain, and the formation of subjectivity is still problematic. All that alters is the context within which such negotiation occurs.

SECTION 2
Phenomenology

CHAPTER 3

'With a word they could begin to grid the world'[1]: Denotation and the Language of Self

As Cowart observes of DeLillo's use of language, the novelist's closest philosophical connections are with Ludwig Wittgenstein, Walter Benjamin and Martin Heidegger (Cowart, 2002, p. 11). What is significant about such a selection of philosophical influences is the divergent conceptions of language which they represent. While Heidegger's linguistic theory, and resulting conception of subjectivity, is rooted in his phenomenological conception of the inextricability of λόγος and phenomenon (Φαινόμενον) – the impossibility of perception without language – Wittgenstein and Benjamin both argue for an a-linguistic conception of thought as occurring prior to denotation. Even this shared conception, however, does not result in comparable conceptions of either language or Self. While Wittgenstein refrains from exploring what he considers to exist beyond the linguistic, for Benjamin it is this externality which comprises his own philosophical focus. All three philosophers therefore represent fundamentally irreconcilable conceptions of language and subjectivity which raises the question that if Cowart's assertion is correct, how can DeLillo's fiction reconcile or synthesize such divergent views of λόγος, subjectivity and their interrelation?

To being to address this question, this chapter explores how these three conceptions of language and subjectivity manifest themselves in DeLillo's fiction, arguing that while there is a degree of overlap within particular novels, a clear progression can still be observed. It will then be shown that it is the differing suitability of each philosophy of language as a vessel for the establishment and transmission of the language of Self which drives

[1] Don DeLillo, *Libra*, p. 414.

linguistic evolution in DeLillo's texts, shaping the possible enunciations which the Self can adopt and leading to the primacy of a phenomenological conception of language and subjectivity.

In the *Tractatus Logico-Philosophicus*, Wittgenstein emphasizes the logical elements of language and its internal structure. As he observes, the purpose of his work 'is to draw a limit to thought', or rather 'to the expression of thoughts'.[2] For Wittgenstein it can 'only be in language that the limit can be drawn, and what lies on the other side of the limit will simply be nonsense' (Wittgenstein, 2006, pp. 3–4). It is this emphasis upon language as a means of both understanding, and excluding what cannot be understood – sorting it into sense and nonsense, factual and nonfactual – which is the defining philosophical position of the *Tractatus*.

For Wittgenstein, language is seen as predominantly a means of conveying information and understanding facts, judged according to issues of truth and falsity, determined by the accordance of a proposition with the 'real' world of objects and each statement's internal, logical relations:

> (1.1) The world is the totality of facts, not of things. (1.11) The world is determined by the facts, and by their being all the facts. (1.12) For the totality of facts determines what is the case, and also whatever is not the case. (1.13) The facts in logical space are the world. (1.2) The world divides into facts. (Wittgenstein, 2006, p. 5)

As Wittgenstein observes, facts are determined by the appropriateness of the correlation between language and object, since, as he observes, '(2.021) [o]bjects make up the substance of the world' (Wittgenstein, 2006, p. 7):

> (2.0211) If the world had no substance, then whether a proposition had sense would depend on whether another proposition was true. (2.0212) In that case we could not sketch any picture of the world (true or false). (2.022) It is obvious that an imagined world, however different it may be from the real one, must have *something* – a form – in common with it. (2.023) Objects are just what constitute this unalterable form. (Wittgenstein, 2006, p. 7)

---

2   Ludwig Wittgenstein, *Tractatus Logico-Philosophicus*, D.F. Pears and B.F. McGuinness (trans.) (London: Routledge, 2006), pp. 3–4. Further references are given after quotations in the text.

For Wittgenstein, what prevents language from simply becoming self-referential and postmodern – words merely referring to other words – is whether or not they are 'true or false' in relation to the 'substance' of the world (Wittgenstein, 2006, p. 12).

Such an emphasis upon language as facts and reason can be seen to predominate in DeLillo's early fiction as language is used as a means of establishing and policing a verifiable 'picture of the world'. The Wittgensteinian conception of the λόγος accordingly functions as a means of defending against alterity and the concomitant vulnerability to wounding, stressing the 'logical' and 'factual' over the emotional and (inter)subjective. Such a conception can be observed in DeLillo's second novel, *End Zone*, in which the narrator, Gary Harkness, describes how he is 'fascinated by the way the state troopers copied from each other's little books' in an attempt to reassure themselves as to the factual veracity of their information.[3] Creating a single, unified perspective of events – a 'totality of true thoughts' which form a 'picture of the world' – and eliminating difference, the state troopers 'checked each other out until it was apparent that they had reached an accord'. Through such an effort they could 'safeguard against errors and stray facts', ensuring a fortress-like enunciation undisturbed by doubt or question, centred upon the λόγος (Don DeLillo, *End Zone*, p. 72).

This Wittgensteinian perspective of the 'truth' of a sentence being determined by 'factual' agreement in turn informs Gary's own writing and enunciation, as shown by his use of the same metaphor:

> Maybe the failure was mine, the ill health mine, that blank life a kind of notebook in need of somebody else's facts, those facts a mass of jargon for the military mind, this jargon resembling clichés passed from mourner to mourner in the form of copied notes. But it was just another of my philosophic speculations, to think his life depended on what my mind could make of him, existence turning on a wheel, numerical, nonbuddhist, the notes comforting the notebook, numbers covering the words used to cover silence. (Don DeLillo, *End Zone*, pp. 72–3)

---

[3] Don DeLillo, *End Zone* (London: Penguin, 1986), p. 72. Further references are given after quotations in the text.

Through this inscription of language as a means of 'clothing' thought, the Self can become intelligible, verifiable and comforted, susceptible only to logical relations rather than the unknowability of the silence beyond language. The λόγος thus becomes a solid, unchanging vessel, through which the individual can enunciate his language of Self, evading the emptiness of silence which, as void space, is signifiable by the Other.

This desire to stress logical relations over the chaotic unknowability of what lies beyond language is accordingly a pervasive force in DeLillo's early fiction, receiving further exploration in DeLillo's fifth novel *Players*. As Lyle observes, he 'sometimes carried yellow teleprinter slips with him for days', seeing 'in the numbers and stock symbols an artful reduction of the external world to printed output', one in which '[a]ggression was refined away', along with 'the instinct to possess'.[4] Rather than such subjective phenomena, all Lyle perceives in the teletype are 'fractions, decimal points, plus and minus signs' embodied on a 'paper contain[ing] nerve impulses: a synaptic digit, a phoneme, a dimensionless point', devoid of any representation 'of the competitive mechanism of the world, of greasy teeth engaging on the rim of a wheel' (DeLillo, *Players*, p. 70). Instead of the urges of language's externality, or the incomprehensible, threatening vastness of an unmediated perception of the 'world', immersion in the λόγος allowed the '[i]nked figures' inscribed on the yellow slip to be all that Lyle 'saw', a 'property in its own right, tucked away, his particular share (once removed) of the animal body breathing in the night' (DeLillo, *Players*, p. 70). It is precisely this ordering force which the terrorists in *Players* ostensibly attempt to resist, striving 'to break the inhumanity of power translated into electronic data'.[5]

As both of the above passages indicate, however, while Wittgensteinian language may provide a means of establishing 'a picture of the world', defending against the alterity of the Other and the *Angst* of being-towards-the-end

---

4   Don DeLillo, *Players* (New York: Vintage, 1989), p. 70. Further references are given after quotations in the text.

5   Steffen Hantke, '"God save us from bourgeois adventure": The figure of the terrorist in contemporary American conspiracy fiction', *Studies in the Novel*, 28:2 (1996): pp. 219–44, p. 225.

(*Sein zum Ende*), in so doing, it denies the possibility of authentic intersubjectivity. Such ambiguity was noted, in part, by Wittgenstein, who observed that language was a phenomenon which 'disguises thought', even as it allows the possibility of its communication (Wittgenstein, 2006, p. 22). The metaphor which Wittgenstein utilizes to explore this is that of 'clothing':

> [...] from the outward form of the clothing it is impossible to infer the form of the thought beneath it, because the outward form of the clothing is not designed to reveal the form of the body, but for entirely different purposes. (Wittgenstein, 2006, p. 22)

For the Wittgenstein of the *Tractatus*, language is thus a phenomenon which occurs after cognition, 'clothing' and obscuring a supposedly 'deeper', logical truth of the subject's thought processes, though in return allowing these 'thoughts' to be at least partially communicable. It is precisely this ambiguity which allows DeLillo's characters to use the protective qualities of Wittgensteinian language to turn the λόγος into a fortress-like enunciation of Self which seemingly occupies every contestable space.

The Wittgensteinian conception of language present in DeLillo's texts is not solely limited to the theories advanced in the *Tractatus*, however, and the *Philosophical Investigations* can also be seen to have considerable impact. Focusing upon the manner in which 'individual words in language name objects' and positing sentences as 'combinations of such names',[6] the *Philosophical Investigations* coins the term '"language-games"' (Wittgenstein, 2000, p. 5), arguing that '[f]or a *large* class of cases – though not for all – in which we employ the word "meaning" it can be defined thus: the meaning of a word is its use in the language' (Wittgenstein, 2000, pp. 20–1). It is no longer the accordance with the world of objects which is pre-eminent but instead language's relativism, its accommodation of meaning.

Using the metaphor of American football, *End Zone* also explores this latter conception of language, focusing upon the ways in which plays come into existence and evolve, in a manner analogous to Wittgenstein's

---

6   Ludwig Wittgenstein, *Philosophical Investigations*, G.E.M. Anscombe (trans.) (London: Blackwell, 2000), p. 2. Further references are given after quotations in the text.

use of the metaphor of a stonemason, his apprentice, and the tools with which they interact.[7] As DeLillo observes, football 'is the one sport guided by language, by the word signal, the snap number, the color code, the play name' (DeLillo, *End Zone*, pp. 111–13). Just as with the stonemason's tools, the plays are pre-existing forms, since, as Gary observes, '[a]ll teams run the same plays'. What differs is that 'each team uses an entirely different system of naming', correlating to Wittgenstein's concept of 'language-games' in which the word used is nominal and meaning arises through mutual accord (DeLillo, *End Zone*, p. 118).

Through this sporting metaphor Gary is able to show how the importance of the Wittgensteinian conception of λόγος is not just valuable as a means of establishing 'order', but that it also provides an exemplar of how the act of naming fulfils 'part of the spectator's need' to 'sort the many levels of material: to allot, to compress, to catalogue', thereby providing social cohesion through a collective representation of the world; a supposedly 'benign illusion' in which meaning is established through collective use (DeLillo, *End Zone*, pp. 111–13). The corollary, however, of this collective naming and participation, is that less room is left for individual expression. Communal naming can instead facilitate the publicness of *das Man*, rather than the mediated intersubjective production of care (*Sorge*) and concern (*sorgen*).

The inherently political dimension of such fetishizing of λόγος and reason has also been noted in the writing of Jacques Lacan, who observes that it is the ostensible universality of the proper name and its relation to the 'substance' of the world which shapes 'the value of a language as speech', measured 'by the intersubjectivity of the "we" it takes':[8] namely the extent to which language can encompass, define and absorb individual forms of

---

7   The name of the institution of higher learning which Harkness attends is Logos college, highlighting the centrality of language and reason in DeLillo's novel. In addition, it also alludes to the extent to which its students are characters who comprise a larger form of denotation.

8   Jacques Lacan, 'The Function and Field of Speech and Language in Psychoanalysis', in *Ecrits*, Alan Sheridan (trans.) (London: Routledge, 2005), pp. 23–86, p. 64. Further references are given after quotations in the text.

subjectivity and expression, and offer access instead to a seemingly universal, symbolic subjectivity.

In thus 'lay[ing] down the elementary structures of culture'[9] language becomes a site of contestation since, as Lacan observes, 'language and its structure exist prior' to the subject's 'entry', and, as a result, 'the subject, too, if he can appear to be the slave of language is all the more so of a discourse in the universal movement in which his place is already inscribed at birth' (Lacan, *The Agency of the Letter*, pp. 112–13). Policed through the phallologocentric dominance of the 'law,' Lacan observes that the *nom du père* 'revealed clearly enough as identical with an order of language', which through the act of naming, functions as a deployment of such power. As Lacan notes, 'without kinship nominations, no power is capable of instituting the order of preferences and taboos that bind and weave' the relations between subject, culture and environment (Lacan, *The Field and Function of Speech*, p. 49).

Such an attempt at phallologocentric policing can also be observed in *End Zone*'s portrayal of Gary's college football coach:

> Emmett Creed moved his right foot over the grass, a few inches either way. This was his power, to deny us the words we needed. He was the maker of plays, the namegiver. We were his chalk-scrawls. (DeLillo, *End Zone*, p. 135)

Through his control of the language they can use, Emmett dominates Gary and the other footballers, denying or allowing words with which to express thought and thereby shaping the 'picture of the world' to which they have access.[10] Through the 'clothing' of thought by language, the Other can accordingly be transformed into a text, subject to phallologocentric editing and authorial control, reduced to 'chalk-scrawls' to be erased and re-patterned at will. As Gary notes, within such a context '[w]ords move

---

9 Jacques Lacan, 'The Agency of the Letter in the Unconscious or Reason Since Freud', in *Ecrits*, Alan Sheridan (trans.) (London: Routledge, 2005), pp. 111–36, p. 11. Further references are given after quotations in the text.
10 The description of individuals as chalk scrawls also links to the discussion of character as graven mark advanced in *The Names*.

the body into position' and '[i]n time the position itself dictates events', becoming almost mathematical in its indifference to subjective experience (DeLillo, *End Zone*, p. 45).

While Wittgenstein may not have explored the externality of language, he did build upon the concept of language-games and proposed two further interrelated terms – 'grammar' and 'private language' – which emphasize the social significance of the gap between thought and λόγος. Arguing for the concept of a private language, Wittgenstein demonstrates the relativity of sensation, stating that while everyone can feel pain and can use the same word to describe the experience, the particularity of a particular instance of the phenomenon is non-transferable.[11] While the same word appears to refer to the same thing – and according to the factual emphasis of the *Tractatus* would be treated identically – the *Philosophical Investigations* argues that it merely refers to something comparable and that such comparability is determined through the play of language-games:

> [...] imagine a language in which a person could write down or give vocal expression to his inner experiences – his feelings, moods, and the rest – for his private use? – Well, can't we do so in our ordinary language? – But that is not what I mean. The individual words of this language are to refer to what can only be known to the person speaking; to his immediate private sensations. So another person cannot understand the language. (Wittgenstein, 2000, pp. 88–9)

Any act of denotation thus simultaneously functions on two levels of discourse, a private and a public strata, paralleling the basic paradigm of Julia Kristeva's theory of poetic language,[12] that of the symbolic and semiotic.

Whereas for Kristeva, the 'private language' of the semiotic operates at a largely subconscious level, only revealing itself in the kinetic motility of rhythm and pause, for Wittgenstein it exists instead in the gap between subject and object – the predicate – across which any communication is always an act of translation: an idiosyncratic specificity of meaning which

---

[11] Interestingly, Heidegger's argument for the untransferable nature of being-towards-death (*Sein sum Tode*) follows the same basic form as that of Wittgenstein.
[12] Julia Kristeva, *Revolution in Poetic Language* (New York, NY: Columbia University Press, 1984). Further references are given after quotations in the text.

is sacrificed for social intelligibility. The process by which this latter effect occurred was what Wittgenstein termed as 'grammar', a process superficially similar to the action of Kristeva's symbolic. As with the latter concept, Wittgenstein argues that 'grammar' is determined by logical relations and 'does not tell us how language must be constructed in order to fulfil its purpose', which instead 'only describes and in no way explains the use of signs' (Wittgenstein, 2000, p. 138).

Just as with Kristeva's symbolic, Wittgenstein's philosophy seems to propose that social relations and regulations are encoded in the structuring forces of language. As he observes, '*[e]ssence* is expressed by grammar' and it is '[g]rammar [which] tells what kind of object anything is', combining to create what Wittgenstein terms '[t]heology as grammar' (Wittgenstein, 2000, p. 116). Unlike Kristeva's theory, however, Wittgenstein's concept of this social dimension remains within the boundaries of his focus upon language. While the former proposed that the symbolic was rooted in the Oedipal structures surrounding the mother's body, and the social prohibitions which restrain the subject's access to the *jouissance* which only her corporeality can provide, Wittgenstein's concept of grammar is carefully circumspect. As he observes, to 'say "This combination of words makes no sense" excludes it from the sphere of language and thereby bounds the domain of language' (Wittgenstein, 2000, pp. 138–9), but he chooses not to speculate upon what motivates this exclusionary practice.

Unlike Kristeva, Wittgenstein is reluctant to apply his observation beyond the sphere of language and its relation to thought:

> [...] when one draws a boundary it may be for various kinds of reason. If I surround an area with a fence or a line or otherwise, the purpose may be to prevent someone from getting in or out; but it may also be part of a game and the players be supported, say, to jump over the boundary; or it may shew where the property of one man ends and that of another begins; and so on. So if I draw a boundary line that is not yet to say what I am drawing it for. (Wittgenstein, 2000, pp. 138–9)

It is this careful – and self-conscious – unwillingness to speculate upon the social impact of grammar which sets his work apart from the later theories of Kristeva. As he observes, the 'rules of grammar may be called "arbitrary", if that is to mean that the *aim* of the grammar is nothing but that of the language' (Wittgenstein, 2000, p. 138). In an analogue to his maxim at the end of the *Tractatus* Wittgenstein again chooses to leave unexplored what exists beyond language.

While Wittgenstein may be reluctant to apply his theories beyond the strict parameters which he sets, such hesitancy is not present in DeLillo's novels. The former's concept of private language finds its analogue in *End Zone* during the prelude to a football game. As Gary observed, '[i]n the runway a few people made their private sounds, fierce alien noises having nothing to do with speech or communication of any kind', yet still their 'frantic breathing' contained 'elements of chant, each man's sound unique', literally a private language which gives form to the idiosyncratic, untransferable sensation of heading out for a match. Each 'unique' utterance, however, 'mated to the other sounds,' becoming 'a mass rhythmic breathing that became more widespread as we emerged from the runway and trotted onto the field' (DeLillo, *End Zone*, pp. 106–7). Becoming part of a wider social grammar, such utterances form the basis of a public language and a fallen language of Self, emphasizing collectivity, yet simultaneously limiting the possibility of wounding through an imposition of an 'arbitary' logical structure upon the chaos of silence.

The externality of Wittgenstein's concept of grammar is also explored within the novel and its application is taken far beyond the limits which the philosopher imposed upon his own project. Through the figure of Anatole, who has headed to Logos College in an attempt to 'unjew' himself, grammar is explored as a means of ensuring hegemony and eliminating difference. Heading 'to a place where there aren't any Jews', Anatole attempts to 'revise' his 'way of speaking' in the hope that by so doing he can alter his enunciation. Through this extrapolation of the idea of grammar into a wider conception of social externality, the interrelation of power and ethnic difference is explored in relation to a homogeneous (ideologically White, Anglo-Saxon, Protestant) campus community. Through the removal of the 'urbanisms', 'folk wisdom', 'melodies' and 'inverted sentences' from his speech and their replacement by 'a completely different set of words and phrases', Anatole hopes to 'transform' his 'mind into a ruthless instrument' which 'reject[s] certain categories of thought' (DeLillo, *End Zone*, pp. 46–7). Correlating to an uninflected understanding of the

Wittgensteinian conception of language, Anatole highlights the danger posed by an insensitivity to the relationship between power and the λόγος central to language's externality and to phallologocentricism.

Such a conception is echoed by Bobby Brand in *Americana* who has also undertaken a comparable project of grammatical cleansing, believing that his 'brain needs cleaning out', since, as he observes, 'I think the way I talk' (DeLillo, *Americana*, p. 113). Adopting a conventional, dominant form of language, Bobby is attempting to re-inscribe his Self to fit within a majority pattern and hegemonic power, abandoning the authenticity of his own racial and individual difference. As Bobby observes, since he 'want[s] to be colorless' he has gone into 'exile' in an attempt to remove the 'insidious' racial argot from his Self, since, in his opinion, it is such difference which 'leads to violence' (DeLillo, *Americana*, p. 113):

> The old violence. I thought it was gone but I can feel it coming back. Correctly or not I associate blandness with non-violence. That's why I want to be bland. To use bland words. Do bland things. I've been trying not to arouse the old instincts. You can arouse them with words, mainly slang words. (DeLillo, *Americana*, pp. 251-2)

Problematically, however, the 'blandness' to which Bobby refers is simply the homogenization of the language of the white majority, that of *das Man*, consisting of the elimination of difference and an uncritical imposition of Wittgenstein's conception of grammar.

The failure of Bobby's 'blandness' and Anatole's process of 'unjewing' shows how the phallologocentrism of Wittgenstein's theory of language and its rejection of metaphysics proves to be an inadequate vessel for a fulfilling language of Self. Though Anatole may have headed to the desert in an attempt at 'straightening out' his 'grammar' – to begin 'to think more clearly, to concentrate, to leave behind the old words and aromas and guilts' – the impossibility of such an endeavour is shown by the aftermath of his mother's death and the confrontation it forces with his historicity (*Historizität*), just as Nick was forced to confront the legacy of his own past. Once Anatole hears that she has been killed '[i]t all came back, who I was, what I was, where the past crossed over into the present and from being to being' – a succinct summary of Heidegger's theory of historicity (*Historizität*). It is precisely this issue of Being which was inimical to Wittgenstein's project, revealing how far death has taken Anatole from his previous absorption within Wittgensteinian grammar (DeLillo, *End Zone*, pp. 187–8).

Confronting his historicity in the aftermath of his mother's demise, Anatole abandons verbal language and his pursuit of an immersion within the limiting forms of Wittgensteinian grammar. While he refused to 'go home to look at her small dead body' since it 'would have been too much of a bringing back', leaving him 'sure' that he 'would never recover from the unspeakable heartbreak and Jewishness of her funeral', the effect still lingers within him, shaping his present and future. Rather than attending the ceremony, he instead 'went into the desert with a paintbrush and a can of black paint', finding amongst 'all those flat stones' 'a single round one'. Rather than using a language governed by Wittgensteinian grammar to engage with this loss, Anatole instead takes this unique stone and 'painted it black', denoting it from amongst the others to form his 'mother's burial marker', a personal act of signification, and an implicit rejecting of Wittgensteinian limitations (DeLillo, *End Zone*, pp. 187–8).

A similar non-comformity can also be observed in Gary Harkness' relationship with Myna. Together they attempt to shape a new form of language, one which, rather than being governed by phallologocentricism, instead attempts to explore alternative ways of Being. As Lacan argues, the phallus forms 'the privileged signifier of that mark in which the role of the logos is joined with the advent of desire',[13] ensuring that, as Hélène Cixous notes, the majority of male subjects remain 'bound' to this phallolinguistic order through their 'antiquated relation – servile, calculating – to mastery'.[14] Such a relation, however, requires male subjects such as Gary to 'engag[e] only the tiniest part of the body', their phallus, in the sustaining such a public enunciation (Cixous, 1976, p. 881). To maintain this investment,

---

13   Jacques Lacan, 'The Signification of the Phallus', in *Ecrits*, Alan Sheridan (trans.) (London: Routledge, 2005), pp. 215–22, p. 220. Further references are given after quotations in the text.
14   Hélène Cixous, 'The Laugh of the Medusa', Keith Cohen and Paula Cohen (trans.), in *Signs*, 1:4 (1976), pp. 875–93, p. 881. Further references are given after quotations in the text.

'With a word they could begin to grid the world' 83

however, individuals such as Gary must be willing to restricting themselves to a 'glorious phallic monosexuality' (Cixous, 1976, p. 884) in which the 'function of the phallic signifier touches here on its most profound relation: that in which the Ancients embodied the Νους [mind] and the Λογος' (Lacan, *The Signification of the Phallus*, p. 222).

As Cixous notes, however, while conventional 'masculine sexuality gravitates around the penis', ensuring the phallologocentricism of language, 'woman does not bring about the same regionalization which serves the couple head/genitals and which is inscribed only within [such] boundaries' (Cixous, 1976, p. 880). It is in this respect that Cixous considers the potential entry of the female body into language as a means by which 'the strength of women' can be responsible for 'sweeping away syntax, breaking that famous thread (just a tiny little thread, they say) which acts for men as a surrogate umbilical cord, assuring them' of their continued dominance and centrality (Cixous, 1976, p. 886). In order to prevent such potential destabilization, 'the repression of women' has formed a 'locus' by which any 'space that can serve as a springboard for subversive thought', or as 'the precursory movement of a transformation of social and cultural structures', is eliminated (Cixous, 1976, p. 886). The means by which this policing and elimination has occurred is through the dominance of 'a libidinal and cultural – hence political, typically masculine – economy' (Cixous, 1976, p. 879). The co-extensive role of both phallus and λόγος in this process of policing is underlined by Cixous who notes that '[n]early the entire history of writing is confounded with the history of reason, of which it is at once the effect, the support, and one of the privileged alibis' of the prevailing social order, forming the cornerstone of a 'self-admiring, self-stimulating, self-congratulatory phallocentrism' (Cixous, 1976, p. 879).

Yet, as Cixous proceeds to note, '[t]here are some men (all too few) who aren't afraid of femininity' (Cixous, 1976, p. 885), men who are 'capable of loving love and hence capable of loving others and of wanting them, of imagining the woman who would hold out against oppression and constitute herself as a superb, equal, hence "impossible" subject, untenable in a real social framework' (Cixous, 1976, p. 879). Rather than fearing this capacity to 'brea[k] the codes that negate her', for such men this destabilization is instead something to celebrate as it offers the possibility of 'bring[ing] on, if not revolution – for the bastion was supposed to be immutable – at least harrowing explosions' in the edifice of a limiting, phallologocentric order (Cixous, 1976, p. 879). For Cixous, the means by which women can bring about such destabilization is through the female body and its drives, and, as Cixous notes of such a woman, 'she doesn't deny' the 'prodigious' and transgressive '"economy" of her drives' and 'the intractable and impassioned part' which they play in her discourse (Cixous, 1976, pp. 881–2). Such an individual, as Cixous notes, thus 'throws her trembling body forward; she lets go of herself, she flies; all of her passes into her voice, and it's with her body that she vitally supports the "logic" of her speech' and '*inscribes* what she's saying', 'signif[ying] it with her body' (Cixous, 1976, p. 881). As a result, such trangressive female 'libido will produce far more radical effects of political and social change than some might like to think' (Cixous, 1976, p. 882), creating a space and a permeability which 'break[s] the old circuits' of a phallologocentric order, 'render[ing] obsolete the former relationship and all its consequences', whilst 'launching' a 'brand-new subject, alive, with defamilialization' which characterizes 'a thrilling era of the body' (Cixous, 1976, p. 890).

While for the majority of the novel Gary struggles to conform himself to a phallic sexuality centred upon λόγος as reason, the evolving nature of his relationship with Myna offers the possibility of alternative forms of being. Sitting in the library with Myna, Gary transgresses the boundaries of his limited, phallocentric enunciation. As he observes, together they 'selected certain words to read aloud' (DeLillo, *End Zone*, pp. 216–17):

> We read them slowly, syllable by syllable, taking turns, using at times foreign or regional accents, then replaying the sounds, perhaps backward, perhaps starting with a middle syllable, and finally reading the word as word, overpronouncing slightly, noses to the page as if in search of protomorphic spoor. (DeLillo, *End Zone*, pp. 216–17)

Through their deconstruction of the sounds of language, they separate each word from its assigned meanings – the Wittgensteinian, symbolic formulation of meaning as general use – instead reconfiguring them into something that resembles a private language which they share and create together: a means of expressing not just a purely idiosyncratic sensation but also a mutual experience of Heideggerian intersubjectivity rooted in care (*Sorge*) and being-with-others (*Mitsein Andere*). There is no factual information to be conveyed in their shared speech, no logical relations, no 'picture of the world' to be created, or thought to be 'clothed'. The focus of their language is instead purely one of emotion and sensation, as shown by Myna's reaction to '[s]ome of the words' which 'put' her 'into a state of mild delirium' through their 'almost excessive' 'beauty' (DeLillo, *End Zone*, pp. 216–17).

As with Anatole, it is again Being and externality which characterizes the language Gary and Myna create. As Gary observes, the 'words were ways of touching and made us want to speak with hands', to develop new forms of signification unbounded by Wittgensteinian grammar and which, as Cixous proposed, allow the entry of the female body and its drives into the phallocentric realm of the symbolic. The sexual congress which follows, while still a form of denotation, is no longer centred upon the phallus, dominated by logical relations, and Gary instead made 'bubbling' sounds and 'strange noises of anticipation (*gwa, gwa*)'. As he observes, '[t]o mark the event I brought new noises to the room, vowel sounds predominating', and in return, as 'Myna stepped away from the clothes, aware of the moment's dynamics' she in turn 'positing herself as the knowable word, the fleshmade sigh and syllable.' It is this concept of the inextricability of the body and language, which marks a significant break from the rigours of the Wittgensteinian anti-metaphysical turn and towards Cixous' *Écriture féminine*. Emotive and existential, the form of language which Gary and Myra create opens the Self to the alterity of the Other, abandoning phallic mastery, and engendering an enunciation which stresses connection and rejects the logic of Wittgensteinian linguistic philosophy (DeLillo, *End Zone*, pp. 216–18).

In DeLillo's 'middle' period, this concern with language's sensitivity to ontological concerns encouraged a gradual transition to a conception of denotation which correlates to the *linguistic* philosophy of Walter Benjamin. Rather than the distinction between the two philosophers originating from radically differing foundational principles, it is instead in terms of their divergent conclusions that the contrast becomes apparent. The most central of their shared ideas is that language 'clothes' thought in a manner which makes it apprehendable. As Benjamin observes, '[l]inguistic "transference" enables us to give material form to the invisible – "A mighty fortress is our God"' – and thus to render it capable of being experienced.[15] It is for this reason that he observes that '[e]very expression of human mental life can be understood as a kind of language' (Benjamin, 1997, p. 62). While the initial purpose of language to make visible the invisibility of 'mental life' may be the same as in Wittgenstein's linguistic theory, the conclusion which is drawn is radically different.

While denying what he terms as a 'mystical linguistic theory' in which 'the word is simply perceived as the essence of the thing' (Benjamin, 1997, p. 69), Benjamin equally considers such logocentric views as those of Wittgenstein's meaning-as-use to be an inadequate conception of language. Terming such a perspective as a 'bourgeois conception' which perceives the sole 'addressee [as] a human being' (Benjamin, 1997, p. 65), Benjamin argues for a more diffuse understanding:

> [...] it is no longer conceivable, as the bourgeois view of language maintains, that the word has an accidental relation to its object, that it is a sign for things (or knowledge of them) agreed by some convention. Language never gives *mere* signs. (Benjamin, 1997, p. 69)

Proposing a hybridized conception of language, Benjamin lays the groundwork for a distinction between different 'levels' of denotation, observing that 'the German language, for example, is by no means the expression of everything that we could – theoretically – express *through* it, but is instead the direct expression of that which communicates *itself* in it' (Benjamin, 1997, p. 63). Like Kristeva's symbolic/semiotic divide, such a nuance provides Benjamin's theory with a way of exploring how different social and personal levels of meaning can exist within a single utterance.

---

15 Walter Benjamin, 'On Language as Such and on the Language of Man' in M. Bullock and M. Jennings (eds) *Selected Writings Volume 1 1913–1926* (London: The Belknap Press of Harvard University Press, 1997), pp. 62–74, p. 20. Further references are given after quotations in the text.

Unlike the personal urges versus social order of Kristevan theory, or the factual versus the untransferable of Wittgenstein's private language, what is conveyed in Benjamin's theory is 'the mental entity that communicates itself in language', 'not language itself but something to be distinguished from it' (Benjamin, 1997, p. 63). Within such a conception, '[l]anguages, therefore, have no speaker, if this means someone who communicates *through* these languages' since it is instead '[m]ental being [which] communicates itself in, not through, a language, which means that it is not outwardly identical to linguistic being' (Benjamin, 1997, p. 63). As Benjamin observes:

> [...] because nothing is communicated through language, what is communicated in language cannot be externally limited or measured, and therefore all language contains its own incommensurable, uniquely constituted infinity. Its linguistic being, not its verbal contents, defines its frontier. [...] man communicates his own mental being *in* his language. Man therefore communicates his own mental being (insofar as it is communicable) by *naming* all other things. (Benjamin, 1997, p. 64)

Rather than 'verbal contents' defining the horizon of language – as in Wittgenstein's theory – it is linguistic being – what is communicated in language – which is instead 'its frontier', realized through the process of 'transference'.

It is in this theorizing beyond the 'bourgeois conception of language' to questions of Being that Benjamin's thought shows the greatest divergence from Wittgenstein's conception. As the latter noted:

> You always hear people say that Philosophy makes no progress and that the same philosophical problems which were already preoccupying the Greeks are still troubling us today. But people who say that do not understand the reason why it has to be so. The reason is that our language has remained the same and always introduces us to the same questions. As long as there is a verb 'be' which seems to work like 'eat' and 'drink'; as long as there are adjectives like 'identical', 'true', 'false', 'possible'; as long as people speak of the passage of time and of the extent of space, and so on; as long as all this happens people will always run up against the same teasing difficulties and will stare at something which no explanation seems able to remove.[16]

---

16   Ludwig Wittgenstein, 'The Nature of Philosophy', *The Wittgenstein Reader*, Anthony Kenny (ed.) (London: Blackwell, 2006), pp. 46–69, pp. 55–6.

While Wittgenstein dismisses such confusion as an error of language – which philosophy can explore and clarify – for Benjamin this confusion is the result of the residue of 'linguistic being' which communicates itself *in*, rather than *through*, language. In a manner similar to that of Kristeva, Benjamin argued that '[w]ithin all linguistic formation a conflict is waged between what is expressed and expressible and what is inexpressible and unexpressed' (Benjamin, 1997, p. 66). It is this 'other conception of language', of the 'inexpressible and unexpressed' which, in Benjamin's view, 'knows no means, no object, and no addressee of communication' (Benjamin, 1997, p. 65).

Such a struggle between the effable and the ineffable can be observed in *Players*, a transitional text in DeLillo's depiction of the λόγος. While Lyle's absorption in the teleprinter strip represents an attempt to embrace Wittgensteinian grammar as a means of defending the Self, Jack's use of language instead correlates to a Benjaminian conception, conveying his yearning enunciation of Self. As his partner Ethan notes, periodically Jack gets obsessed with places to which he's never been:

> 'It's the driving force of his life, suddenly, out of nowhere, this thing, Maine, this word, which is all it is, since he's never been there.' (DeLillo, *Players*, p. 20)

While Ethan analyses Jack's obsession with the word Maine on a Wittgensteinian, factual level, what is significant about his wish is the sudden 'driving force' which is conveyed *in* rather than *through* the word. Unlike Ethan, Pammy is able to appreciate Jack's utterance on this Benjaminian level as a means of conveying the force, longing and idiosyncracy of his language of Self. As she observes, '[i]t's simple maybe, Ethan, but it has a strength to it', a 'sort of core, the moral core' (DeLillo, *Players*, p. 20). Rather than Ethan's literal interpretation, Pammy knows that 'Jack has the inner meanings of it, the pure parts' and while she claims that they 'both know this about Jack', it is seemingly something which only she appreciates (DeLillo, *Players*, p. 20):

> To forge a change that you may be reluctant to forge, that may be problematical for this or that reason, you have to tell people. You have to talk and tell me. Jack sees what I'm getting at. You have to bring it out. Even if you have no intention at the

> time of doing it out of whatever fear or trembling, you still must make it begin to come true by articulating it. This changes the path of your life. Just telling people makes the change begin to happen. If, in the end, you choose to keep going with whatever you've been doing that's been this problematical thing in your life, well and good, it's up to you. But if you need to feel you're on the verge of a wonderful change, whether you are or not, the thing to do is tell people. 'I am on the verge of a wonderful change. I am about to do something electrifying. The very fibres of your being will be electrified, sir, when I tell you what it is I propose to do.' To speak it in words is to see the possibility emerge. (DeLillo, *Players*, p. 43)

Using the λόγος as a repository, the 'electrified' 'fibres' of 'being' find expression *in*, rather than *through* language – the Benjaminian 'mental being' as a conduit for the language of Self.

A similar appreciation of this transmission of 'mental being' is also shown by Pammy in her reaction to a TV talk show:

> On the screen some people on a talk show discussed taxes. Something about the conversation embarrassed her. She didn't know what it was exactly. Nobody said stupid things or had speech defects. There were no public service commercials showing athletes teaching retarded children to play basketball. It wasn't a case of some woman in a news film speaking ungrammatically about her three children, just killed in a fire. (She wondered if she'd become too complex to put death before grammar.) These people discussed taxes, embarrassingly. What was happening in that little panel of light that caused her to feel such disquiet and shame? She put her hands over her ears and watched Lyle read. (DeLillo, *Players*, p. 57)

Sensing their 'linguistic being' conveyed *in* the language they use, Pammy is exposed to their alterity, opening herself to a wounding which she has no desire to experience.

For Benjamin, however, this concept of the transmission of 'linguistic being' is not solely limited to alterity, but instead, through the utilization of '*the name*', is also granted a theistic dimension. Language is thus perceived as the means by which '*the mental being of man communicates itself to God*' (Benjamin, 1997, p. 65). Using scriptural justification, Benjamin refers to the Talmudic story of creation to argue that '[t]he paradisiacal language of man must have been one of perfect knowledge, whereas later all knowledge is again infinitely differentiated in the multiplicity of language, was indeed forced to differentiate itself on a lower level as creation in name'

(Benjamin, 1997, p. 71). This concept of fallen, human-word as something separate from the language of God allows the creation of these two levels of language, one of perfect knowledge and an essential relationship between name and object – that of the divine – and a lapsarian human province of name which is nominal and referential:

> For according to mystical theory, the word is simply the essence of the thing. That is incorrect, because the thing in itself has no word, being created from God's word and known in its name by a human word. (Benjamin, 1997, p. 69)

As Benjamin observes, 'the Fall marks the birth of the *human word*, in which name no longer lives intact and which has stepped out of name-language,' making 'language a means (that is, a knowledge inappropriate to him), and therefore also, in one part at any rate, a *mere* sign' (Benjamin, 1997, pp. 71–2).

In spite of this 'bourgeois' dimension, signification is not perceived as a wholly nominal process of meaning as use, but instead a 'translation of the language of things into that of man', transposing 'the nameless into name'. 'The objectivity of this translation', for Benjamin, is 'guaranteed by God', since, within the Talmudic perspective, 'God created things' and 'the creative word in them is the germ of the cognizing name, just as God, too, finally named each thing after it was created.' This relation between a germ of divine language and that of the language of man is the means by which a name can communicate both factual information and the mental Being of man, inexpressible, yet communicated *in* language due to its relation to the divine (Benjamin, 1997, pp. 69–70).

While *Players* began to explore this conception of 'linguistic being', it was DeLillo's later novel, *The Names*, which fully engaged with this religious dimension of the λόγος. As Owen Brandamas observes, '[i]f you play with the word 'metempsychosis long enough I think you find not only *transfer-of-soul* but you reach the Indo-European root *to breathe*.'[17] It is within this connection between breath and the *transfer-of-soul* that the

---

17 Don Delillo, *The Names* (London: Picador, 1987), pp. 112–13. Further references are given after quotations in the text.

Benjaminian concept of the religious dimension of language is rooted in DeLillo's texts. Language is thus 'the experience that goes deeper than the sensory apparatus will allow', accessing the '[s]pirit' and 'soul' which 'is tied up with self-perception somehow'. As Owen observes, 'the air is full of words' and through this relation between breath and the *transfer-of-soul* he comes to the conclusion that '[m]aybe it's full of perceptions too, feelings, memories' (DeLillo, *The Names*, pp. 112–13).

Such a conception is also shared by James Axton, the novel's narrator. Imagining a group of holy men, he stresses how 'beautiful' they would be 'to see, leaning on staffs, mind-scorched, empty-eyed, men in the dust of India, lips moving to the endless name of God', which, as James speculates, is that of '[t]he alphabet' (DeLillo, *The Names*, p. 92). While the reference James uses is from the Asian subcontinent, evoking for an American of his socio-economic status a pleasing oriental exoticism, the allusion also has Judaeo-Christian connotations. As John of the Revelation states, '"I am Alpha and Omega", says the Lord God, "who is and who was and who is coming, the Almighty"',[18] echoing the opening of John's Gospel which states that '[i]n the beginning was the Word, and the Word was with God, and the Word was God.'[19] Thus, from both an Eastern and a Christian, Western context, *The Names* advances the sense of God as the start and endpoint of existence and Being – the horizon of the language of Self as well as that of the λόγος – and it is this which is expressed by the medium of language and its ability to convey 'linguistic being' *in* the word.

Observing the cult's fascination with ancient languages, Owen notes that they 'wanted to hear about ancient alphabets' and their evolution, of 'the Pylos tablet', 'Linear B', which constituted a 'plea for divine intercession', taking the form of a 'list of sacrifices that included ten humans' (DeLillo, *The Names*, p. 116). While as Longmuir observes, much 'existing academic criticism reduces *The Names* to an abstract analysis of language',[20] margin-

---

18 'Revelation', *The Bible* (Swindon: Bible Society, 1994), 1:8.
19 'The Gospel According to St. John', *The Bible* (Swindon: Bible Society, 1994), 1:1.
20 Anne Longmuir, 'The Language of History: Don DeLillo's *The Names* and the Iranian Hostage Crisis', *Critique*, 46:2 (2005): pp. 105–23, p. 106.

alizing the extent to which such exploration is set 'within a very specific location and period',[21] an appreciation of Benjaminian linguistic theory demonstrates that such seemingly abstract analysis is neither a-political nor a-historical. Rather than merely the historical intertexts which Longmuir stresses, it is also the *Historizität* of linguistic theory which provides such nuance and context, leading James to pose the question of whether 'this murder [could] be a latter-day plea to the gods' (DeLillo, *The Names*, p. 116), tied to a historicity of language which continues to shape behaviour in the present, grounded in the same perceived 'inseparability of pattern and power'.[22] Conceiving of pattern as the 'secret power' of the λόγος, 'Nameforms' become 'an important element' in the cult's 'program', 'a way of escaping the world' and 'opening into the self' (DeLillo, *The Names*, p. 210). It is precisely through their conception of God as '[t]he river of language', correlating with Benjaminian theory, that the cult attempts to create an enunciation of Self which connects with a conception of the divine rooted in a particular *Historizität* of abstract theology and linguistic theory (DeLillo, *The Names*, pp. 151–2).

While the cultists live at the extreme margins of society, this link between language and religion within the novel is not solely limited to the distant past or to the foreign occult. As James observes, when they 'entered through the Damascus Gate and were caught at once in the polyglot surge', they were left feeling 'crowded by languages' (DeLillo, *The Names*, p. 145). This sense of the λόγος as something which surrounds the Self, the river enveloping Dasein's Being, is even more pronounced at the end of the novel when James finally relents and visits the Parthenon:

> People come through the gateway, people in streams and clusters, in mass assemblies. No one seems to be alone. This is a place to enter in crowds, seek company and talk. Everyone is talking. I move past the scaffolding and walk down the steps, hearing one language after another, rich, harsh, mysterious, strong. This is what we bring to the temple, not prayer or chant or slaughtered rams. Our offering is language. (DeLillo, *The Names*, p. 331)

21 Ibid., p. 106.
22 Matthew J. Morris, 'Murdering Words: Language in Action in Don DeLillo's *The Names*' in *Contemporary Literature*, 30:1 (1989), pp. 113–27, p. 114.

Language as an 'offering' thus raises the question of whether 'religion [was] the point or language?' or merely a 'costume' (DeLillo, *The Names*, p. 145).

Meditating upon this issue, Owen and James debate the historical fate of the Aramaic alphabet. As the former observes, all that remains are 'sounds' which 'travelled in history with the Jews', 'mixed with other languages' and 'carried by religion'. As Owen proceeds to note, 'now it [also] fades because of religion, because of Islam, Arabic'. It is thus 'religion that carries a language', and it is for this reason that Owen proposes that '[t]he river of language is God.' While a word may convey meaning *through* its form, it is sound which is the means *in* which 'linguistic being' is conveyed, taking the form of the language of Self, embedded in words which plead to the divine for support and intercession (DeLillo, *The Names*, pp. 151–2).

While the unprecedented exoticism of *The Names* allows for an exploration of this religious dimension largely free from issues of Middle American materialism, the novel's depiction of the connection between language and religion is not solely limited to a Mediterranean or Eastern context.[23] Describing his own upbringing in the continental US, Owen observes how he and his parents used to attend a 'congregation of poor people and most of them spoke in tongues' (DeLillo, *The Names*, p. 173). Significantly, however, the language which he uses to describe the scene still has connotations of an alien experience within which he is observing, rather than participating, rooted in issues of socio-economic status. As he notes, it 'was an awesome thing to see and hear' as '[h]is father fell away to some distant place' (DeLillo, *The Names*, p. 173). What is key to this speaking in tongues, from a Benjaminian perspective, is that the words used are contextually nonsensical, an 'insideoutness' of 'sound' and a 'tumbling out of found words' (DeLillo, *The Names*, p. 173). While they may lack meaning conveyed *through* their usage, they represent an attempt at a different type of communication *in* language, a plea through the medium of '*the name*' by which '*the mental being of man communicates itself to God*' (Benjamin,

---

23 *Americana* (1971), *Great Jones Street* (1973), *Players* (1977) and *Running Dog* (1978) were all largely set in New York. All other sections of the novels, as well *End Zone* (1972) and *Ratner's Star* (1976), were located within the continental US.

1997, p. 65). Owen, however, cannot bring himself to communicate in such a direct way with the divine, and is instead left with a self-conscious appreciation of the 'strangeness' of the sight for a boy who 'didn't know the experience'. His desired form of enunciation being one of partial publicness, Owen attempts to resist unmediated connection by perceiving what occurs through a 'bourgeois conception of language'. In so doing, however, he is left with 'his lonely wanting, his need for safety and twice-seen light.' Since Owen's language of Self remains within a largely Middle American context, he is left feeling lonely by the experience, desiring an authenticity of existence which only a connection with the divine can provide (DeLillo, *The Names*, p. 173).

However, while Benjamin's introduction of a religious dimension to the λόγος opened his theory to issues of externality, his philosophy, like that of Wittgenstein, still conceived of thought as extra-linguistic. Like the *Tractatus* which argued that language clothed a peculiarly a-linguistic conception of sentience – simultaneously obscuring yet rendering it visible to others – Benjamin also argued that 'all communication of the contents of the mind is language, communication in words being only a particular case of human language and of the justice, poetry, or whatever underlying it or founded on it' (Benjamin, 1997, p. 65). By arguing that all communication of the mind's contents is language, rather than proposing that it is the contents itself which is linguistic, there is an implicit assumption, like that of Wittgenstein, that thought exists as something extra-linguistic, prior to language.

It is in this respect that both Wittgensteinian and Benjaminian linguistic conceptions reveals their limitations as a vessel for an authentic (*eigentlich*) language of Self. Through their theory of thought as extra-linguistic, preceding language, they both hint at a more stable conception of subjectivity which exists prior to the linguistic, and which, presumably, is a text largely beyond the individual's ability to reinscribe and author. As I have argued, however, for DeLillo's characters the Self is not something stable, preceding interaction and engagement, a-linguistic in nature, but rather something constructed and negotiated, mediated and structured along the fasciae of isolation and connection that are integral to the very possibility of Self. In this respect, Heidegger's phenomenological philosophy of language becomes crucial for an understanding of the way in which the language of Self interacts with the λόγος, allowing it to function as a signifying medium.

It is through a correlation with a Heideggerian conception of language and subjectivity that Nick Shay is able to begin a process of 'minting intellect and shiny soul' after having shot a man (DeLillo, *Underworld*, p. 450). This is best illustrated in Nick's meeting with Father Paulus, who states that one of the central aims of the Jesuit mission in Minnesota is to produce 'decisive', 'serious men' in possession of an 'ethical strength', and the knowledge of 'precisely who [they are and] how [they are] meant to address the world'; individuals possessed of a stable, secure and self-constructed enunciation (DeLillo, *Underworld*, p. 538). In order to achieve this aim, and develop these qualities, Paulus recommends an immersion in the study of the λόγος which, as the Jesuit observes, provides a means of reconceptualizing the self. For Father Paulus, it is because the young Nick does not 'know the names' that he cannot conceive differently of either himself or his environment (DeLillo, *Underworld*, p. 540).

Embracing the discipline of linguistic enquiry as a means of shaping the Self, Nick observes that a mastery and immersion in language is 'the only way in the world you can escape the things that made you' (DeLillo, *Underworld*, p. 543), preventing the Self from 'living in the shallowest turns and bends' of its 'own preoccupations' (DeLillo, *Underworld*, p. 539). Through an immersion in a Heideggerian conception of language, Paulus believes that what he terms as 'the basic human tubing' can be 'unnarrow[ed]' and a new, *eigentlich* form of the language of Self can be devised (DeLillo, *Underworld*, p. 538). Nick is thus able to make 'attempts at analytical insight' in a way that was not possible for him before he possessed the names with which to do so, allowing him to create what Nick's brother, Matt, refers to as a 'self-conscious correctness' – a particular manifestation of the language of Self and the means by which he begins to reconstruct his subjectivity in the wake of his debilitating historicity (*Historizität*) (DeLillo, *Underworld*, p. 450).

It is in DeLillo's subsequent novel, *The Body Artist*, however, that his Heideggerian dimension of the λόγος receives its most extensive exploration. As Lauren observes of Mr Tuttle, there 'was something at the edge' of his voice that was 'unconnected to income levels or verb tenses or what his parents watch on TV'.[24] Rather than everyday, factual information, he instead 'talked about objects in the room, stumblingly, and she wondered what he saw, or failed to see, or saw so differently she could never begin to conjure its outlines' (DeLillo, *The Body Artist*, p. 50). This inability to use language to 'clothe' or 'translate' cognitive processes is linked by Lauren to an equal failure of thought and perception, correlating to the Heideggerian concept of phenomenology as the inextricable interrelation of λόγος and phenomenon (Φαινόμενον). It is thus a concomitant failure of both perception and thought which constituted the 'something at the edge' of Mr Tuttle's voice:

> There was a certain futility in his tone, an endlessness of effort, suggesting things he could not easily make clear to her no matter how much he said. Even his gestures seemed marked by struggle. (DeLillo, *The Body Artist*, pp. 46–7)

Rather than merely suffering a form of agnosia, however, grammatical structures prove as troubling for Mr Tuttle to master. Just as time constitutes the horizon of Being in *Sein und Zeit*, it is also temporality, in *The Body Artist*, which structures the subjectivity formed through the interconnection of λόγος and phenomenon, achieved through the use of tense. As Lauren observes, his 'shift from past tense to present had the sound of something overcome, an obstacle or restriction' (DeLillo, *The Body Artist*, p. 49). In order to transcend this limitation he 'had to extend himself to get it out' and as he struggles 'she heard something in his voice', a striving to master tense in order to understand the role of time in perception, λόγος and the language of Self (DeLillo, *The Body Artist*, p. 49).

For Lauren, time was 'a continuous whole, and the only way to distinguish one part from another, this from that, now from then, is by making arbitrary divisions' through the deployment of tense, preposition and case within the medium of the λόγος. As she notes, '[t]his is exactly what' Mr Tuttle 'doesn't know how to do.' From her perspective it thus seems as if he 'drifts from one reality to another, independent of the logic of time' and as a result of his inability to use language he is also unable to deploy any

---

24 Don DeLillo, *The Body Artist* (London: Picador, 2001), p. 50. Further references are given after quotations in the text.

successful, authentic enunciation of Self. It is only by imposing divisions in time through the λόγος that the subject can engage with its own historicity, shaping its enunciation of Self. For Lauren, as for Heidegger, an individual is consequently 'made out of time' and it is this which is 'the force that tells you who you are' and which 'defines your existence' (DeLillo, *The Body Artist*, p. 107). Through the mediation of tense, it is the λόγος which allows engagement with temporality, structuring and shaping the language of Self.

Without the ability to impose artificial temporal divisions, the λόγος escapes competent use in the formation of the language of Self, resulting in a signification of Being which takes a fluid, uncertain form. Without a proficiency at using the λόγος, Mr Tuttle's language of Self 'laps and seeps, somehow, into other reaches of being, other time-lives, and this is an aspect of his bewilderment and pain' (DeLillo, *The Body Artist*, pp. 91–2):

> Time is the only narrative that matters. It stretches events and makes it possible for us to suffer and come out of it and see death happen and come out of it. But not for him. He is in another structure, another culture, where time is something like itself, sheer and bare, empty of shelter. (DeLillo, *The Body Artist*, pp. 91–2)

Without time as a narrative, a structure, engineered through the λόγος, Mr Tuttle 'didn't know how to measure himself to what we call the Now' (DeLillo, *The Body Artist*, p. 66). Even confronted with the realization of his own existence, the competence with tense that would allow him to shape and structure his enunciation is still elusive:

> 'Being here has come to me. I am with the moment, I will leave the moment. Chair, table, wall, hall, all for the moment, in the moment. Chair, table, wall, hall, all for the moment, in the moment. It had come to me. Here and near. From the moment I am gone, am left, am leaving. I will leave the moment from the moment. [...] Coming and going I am leaving. I will go and come. Leaving has come to me. We all, shall all, will all be left. Because I am here and where. And I will go or not or never. And I have seen what I will see. If I am where I will be. Because nothing comes between me.' (DeLillo, *The Body Artist*, p. 74)

Without such proficiency of tense, preposition and case, he cannot gain the perspective necessary to successfully engage with his own potential for subjectivity.

In the absence of such competence, and deprived of the language of Self, all Mr Tuttle is capable of is the mimicry of the Being of an Other, a desperate attempt to assuage the absence of his own subjectivity. As Lauren notes, 'it wasn't outright impersonation but she heard elements of her voice, the clipped delivery, the slight buzz deep in the throat, her pitch, her sound, and how difficult at first, unearthly almost, to detect her own voice coming from someone else, from him, and then how deeply disturbing' (DeLillo, *The Body Artist*, p. 50). While Lauren concedes that Mr Tuttle is neither her, nor Rey reborn, in the instability of his language of Self Mr Tuttle still 'knew how to make her husband live in the air that rushed from his lungs into his vocal folds – air to sounds, sounds to words, words the man, shaped faithfully on his lips and tongue' (DeLillo, *The Body Artist*, p. 62). It is precisely this concept of transition from breath to sound to word to Self which is the basis of the relationship between the λόγος and the language of Self, linking to the exploration undertaken in *The Names*. As Lauren observes, '[s]he thought in words sometimes, outright and fully formed' and '[s]he wasn't sure when this began to happen, a day or a month ago, because it seemed to have been the case forever' (DeLillo, *The Body Artist*, pp. 113–14). It is this inability to separate thought and λόγος which reveals cognition as inherently linguistic. Any division will by necessity be artificial, a breaking of 'the logistics of word and thought', of λόγος, appearance and subjectivity (DeLillo, *The Body Artist*, pp. 113–14).

In DeLillo's subsequent novel, *Falling Man*, this Heideggerian conception of the λόγος and its relation to the language of Self is explored through the portrayal of Alzheimer's. Key to an understanding of the condition is the relationship between λόγος and the language of Self, captured through 'the first signs of halting response, the losses and failings, the grim prefigurings that issued now and then from a mind beginning to slide away from the adhesive friction that makes an individual possible'.[25] As Lianne observes, this loss of Self 'was in the language, the inverted letters, the lost word at the end of a struggling sentence', visible 'in the handwriting that

---

25   Don DeLillo, *Falling Man* (London: Picador, 2007), p. 30. Further references are given after quotations in the text.

might melt into runoff' (DeLillo, *Falling Man*, p. 30). Just as the loss of language accompanies a loss of the enunciation of Self and the possibility of subjectivity, so too does the λόγος provide 'a chance to encounter the crossing points of insight and memory that the act of writing allows' (DeLillo, *Falling Man*, p. 30). Formulating a containing enunciation of Self against her inexorable decline, Rosellen can only slow rather than halt the 'inevitably' of 'diminishing returns' through an attempt to 'write everything, say everything before it's too late', to enunciate the Self against the inevitability of its eventual destruction (DeLillo, *Falling Man*, p. 60). The condition accordingly provides a microcosm of being-towards-the-end (*Sein zum Ende*), of the construction of an enunciation of Self in the face of the inexorability of the end and the *angst* which such inevitability evokes. After Rosellen has forgotten where she lived, she is left with a sense that '[t]he world was receding' and that she was losing 'the simplest recognitions' (DeLillo, *Falling Man*, pp. 93–4). Fearing that it would continue until '[n]othing lay around her but silence and distance', Rosellen embodies the manner in which the two states of the loss of language and the loss of subjectivity are equated (DeLillo, *Falling Man*, pp. 93–4). It is for this reason that when Lianne looks at her group and sees the members groping towards expression, she perceives them to be equally 'staring into a memory or a word', to the name which makes possible the appreciation of an appearance and of subjectivity (DeLillo, *Falling Man*, p. 141).

It is this Heideggerian interrelation of the λόγος and the enunciation of Self which Lianne considers when '[s]he thought of the language that Rosellen had been using at the last sessions' (DeLillo, *Falling Man*, p. 156). As Lianne observes, Rosellen 'developed extended versions of a single word, all the inflections and connectives, a kind of protection perhaps, a gathering against the last bare state, where even the deepest moan may not be grief but only moan', when the language of Self is finally stripped away in the loss of language and the surrender of the λόγος (DeLillo, *Falling Man*, p. 156). It is this end which Lianne perceives as awaiting her own being, motivating her to work with the group and confront her own *Sein zum Ende*. As she observes, '[t]hese people were the living breath of the thing that killed her father' (DeLillo, *Falling Man*, p. 61). Reflecting upon his loss, Lianne sees herself as 'bearing her father's mark' (DeLillo, *Falling Man*,

p. 125). Rather than death itself being the source of distress, it is instead 'the loss of memory, personality and identity, the lapse into eventual protein stupor' which she fears; the collapse of her enunciation of Self enabled by a Heideggerian, phenomenological conception of the interrelation of λόγος and appearance (DeLillo, *Falling Man*, p. 125).

While DeLillo's texts thus initially correlate to a predominantly Wittgensteinian conception of the λόγος, the unsuitability of his theories for an *eigentlich* language of Self ultimately results in an abandonment of such a conception. Through the exploration of issues of externality, the novels show a transition towards a more Benjaminian philosophy of language, one which focuses upon issues of Being and the distinction between what is communicated *through* versus *in* language. In his presumption, however, of thought as a-linguistic, Benjamin's linguistic theories proves insufficient in conceptualizing the inextricability of λόγος and subjectivity in DeLillo's later novels. A further transition accordingly occurs, analogous to a predominantly Heideggerian conception of language which emphasizes a phenomenological perspective that inextricably links λόγος and phenomenon, positing time as the horizon for Being, manipulated through tense, preposition and case.

The next chapter, entitled '"[T]o smash my likeness, prism of all my images"[26]: Hyperreality, ἀλήθεια (truth) and the Language of Self', will explore the alternate influence of phenomenon and image, and in particular the role of the Baudrillardian simulacra. Building upon a postmodernist/ poststructualist perspective and exploring its relation to the λόγος, image will be discussed as an alternate site for the expression of the language of Self.

---

26 Don DeLillo, *Americana*, p. 236.

CHAPTER 4

'[T]o smash my likeness, prism of all my images'[1]: Hyperreality, ἀλήϑεια (truth) and the Language of Self

Just as the λόγος provides a vessel for an enunciation of Self, so too does the coextensive presence and possibilty of image play a significant role in the formation of subjectivity. Accompanying the gradual evolution of the λόγος, is a change in the nature, perception and role of the image in DeLillo's texts. This chapter analyses this changing impact, exploring the Baudrillardian concept of hyperreality and image upon the three conceptions of the λόγος discussed previously, showing that while image as simulacrum contests the validity of Wittgenstein's and Benjamin's conception of the λόγος, the linguistic theory advanced in Heidegger's later philosophy – and in particular his concept of truth (*aletheia*) – allows a phenomenological conception of the λόγος to continue to function as a suitable vessel for a stable, public enunciation of Self.

For Jean Baudrillard, contemporary society has entered a postmodern, 'hyperreal' age, dominated by 'models of a real without origin or reality'.[2] Rather than images as referential, he proposes that an 'imperialism' has emerged in which 'present-day simulators invert such a relationship and attempt to make the real, all of the real, coincide with their models of simulation' (Baudrillard, 2006, pp. 1–2). Through the implementation of this 'imperial' endeavour, '[s]omething has disappeared', 'the sovereign differ-

---

[1] Don DeLillo, *Americana*, p. 236.
[2] Jean Baudrillard, 'The Precession of Simulacra' in *Simulacra and Simulation*, Shelia Faria Glaser (trans.) (Ann Arbor: The University of Michigan Press, 2006), pp. 1–42, p. 1. Further references are given after quotations in the text.

ence, between one and the other' (Baudrillard, 2006, pp. 1–2). Without this difference, Baudrillard argues, 'all of metaphysics' is 'lost', and once this demise has occurred there is '[n]o more mirror of being and appearances, of the real and its concept' which would allow certainty in representation (Baudrillard, 2006, p. 2). In the absence of such a guarantee, the 'real is [instead] produced from miniaturized cells, matrices, and memory banks, models of control – and it can be reproduced an indefinite number of times from these' since it 'no longer needs to be rational, because it no longer measures itself against either an ideal or negative instance' (Baudrillard, 2006, p. 2).

If Baudrillard's theory of the hyperreal is accepted, an accompanying destabilization occurs in the Wittgensteinian conception of language. While Wittgenstein also rejected the validity of the metaphysical, the conception of the λόγος which he advances is of a language as a vehicle for factual assertions which provides the means by which the conceptualization and creation of '[t]he world [a]s the totality of facts, not of things' can occur (Wittgenstein, 2006, p. 5). Since it is precisely this conception of language as factual representation – rather than according with the 'truth' of the 'things' themselves – which is crucial for Wittgenstein's theory of how the 'world' is established, the concept of hyperreality is accordingly problematic for denotation as a vessel for a rigid, phallologocentric language of Self.

Rather than the factual surety of the λόγος and image proposed in the *Tractatus*, with the emergence of the hyperreal a 'crossing' occurs 'into a space whose curvature is no longer that of the real, nor that of truth'. Once this transition has taken place, Wittgenstein's conception of the λόγος as a means of sorting representations into factual and non-factual, sense and nonsense, true and false, is contested. The 'era of simulation' 'inaugurated' a 'liquidation of all referentials' and a subsequent 'artificial resurrection in the systems of signs'. In place of representational certainty is 'a material more malleable than meaning,' which 'lends itself to all systems of equivalences, to all binary oppositions, to all combinatory algebra'. The hyperreal is thus 'no longer a question of imitation, nor duplication, nor even parody' but instead is the 'substituting' of 'signs of the real for the real', the creation of 'a programmatic, metastable, perfectly descriptive machine that offers all the signs of the real and short-circuits all its vicissitudes' (Baudrillard, 2006, p. 2).

While Wittgenstein's theorizing in the *Tractatus* is obviously vulnerable to the hyperreal, the *Philosophical Investigations* marginalized the necessity of a secure representation with which to create 'the world' of the subject. Rather than emphasizing the factual and the logical, the focus of *Philosophical Investigations* is instead upon meaning as use. The assertion, however, that 'individual words in language name objects' and that 'sentences are combinations of such names' still results in a conception of the λόγος which is predominantly concerned with the utilization of concrete nouns (Wittgenstein, 2000, p. 2). Rather than insulating Wittgenstein's theory of language, the concept of meaning as use instead makes it more susceptible to the effects of the hyperreal. In the metaphor of the stone mason and his apprentice pointing at tools and ascribing names to each, the certainty that each is perceiving a representation anchored to the real can be seen to be of crucial, foundational importance.

This susceptibility has far-reaching consequences for the externality of the λόγος extrapolated from the *Philosophical Investigations* and discussed in the previous chapter. Through proposing an idiosyncratic conception of 'grammar' which stresses a social construction of linguistic boundaries in which certain words and ideas are excluded 'from the sphere of language' (Wittgenstein, 2000, pp. 138–9), the hyperreal enters the social through such deployment. When a Wittgensteinian conception of grammar is used as a vehicle for a phallologocentric language of Self, such as that of Anatole, it thus inevitably introduces a simulacral dimension which undermines the very certainty to which such signification strives, reflecting Baudrillard's conception that the simulacral destabilizes the real which underpins the social.[3]

Such an impact can be observed in David Bell's fascination with the image in *Americana*. Rather than the λόγος providing the basis for a stable, fulfilling enunciation of Self, it is instead towards the visual that David is

---

3   The interrelation of the hyperreal, real, social and political will receive in-depth analysis in chapters 7 and 8.

drawn for much of the novel, in particular the medium of film. Key to appreciating this fascination is an understanding of what is lost in the transition from Wittgensteinian grammar to the hyperreality of the cinematic image. Unlike the realm of the Wittgensteinian λόγος, with its emphasis upon logical relations and the creation of the 'world' through an accumulation of 'facts', socially mediated by grammar, the Baudrillardian hyperreal is instead a medium free of regulation, structure or order, allowing for the unconstrained expression of instincts and urges. As David observes:

> When I was a teenager I saw Burt in *From Here to Eternity*. He stood above Deborah Kerr on that Hawaiian beach and for the first time in my life I felt the true power of the image. Burt was like a city in which we are all living. He was that big. Within the conflux of shadow and time, there was room for all of us and I knew I must extend myself until the molecules parted and I was spliced into the image. Burt in the moonlight was a crescendo of male perfection but no less human because of it. Burt lives! I carry that image to this day, and so, I believe, do millions of others, men and women, for their separate reasons. (DeLillo, *Americana*, pp. 12–13)

It is precisely this 'true power of the image', so strong that David continues to 'carry' it 'to this day', which is rooted in an emotional context of longing which remains beyond the prescriptions of the Wittgensteinian theory of the λόγος and of any interrelated form of the language of Self. Rather than solidifying the enunciator into a singular, self-contained subject, an engagement with an unfettered image instead has the opposite effect. Investing himself within the simulacrum of Burt Lancaster's image, David 'extend[s him]self until the molecules parted and [he] was spliced into the image', opening the Self to the fragmentation of the hyperreal and eliminating the supposed modernist unity of the subject. This leads to a postmodernist fragmentation and impermanence of the subject, rather than the authored, redraftable enunciator of a phallologocentric language of Self. Such a concern is pervasive throughout DeLillo's novel where the deployment of the image results in a fear of fragmentation. As David observes:

> There were times when I thought all of us at the network existed only on videotape. [...] there was the feeling that somebody's deadly pinky might nudge a button and we would all be erased forever. (DeLillo, *Americana*, p. 23)

Rather than an initially stable subjectivity derived from a Wittgensteinian conception of the λόγος, when David splices himself into the image he is left with the feeling that he and his coworkers 'seemed to be no more than electronic signals' which 'moved through time and space with the stutter and shadowed insanity of a TV commercial' (DeLillo, *Americana*, p. 24).

As well as allowing the unfettered expression of urges, the hyperreal also seemingly offers the possibility of escaping beyond the subject's historicity (*Historizität*). As David observes, '[t]hrough the camera lens passed the light of a woman's body' and once this process of transformation has occurred David is convinced that he had 'plucked' her image 'out of space and placed it in the new era, free of history and death' (DeLillo, *Americana*, p. 33). Without stable reference to the real, the Baudrillardian hyperreal is free of the context or burden that arises from historicity. Rather than creating an authentic (*eigentlich*) enunciation, David thus uses images to escape the particularity of his Self and to enter what he terms as the 'third person singular' (DeLillo, *Americana*, p. 270)[4]: 'the man we all want to be' which '[a]dvertising has discovered' (DeLillo, *Americana*, p. 270) and which Cowart terms as 'the American mass brain.'[5] Such publicness thus represents a freedom from the necessity of evolving an idiosyncratic language of Self, instead offering an externally constructed, *das Man* enunciation which seemingly no longer requires the λόγος as a vessel, nor for the subject to have to engage with their own historicity.

While a seeming freedom may be concomitant with immersion in the simulacra and the third person singular, the novel ultimately shows this to be unfulfilling due to the hyperreal's unsuitability for an authentic enunciation of Self. Though David's film appears to be a paradigmatic example of such an endeavour, he is forced to admit that '[p]erhaps it wasn't a movie I was creating so much as a scroll, a delicate bit of papyrus that feared discovery', an ultimately futile and unfulfilling attempt to shape comparable certainties

---

4   The consumerist dimension of this statement will be returned to in greater detail in the next chapter.
5   David Cowart, 'For Whom Bell Tolls: Don DeLillo's *Americana*', *Contemporary Literature*, 37:4 (1996), pp. 602–19, p. 608.

within a simulacral medium to that offered by the phallologocentricism of the Wittgensteinian λόγος (DeLillo, *Americana*, p. 238). Such ambivalence regarding the image's capacity as a medium of expression has been present for David since his earliest attempts to shape the visual while studying film in California. While he tried to immerse himself within Burt Lancaster's image, David also wanted 'to learn to read the mind and body of my mate', rather than spend time with Wendy Judd 'who continued to hunger after my shadow, my image, the thrust and danger of my car' (DeLillo, *Americana*, p. 33). Though David rejected the Wittgenstianian λόγος as a vessel for his language of Self, and seemingly embraced the simulacral, he still wishes to use the former to construct a mediated enunciation, limiting the impact of the Other. As he observes, just as he wished to be part of Lancaster's image, 'I [also] wanted to free myself from that montage of speed, guns, torture, rape, orgy and consumer packaging which constitutes the vision of sex in America' (DeLillo, *Americana*, p. 33). Even once David has left the desert and taken a job in New York the connection Wendy evokes between simulacral sex and simulacral image still remains:

> Wendy's mouth, enormous and frenzied, was burning at my ear; as I listened, my hand moved to that part of my thigh which corresponded to the area below the hem of Binky's skirt which my eyes had selected a moment before. My senses, it seemed, were scattering, eyes and hand allied, mouth and ears receding into the phone, drawn by the urgent voice, by the image I could not envision; and then, fiercely and strangely excited, I moved my hand across my lap and did a mad kind of loin dance, not moving from the chair, not taking my eyes from that land and sea arrangement of dress and leg, not resisting the tunnelling lure of the telephone, the place where Wendy dwelt, unimaginably desirable, a victory of mouth and ear. It was my secretary who gave flesh to the disassembled words, who modelled for me the image on the other end of the wire [...] (DeLillo, *Americana*, pp. 96–7)

The hyperreality of such an encounter is shown by the way in which the image shatters the physical unity between the subject and the Other, scattering the senses and rendering Binky's physicality equivalent and interchangeable to a disembodied Wendy, as both women become simulacra

'[T]o smash my likeness, prism of all my images'

without original or real, freeing within David a 'mad', unfettered *jouissance*.[6] As David's experience shows, rather than leading to a new freedom for the language of Self, all that immersion within the hyperreal achieves is the shattering of the unity of Self and Other and with it the viability of modernist/romantic subjectivity.

It is within this context that David attempts to capture the one thing he truly desires, the incestuous connection with his dead mother, something which is obviously only feasible through the hyperreal medium of image:

> Then I thought of my mother's blue apron, the old chipped stove, so terribly real, the blue apron with the flowers, the way she stood there stirring the pudding, her hand a small limp triumph of continuity and grace, an assertion of order in the universe. In the morning I loaded the camera. (DeLillo, *Americana*, p. 237)

In terms of the language of Self, David's actions reveal the expression of a desire which is not mediated through the shaping of an enunciation rooted in the λόγος, yet which still longs for 'order in the universe'. Rather than the '"[t]he broken neck of the alphabet"', what is instead embraced is a concept of the image as 'something to play', '[a]n idea, a role, a masquerade', which 'the camera will understand even if no one else does' (DeLillo, *Americana*, p. 251). Though seemingly simulacral, such production is still scripted and structured, an attempt at an enunciation of Self using the medium of images. As the ultimate failure of David's film shows, however, such an endeavour proves to be unrealizable, just as escaping from the unfettered desires of the Self and the Other is impossible without a stable enunciation. It is such a conclusion which David ultimately arrives at, choosing to flee to an isolated island where he can turn once more to the λόγος as a means of recounting his experience, insulated from the hyperreality of the image.

While both strands of Wittgenstein's theory are equally contested by the hyperreal, Benjamin's conception of the λόγος would seem to offer greater resistance. The dual nature of the Benjaminian conception of language would appear to provide a partial escape from the effect of the

---

6   The interaction of image, *jouissance* and the language of Self will be explored in greater detail in chapter 6.

hyperreal, due to the emphasis placed upon language's potential to give voice to the ineffable as opposed to solely representing the 'real'. This seeming resistance to the simulacra is ultimately shown to be illusory, however, due to the way in which Benjamin's conception of the λόγος depends upon its religious context. It is the theological dimension of his theory that man '*communicates itself to God*' which allows Benjamin to argue for the existence of different levels within the λόγος (Benjamin, 1997, p. 65). Such duality is only engendered, as discussed above, by the process of a translation whose 'objectivity' is 'guaranteed' by the God which 'created things' through 'the creative word', 'the germ of the cognising name, just as God, too, finally named each thing after it was created' (Benjamin, 1997, pp. 69–70).

It is precisely this 'germ of the cognising name' which is threatened by the evolution of the simulacra since, as Baudrillard notes, the 'omnipotence of simulacra' has disastrous consequences for theology, possessing a 'faculty' to 'effac[e] God from the conscience of man' (Baudrillard, 2006, p. 4): opening up the Self to 'the destructive, annihilating truth' that 'deep down God never existed, that only the simulacrum ever existed, even that God himself was never anything but his own simulacrum' (Baudrillard, 2006, p. 4). The hyperreal thus serves to 'inaugurat[e] the era of simulacra and of simulation, in which there is no longer a God to recognize his own, no longer a Last Judgment to separate the false from the true, the real from its artificial resurrection, as everything is already dead and resurrected in advance' (Baudrillard, 2006, p. 5). This accordingly threatens the duality of language conceived by Benjamin, since there is no longer the security of the germ of the divine word, no God to function as the addressee of 'mental being', only a simulacrum. Without this theological dimension Benjamin's theory is reduced to merely the 'bourgeois' conception of language in which the λόγος is 'a *mere* sign' denoting factual relations between word and the object which it represents, dependent upon the certainty of representation (Benjamin, 1997, pp. 71–2).

It is for this reason that Baudrillard proposed that while '[o]ne can live with the idea of distorted truth', the profound 'metaphysical despair' arising 'from the idea that the image didn't conceal anything at all' and the according 'death of the divine referential' has a much more profound impact when it is applied to the divine (Baudrillard, 2006, p. 5):

'[T]o smash my likeness, prism of all my images'

> All Western faith and good faith became engaged in this wager on representation: that a sign could refer to the depth of meaning, that a sign could be exchanged for meaning and that something could guarantee this exchange – God of course. But what if God himself can be simulated, that is to say can be reduced to the signs that constitute faith? Then the whole system becomes weightless, it is no longer itself anything but a gigantic simulacrum – not unreal, but a simulacrum, that is to say never exchanged for the real, but exchanged for itself, in an uninterrupted circuit without reference or circumference. (Baudrillard, 2006, pp. 5–6)

The abolition of the image's divine guarantee is the catalyst of the final stage of this transition to a simulacral state: the initial conception of the image as 'the reflection of a profound reality' which transforms into the idea that it instead 'masks and denatures a profound reality', finally evolving into the profound 'metaphysical despair' that the image 'has no relation to any reality whatsoever' – that it is 'its own pure simulacrum' (Baudrillard, 2006, pp. 5–6).

It is in *White Noise* that the effect of this collapse is most fully explored. Throughout the novel, and in particular in the events surrounding the potential Nyodene-D spill,[7] the factual certainties of the bourgeois elements of Benjamin's conception of language surrender their certainty. As the technician who treats Jack in the wake of his potential exposure observes, Gladney is now 'the sum total' of his 'data' from which no one

---

7 As with the other scenes from *White Noise*, discussed below, the toxic waste spill has received extensive analysis. For Thomas Peyser, it signifies the manner in which such events highlight the constructed, fragile nature of American culture [Thomas Peyser, 'Globalization in America: The case of Don DeLillo's White Noise', *Clio*, 25:3 (1996), pp. 255–72]. In a similar vein, Basu Birman argues that the waste spill highlights the anxieties latent in American society due to the perceived threat of a techno-ethnic Other [Birman, B., 'Reading the Techno-Ethnic Other in Don DeLillo's White Noise' in *The Arizona Quarterly*. 61:2 (2005), pp. 87–103]. By contrast, Matthew J. Packer considers the toxic spill to possess 'anthropological elements' which 'have scarcely been considered – despite the religious awe looming in the airborne toxic event'. [Matthew J. Packer, '"At the Dead Center of Things" in Don DeLillo's White Noise: Mimesis, Violence, and Religious Awe' in *Modern Fiction Studies*, 51:3 (2005), pp. 648–68, p. 649].

'escapes' once 'death has entered' the Self.[8] Rather than such an assertion bringing certainty, however, the information is instead 'rendered graphically' and then 'televised', resulting in a 'sense' of 'eerie separation between' the 'condition' and patient, due to the introduction of the image and the destabilization of any referential with the real (DeLillo, *White Noise*, p. 142). As Jack observes, rather than the supposed certainty of the Benjaminian or Wittgensteinian λόγος, such information instead becomes a foreign 'network of symbols' which 'has been introduced, an eerie awesome technology wrested from the gods' which 'makes you feel like a stranger in your own dying' (DeLillo, *White Noise*, p. 142). As Leonard Wilcox notes, within *White Noise*, 'even death is not exempt from the world of simulation: the experience of dying is utterly mediated by technology and eclipsed by a world of symbols', transforming the body into a simulacrum within which 'death loses its personal and existential resonances.'[9]

It is in this transition – from factual, verifiable representation, dominated by intelligible relations between object and word, to a near endless, hyperreal proliferation of data in which the Self is helpless to mediate or understand – that a failure occurs in the ability of language to adequately sort raw data into information 'through' the medium of the λόγος. The self, accordingly, can no longer securely use the 'bourgeois' aspect of language as a vessel for enunciation, without the possibility of subjectivity being swept away in the proliferation of the hyperreal. In the endless questioning that arises in the wake of this production even such simple things as how to stand or walk or sit become objects of scrutiny, cases to be compared against a mean or norm derived from this wealth of data which is no longer information that constructs 'the world', but instead is an alienating, hyperreal force that dissolves its seeming certainty.

While this destabilization may concern what is conveyed 'through' the Benjaminian λόγος, what is expressed 'in' his conception of language,

---

8   Don DeLillo, *White Noise* (London: Penguin, 1985), p. 141. Further references are given after quotations in the text.
9   Leonard Wilcox, 'Baudrillard, DeLillo's *White Noise*, and the End of Heroic Narrative', *Contemporary Literature*, 32:3 (1991), pp. 346–65, pp. 352–3.

'[T]o smash my likeness, prism of all my images'

as discussed above, is equally susceptible to hyperreal destabilization due to the collapse of the divine referential. Such depiction begins innocuously enough with Wilder 'crying out, saying nameless things in a way that touched' Jack 'with its depth and richness'. Rather than appreciating factual information on the 'bourgeois' level in '[t]he inconsolable crying' – i.e. the child was cold, hungry, tired etc – Jack instead 'let it wash over' him 'like rain in sheets' until he 'entered it, in a sense', attempting to join Wilder 'in his lost and suspended place' where they 'might together perform some reckless wonder of intelligibility.' Such a location is conceived by Jack in explicitly theological terms since, as he states, when Wilder ceases to cry he appears 'as though he'd just returned from a period of wandering in some remote and holy place' which Jack 'regard[ed] with the mingled reverence and wonder we hold in reserve for feats of the most sublime and difficult dimensions.' (DeLillo, *White Noise*, pp. 78–9).

It is not just Wilder who allows Jack to engage with this conception of the spiritual and divine as communicated 'in' language. Steffie, like her brother, also evokes a similar response and upon passing her bedroom in the wake of the toxic waste event Jack felt 'a moment of splendid transcendence' when he heard her repeating 'Toyota Celica' in her sleep (DeLillo, *White Noise*, p. 155).[10] Despite being a product brand name, for Jack the religious dimension of her utterance is something which is conveyed 'in', not through, language and is even more arresting than it was with Wilder's wordless weeping. As Jack observed, '[w]atching children sleep' made him

10 As with the airborne toxic event, the 'Toyota Celica' scene has provided material for extensive critical commentary. For Paul Maltby, Jack's reaction is symptomatic of his investment in '[r]omantic and modernist conceptions of visionary moments', which, under the '"hyperreal" conditions' of postmodernism 'are rendered obsolete' and 'can only reproduce the packaged messages of the mass media' [Paul Maltby, 'The Romantic Metaphysics of Don DeLillo', p. 259], echoed by Paula E. Geyh who also conceived of Jack as 'a believer in traditional conceptions of the real' and of 'truth' as 'he plays the role – and voices the perplexity – of a modern thinker confronting postmodernity' [Paula E Geyh, 'Assembling postmodernism: Experience, meaning, and the space in-between', *College Literature*, 30:2 (2003), pp. 1–29, p. 14].

'feel devout, part of a spiritual system', 'the closest' which he 'can come to God' (DeLillo, *White Noise*, p. 147):

> If there is a secular equivalent of standing in a great spired cathedral with marble pillars and streams of mystical light slanting through two-tier Gothic windows, it would be watching children in their little bedrooms fast asleep. Girls especially. (DeLillo, *White Noise*, p. 147)

Such is the force of what is communicated 'in' language that for Jack a 'long moment passed before' he 'realized this was the name of an automobile', and even following this realization it still remains 'like the name of an ancient power in the sky, tablet-carved in cuneiform', leaving the sense 'that something hovered', a presence in language (DeLillo, *White Noise*, p. 141).

While there is a lingering sense of immanence, linked with the divine, the fear that God is simulacral undermines this spiritual dimension and in both cases the prayer-like utterances of man's linguistic Being communicated 'in' language simply express a fear which is neither abated nor assuaged. Their pleas remain unanswered, only ceasing when the Self is exhausted and unable to continue. This sense of God as at best departed, or at worst simulacral, reaches its apogee in the figure of Sister Marie who does not even attempt a pretence of faith in the presence of the lay community, admitting that even nuns no longer believe in God's existence.[11]

Without a divine guarantee for the Benjaminian conception of the λόγος, both what is communicated 'through' and 'in' language is shown to be susceptible to destabilization, losing its spiritual guarantee. It is at this point that the two strands of depiction become unified through Dylar, a pill which purports to eliminate the fear of death and a concern with such issues as the proliferation of data and the collapse of the divine referential. Rather than placing the Self beyond such concerns, however, Dylar instead proves

---

11   Laura Barrett focuses upon *White Noise*'s intertexts and proposes that 'Jack's conversation with Sister Hermann Marie at the end of *White Noise* is reminiscent of the crisis of faith which sends Stephen out of Ireland at the end of *A Portrait of the Artist*' [Laura Barrett, '"How the Dead Speak to the Living": Intertextuality and the Postmodern Sublime in *White Noise*', *Journal of Modern Literature*, 25:2 (2002), pp. 97–113, p. 104].

'[T]o smash my likeness, prism of all my images'

to be illusory, representative of how the hyperreal causes an '[e]scalation' to occur, a '[p]anic-stricken' attempt at the 'production of the real and of the referential, parallel to and greater than the panic of material production' (Baudrillard, 2006, p. 7). It is this, which, in Baudrillard's conception, is the definitive quality of the hyperreal: the near endless production of the simulacral which is engendered as 'a strategy of the real, of the neoreal and the hyperreal that everywhere is the double of a strategy of deterrence' (Baudrillard, 2006, p. 7). Embodying this phenomenon, Dylar seemingly offers an escape from such confusion, though, significantly, even this function turns out to be illusory as the pill fails to fulfil its intended purpose.

While the evolution of the hyperreal thus destabilizes both Wittgensteinian and Benjaminian conceptions of the λόγος, Heideggerian linguistic theory evidences a more complex relationship. As discussed previously, Heidegger stresses a relationship between λόγος and Φαινόμενον,[12] opening his theory to the influence of the hyperreal. A more detailed analysis reveals, however, that unlike the linguistic theory proposed by Wittgenstein and Benjamin, the Heideggerian λόγος is not principally an attempt at representing a previously observed real through denotive codification. It is instead *denotation* which makes visible the real, in a manner similar to Benjamin's concept of 'translation', yet one which is focused upon the effable rather than the ineffable. Such a concept is rooted in a disparagement of 'the current view' in which 'language is held to be a kind of communication' of 'verbal exchange and agreement' (Heidegger, 2001, p. 71). For Heidegger, language is instead 'not only and not primarily an audible and written expression of what is to be communicated' but 'alone brings what is, as something that is, into the Open for the first time' (Heidegger, 2001, p. 71). It is language's potential for 'naming beings for the first time' which consequently 'first brings beings to word and to appearance' (Heidegger, 2001, p. 71).

This creates a curiously reversed relationship between the λόγος, the real and the hyperreal, compared to the conception of language advanced in Wittgenstein's and Benjamin's theories. In his essay 'The Origin of the

---

12 Phenomenon. cf. Martin Heidegger, *Being and Time*, pp. 49–55.

Work of Art', Heidegger built upon his linguistic work in *Sein und Zeit* and proposed an additional concept rooted in an analysis of Greek philosophy as an example of a primordial understanding which had gradually become obscured by subsequent interpretations and '*trans*lation' (Heidegger, 2001, p. 23).[13] Through his philosophical project, Heidegger attempts a form of linguistic archaeology, striving to excavate to the primordial source of the Greek concepts beneath their Roman and Medieval '*trans*lation[s]'. Of the various Greek ideas which he discusses in his essay it is truth (*aletheia*) which is given the most prominent place and which is particularly relevant in terms of the hyperreal. Through its actions 'an open place occurs' in 'the midst of beings', 'a clearing' and 'a lighting' (Heidegger, 2001, p. 21).

Rather than the certainty and unchangeability of Wittgenstianian or Benjaminian representation, the concept of truth evoked by Heidegger's reworking of Greek ontology is one of ambiguity and doubt, mirroring the problematizing of Being undertaken in *Sein und Zeit*:

> There is much in being that man cannot master. There is but little that comes to be known. What is known remains inexact, what is mastered insecure. What is, is never of our making or even merely the product of our minds, as it might all too easily seem. When we contemplate this whole as one, then we apprehend, so it appears, all that is – though we grasp it crudely enough. (Heidegger, 2001, p. 21)

Instead of the certainty of perception, this 'clearing' only 'grants and guarantees to us humans a passage to those beings that we ourselves are not, and access to the being that we ourselves are' (Heidegger, 2001, p. 21).

Unlike the previous conceptions of truth and knowledge discussed above, the Heideggerian rehabilitation of *aletheia* is not one of rigid disclosure, since, as Heidegger notes, 'being can be *concealed*, too' and such concealment can occur 'only within the sphere of what is lighted'. The 'open place in the midst of beings, the clearing, is never a rigid stage with a permanently raised curtain on which the play of beings runs its course',

---

13   Heidegger stresses a concept of the translation of a word as inevitably resulting in a translation and accompanying distortion of the experience which it denotes. The example used is that of Greek thought translated into subtly different Roman concepts.

but instead a form of 'double concealment'. As a result, '[u]nconcealedness (truth) is neither an attribute of factual things in the sense of beings, nor one of propositions' (Heidegger, 2001, p. 52). Instead, the 'nature of truth' is one of 'primal conflict in which that open center is won' (Heidegger, 2001, p. 53). Truth consequently 'does not mean that something is correctly represented and rendered' but is instead 'brought into unconcealedness and held therein' in the sense of '[t]o hold (*halten*)' which as Heidegger notes 'originally means to tend, keep, take care (*hüten*)' (Heidegger, 2001, p. 54). It is precisely this concept of tending which establishes the crucial dimension of Heidegger's theory of *aletheia* as something which can become both clearer, or more obscure, establishing a concept of truth and representation which, unlike that of Wittgenstein and Benjamin, can capture the way in which knowledge can lose its certainty in the face of the hyperreal, yet simultaneously explain how it can be discovered and regained.

A correlation to such a struggle against the 'imperialism' of the hyperreal through an embracing of the concept of *aletheia* can be observed in *The Body Artist*.[14] As with *White Noise*, the catalyst of such a process is again death, though unlike the earlier work, it is the actuality, rather than being-towards-death (*Sein sum Tode*) which drives Lauren initially to immerse herself within a hyperreal world of images. Before embracing the visual, Lauren attempts to use the λόγος as a means of coping with her loss. Possessed of a stable language of Self rooted in a Heideggerian understanding of language, Lauren begins the novel secure in her enunciation as evidenced in the breakfast scene of the opening chapter. Following Rey's suicide, however, the λόγος is shown to be insufficient for the language of Self to sustain its stable expression under the pressure of her loss.

This is principally shown through Lauren's interactions with the figure of Mr Tuttle and the shattering of the λόγος which occurs in his speech.

---

14   Philip Nel provides an alternate reading of *The Body Artist* as 'a lyrical meditation on language, memory, and the modernist (and romantic) project of bridging the gap between word and world' [Philip Nel, 'Don DeLillo's Return to Form: The Modernist Poetics of *The Body Artist*', p. 736].

In the aftermath of such a breakdown, of a surrender to incoherence, it is the simulacral image which comes to dominate. Once Mr Tuttle's 'physical' presence has disappeared from Lauren's rented house, she 'could not remember what he looked like,' and could only reinvoke a glimpse of his existence when 'she leaned into a mirror and there he was, not really, only hintingly, barely at all' (DeLillo, *The Body Artist*, pp. 112–13). Even then, when she sees a glimpse of his previous existence, a fragment of his image, she is constantly aware of 'the strategies of the glass, with its reversal of left and right, this room or that, because every image in every mirror is only virtual, even when you expect to see yourself', hyperreal (DeLillo, *The Body Artist*, pp. 112–13).

Aware of the simulacral nature of the image, any comfort which Lauren could obtain from hearing Rey's voice through the medium of Mr Tuttle is marginalized, representing the final collapse of the λόγος under the pressure of the simulacra. Lauren's abandonment of her previous strategy can be observed in her fascination with Mariella's answer machine message and the significance of its 'synthesized voice' which states '*[p]lease / leave / a mess/age / after / the / tone*'; symbolically shattering both the connection between words and the word itself, 'separated by brief but deep dimensions', an irruption of the hyperreal which the λόγος cannot restrain (DeLillo, *The Body Artist*, p. 67):

> One voice for each word. Seven different voices. Not seven different voices but one male voice in seven time cycles. But not male exactly either. And not words so much as syllables but not that either. She hung up and called back. (DeLillo, *The Body Artist*, p. 67)

The answer-phone message thus comes to represent the instability which occurs when a language of Self, anchored in linguistic expression, is shattered, just as the signifying medium of the λόγος itself is fragmented.

In the aftermath of the destruction of her previously stable enunciation, Lauren has no defence against the tragedy of Rey's demise. Her pain instinctively finds unfettered expression in the shattered hyperreality of images:

'*[T]o smash my likeness, prism of all my images*' 117

> Then she held the nozzle of the spray gun to her head, seeing herself as doing what anyone might do, alone, without special reference to the person's circumstances. It was the pine-scent bottle, the pistol-grip bottle of tile-and-grout cleaner, killer of mildew, and she held the nozzle, the muzzle to her head, finger pressed to the plastic trigger, with her tongue hanging out for effect. (DeLillo, *The Body Artist*, p. 114)

With the collapse of the λόγος as a vessel for her enunciation, Lauren transforms her Self into an image, a simulacrum of Rey's suicide. Such a deployment, however, only serves to re-emphasize the pain of her loss, rather than providing an escape or insulation from its effect. Such is its sterility that Lauren is forced to find a new space within which to find a release and establish a new, stable, fulfilling language of Self.

Her principal means of achieving this is through watching the live feed from a webcam in Kotka, Finland, which shows an alternate space whose emptiness is capable of containing, at least temporarily, the depth of her loss. Significantly, in regards to Baudrillard's theory, what is 'interesting to her' regarding the image was her belief that 'it was happening now', a supposedly real image (DeLillo, *The Body Artist*, pp. 38–9). As she notes:

> It was simply the fact of Kotka. It was the sense of organization, a place contained in an unyielding frame, as it is and as you watch, with a reading of local time in the digital display in a corner of the screen. Kotka was another world but she could see it in its realness, in its hours, minutes and seconds. (DeLillo, *The Body Artist*, pp. 38–9)

It is precisely the emptiness of the image which is so appealing for Lauren, the reason why '[t]he dead times were best', the 'empty road', since these images of desolation provide the most suitable vehicle for her sense of grief and emptiness. Lauren accordingly 'set[s] aside time every day for the webcam' as while '[s]he didn't know the meaning of this feed', and is unable to place it within the factual, classifying world of the Wittgensteinian λόγος, it became for her 'an act of floating poetry' which 'emptied her mind and made her feel the deep silence of other places, the mystery of seeing over the world to a place stripped of everything but a road that approaches and recedes, both realities occurring at once'; yet still evocative of the hyperreal in its microsecond delay, encoding and appearance of authenticity (DeLillo, *The Body Artist*, pp. 38–9).[15]

The image of the webcam can only provide a temporary release, however, from the pain of her loss and Lauren is forced to construct a new enunciation of Self. Rather than trying to recapture a shattered certainty, however, Lauren instead embraces an outlook which correlates to Heidegger's broader conception of the λόγος, providing her with the possibility of an alternative form of subjectivity. Conceiving its strength as lying in the fact that language can be '[p]rojective', that '[p]rojective saying is poetry' and that '[p]oetry is the saying of the unconcealedness of what is', Heidegger conceived of '[a]ctual language at any given moment' as 'the happening of this saying' which 'simultaneously brings the unsayable as such into a world' (Heidegger, 2001, p. 71). Crucially, for Lauren's enunciation, this conception of poetry is not limited to the verbal or written, but instead encompasses a far broader conception of language as anything poetic in a Heideggerian sense:

> Poetry is thought of here in so broad a sense and at the same time in such intimate unity of being with language and word, that we must leave open whether art, in all its modes from architecture to poesy, exhausts the nature of poetry. (Heidegger, 2001, pp. 71–2)

Through creating a work of art, of poetry, in this Heideggerian sense, Lauren is able to begin shaping a new enunciation capable of providing stable support for her language of Self. As a body artist, Lauren uses her physical form to create simulacral images as Mariella observes in a review of the performance:

> The power of the piece is Hartke's body. At times she makes femaleness so mysterious and strong that it encompasses both sexes and a number of nameless states. In the past she has inhabited the bodies of adolescents, pentacostal preachers, a

---

15   Even here, in the seeming innocuousness of this image, there is a inextricable, explicit connection between drives and the simulacrum. Lauren 'imagined that someone might masturbate to this, the appearance of a car on the road to Kotka in the middle of the night' (Don DeLillo, *The Body Artist*, pp. 38–9).

> one-hundred-and-twenty-year-old woman sustained by yogurt and, most memorably, a pregnant man. (DeLillo, *The Body Artist*, p. 110)

Achieving a simulacral potential in her body, Lauren first strips away the physical legacies of her previous Self which was unable to cope with the loss of Rey. Such a process, however, remains grounded in the Heideggerian conception of the unity of λόγος and image. As the narrator observes, through 'emery boards and files, many kinds of scissors, clippers and creams' Lauren 'activated the verbs of abridgement and excision', excising her former Self through the language which helps form such an enunciation (DeLillo, *The Body Artist*, p. 76). As a result, Lauren becomes 'not pale-skinned so much as colorless, bloodless and ageless', appearing 'rawboned and slightly bug-eyed', almost 'terroristic' in the extent to which she becomes a blank canvas for the clearing of truth (ἀλήθεια), stripped of any markers of her former enunciation of Self (DeLillo, *The Body Artist*, p. 103). As Mariella observes, this was Lauren's 'work, to disappear from all her former venues of aspect and bearing and to become a blankness, a body slate erased of every past resemblance' (DeLillo, *The Body Artist*, p. 84).

While Lauren may transform herself into a slate ready to be rewritten, to be inscribed upon, the authorial content is her own. As the narrator observes, there was a kind of 'solemn self-absorption' to the process and it is this which reveals how it is a poetic artwork in a Heideggerian sense through its paradoxical relationship to *aletheia* (DeLillo, *The Body Artist*, p. 76). While the constituting images of her artwork – and the medium of her new enunciation of Self – may be simulacral, by placing them within her artistic 'routine' Lauren transforms her own body into a living embodiment of this wider conception of the λόγος and of poetry. When Mariella approaches Lauren and attempts to compel her to reduce the wider, Heideggerian concept of the λόγος and the poetic which underpins her artwork, into a narrower, more factual conception of language, Lauren consequently refuses:

> 'How simple it would be if I could say this is a piece that comes directly out of what happened to Rey. But I can't. Be nice if I could say this is the drama of men and women versus death. I want to say that, but I can't. It's too small and secluded and complicated and I can't and I can't and I can't.' (DeLillo, *The Body Artist*, pp. 108–9)

Her artwork ultimately rejects reintegration into a factual, conventional understanding of the λόγος, remaining poetical in its denial of the conversion of *aletheia* into an assertion that would gradually lose its primordiality, decaying slowly into a fallen Being which surrenders its truth and power to the publicness of *das Man*. When Lauren leaves for the bathroom and does not return, clinging to the new vessel for her language of Self, she symbolically rejects any social attempt at constraint.

Thus, while the Wittgensteinian and Benjaminian conceptions of the λόγος are shown – in *Americana* and *White Noise* respectively – to be susceptible to the destabilizing effect of the hyperreal, Heidegger's phenomenological theory of language and image results in a more nuanced interaction. Through a broader conception of what constitutes the λόγος and the poetic, 'The Origin of The Work of Art' establishes a theory of both language and art (and language as art) which is rooted in a rehabilitation of the Greek concept of ἀλήθεια. Broader and suppler, this idea of language builds upon the relationship between λόγος and phenomenon advanced in *Sein und Zeit*, not only allowing the uncertainty of representation to be integrated into Heidegger's conception of the λόγος – without undermining its validity – but also to transform such instability of referent into a theoretical strength. It is this suppleness which allows Lauren to create the authentic enunciation of Self with which she ends the novel, one which had eluded David and Jack due to their enunciations correlating to a principally Wittgensteinian or Benjaminian understanding of language.

Building upon this analysis, the next section, 'Das Man', explores how λόγος and image interact with capital and politics in Dasein's formation of public languages of Self.

SECTION 3

Das Man

CHAPTER 5

'Capital burns off the nuance in a culture'[1]: Consumption, Capital, *Chrimatistikós* and the Middle American Enunciation of Self

Building upon the discussions undertaken above, this third section of the monograph will explore how Dasein's negotiation of isolation and connection, mediated through the phenomenology of denotation and image, helps to form, sustain or contest wider enunciations of Self. It is through participation in collective forms of signification, undertaken in the media of λόγος and phenomenon (Φαινόμενον), that these wider social enunciations occur. The first of these signifiying practices, consumption, will form the subject of this chapter. Proposing an historically contingent model of consumption, the following analysis traces the transition from the signification of local, ethnic commodities, to an increasingly national mediation of taste which is concomitant with the growing hegemony of what DeLillo terms as the Middle American 'land of lawns' (DeLillo, *Mao II*, p. 9); what this chapter will argue is a particular public enunciation of Self and the most prevalent US form of *das Man*. It will be argued, however, that the very mass media and advertising which brought this Middle American, public enunciation to prominence, also contains the seeds of its contestation. The role of the simulacra in mass communication will be shown to create a disjunct between concrete commodity and consumption, leading to the rise of hyperreal capital. An exploration of the concept of *Chrimatistikós* will then demonstrate the manner in which Eric Packer, the protagonist of *Cosmopolis*, attempts to use capital's hyperreality as a vessel for a new,

---

[1] Don DeLillo, *Underworld*, p. 776.

idiosyncratic enunciation of Self which attempts to reject the publicness of *das Man*, characteristic of the Middle American enunciation of Self.

DeLillo's analysis of the historically contingent nature of commodity and consumption receives its most nuanced treatment in *Underworld*, which, due to the novel's length and scope, affords ample opportunity to explore such development. Through multiple depictions in the novel's fragmentary sections, the text shows the changes which occurred in the Italian-American Bronx neighbourhoods of the post-war era. As Kenneth T. Jackson notes in his prize-winning account of US suburbanization, '[b]etween 1950 and 1970, the suburban population doubled from 36 to 74 million, and 83 per cent of the nation's total growth took place in the suburbs.'[2] Such growth in suburbanization was matched by an accompanying decline in urban populations as '[e]ighteen of the nation's twenty-five largest cities in 1950 suffered a net *loss* of population' (Jackson, 1985, p. 283). Such decline was self-perpetuating, and, as Jackson notes, as 'larger numbers of affluent citizens moved out, jobs followed', which in turn 'attracted more families, more roads, and more industries' to the suburbs, whilst 'cities were often caught in a reverse cycle' (Jackson, 1985, pp. 284–5).

In order to defend their community against this escalating dissolution, DeLillo depicts how Italian-American New York neighbourhoods turned to a policing of λόγος and commodity in an attempt to sustain their public enunciation in the face of the growth in suburban living. The unique language of the Italian-Bronx neighbourhood is a means of both cohering the 'social unit' – a struggle to find and maintain a unifying language and consumption based upon concrete relations – and an attempt to try and defend that coherence from external attack through a shared rhythm, inflection, accent, lexicon and tone. While borrowed or corrupted Italian words such as '*Sboccato*' and '*scucciament*' are present in their speech (DeLillo, *Underworld*, p. 680; p. 695), the defining, unique quality of Italian-American Bronx language is equally captured in English expressions

---

2   Kenneth T. Jackson, *Crabgrass Frontier: The Suburbanization of the United States* (Oxford: Oxford University Press, 1985), p. 283. Further references are given after quotations in the text.

such as '[b]e good' and in the rhythm of the English-language dialogue such as 'I'm hearing things that I don't know if it's good or what' (DeLillo, *Underworld*, pp. 665–6).

It is in reference to ethnic forms of consumption, however, that the relationship between the λόγος and the Italian-American enunciation of Self receives its most developed portrayal. As the externality of a phrase 'I'm making gravy' demonstrates (DeLillo, *Underworld*, p. 698), both language and commodities are used in the striving to sustain a community-wide enunciation:

> She heard the women talk about making gravy, speaking to a husband or child, and Rosemary understood the significance of this. It meant, Don't you dare come home late. It meant, This is serious so pay attention. It was a special summons, a call to family duty. The pleasure, yes, of familiar food, the whole history of food, the history of eating, the garlicky smack and tang. But there was also a duty, a requirement. The family requires the presence of every member tonight. Because the family was an art to these people and the dinner table was the place it found expression. (DeLillo, *Underworld*, p. 698)

Through the Old World legacy of their food, the phrase 'I'm making gravy' links families to each other and to the locally owned shops due to a shared historicity, reaffirming the Italian-American values of family, community, sharing, craft, *machismo*, and tradition – the ethos of their 'compact neighborhood' and the defining quality of their enunciation of Self (DeLillo, *Underworld*, p. 661). Rather than merely functioning as an amenity impersonally serving interchangeable consumers, the butcher is an integral part of the neighbourhood, calling 'to people walking by [...] to insult a man or engage a particular woman with knowing references' (DeLillo, *Underworld*, p. 667). Embodying values of craft, tradition and *machismo* in his work, manner and bearing, the butcher accordingly 'looked well-placed amongst the dangled animals', his body possessing 'a burly grace' shaped by his 'belong[ing] to the cutting block, to the wallow of trembling muscle and mess – his aptitude and ease, the sense that he was born to the task': a concrete relation between consumption, commodity and private and public enunciations of Self (DeLillo, *Underworld*, pp. 666–8). Like the gravy that is made, and the vision of family life it represents, the neighbourhood shops embody values in opposition to the clean, 'spick-and-span suburbs'[3] and the bright, hyperreal packages of consumerism and supermarkets, instead connoting the unity of λόγος, commodity and consumption that supported the society which evolved these very traditions. As long as such unity is maintained, the Bronx neighbourhood can resist the hyperreality of mass marketing and its homogenizing effect through '[t]his food, this family meal, this meat sauce simmering in a big pot with sausage and spareribs and onions and garlic' that constituted 'their loyalty and bond and well-being' (DeLillo, *Underworld*, p. 699).

Such unity, however, is only sustainable provided that the connection between local forms of commodity, consumption and λόγος is maintained. Just as eating is an event redolent of the Old World, for Bronzini 'walking was an art', a means by which he can immerse himself within his community and 'pass the time' speaking the Italian-American rhythms and inflections of their shared language. This enthusiasm for walking and remaining within the boundaries of a local community, however, is not shared by the subsequent generation. While 'Bronzini didn't own a car, didn't drive a car, didn't want one, didn't need one, wouldn't take one if somebody gave it to him', for individuals such as the young Nick Shay, the image of the car is something almost infinitely desirable (DeLillo, *Underworld*, pp. 661–2).

While for Bronzini everything that he wishes to consume can be found within the neighbourhood – a part of the connection between λόγος, commodity and community – for Nick, the car is necessary to obtain freedom from the very presence of family and society which Bronzini cherishes. Within the cramped confines of their houses and streets, someone is always present, and for Italian-American adolescents, a car represents an escape from parental and social control, a means to realize their socially constrained desires:

> 'You'll never get laid, Vito. Both you guys. That car is your only hope.' (DeLillo, *Underworld*, p. 693)

---

[3] Sidra Stich, *Made in U.S.A.* (Berkley: University of California Press, 1987), p. 58. Further references are given after quotations in the text.

Such consumer longing is thus not for a car itself, but instead for the possibility of *jouissance* which it represents, a conflation of the image of the vehicle and the possibility of freedom – the dream of the third person singular which governed David Bell's desires. Once Nick's generation begins to share in such Middle American consumerism – the equation of the car with freedom and of the hyperreal with desire – the fabric of the neighbourhood starts to unravel. Whereas Bronzini thought '[s]top walking ... and you die' (DeLillo, *Underworld*, p. 662), the above analysis has shown that it is not the person but rather the neighbourhood which withers into the publicness of 'the American dream', signified in the 'buying [of] a new single-family house and a capacious new car' (Stich, 1987, p. 58).

Such fear of the desire for hyperreal products and the values of Middle America is not solely restricted to Bronzini, and just as with the Italian-American concept of consumption, it, too, can be observed in the community's use of the λόγος. The defensive externality of a phrase such as '[w]ho's better than me', in its 'statement of the importance of small pleasures' such as a 'meal, a coat with a fake-fur collar, a chair in front of a fan on a hot day', becomes evident as a form of resistance to marketed desires which are not simple and which lead away from the neighbourhood and out to the suburbs (DeLillo, *Underworld*, p. 700). When Alfonse asks to be called Alan, the anger of the community is palpable precisely because it is their Italian-American identity, rooted in their shared use of the λόγος, and of local forms of consumption, which he wishes to shed; both his own historicity and that of his community. As he states of his given name, 'I'm not them', revealing his desire to embrace the hyperreal and become immersed within the third person singular where such historicity ceases to apply in any meaningful sense. The community's response of 'Who are you, *stunat*', if you're not them?', in its externality of fear and anger, shows the seductive power of this Middle American dream (DeLillo, *Underworld*, p. 706). In suburbia, with its motility of people and its sundering of traditional communities, an individual does not have to subscribe to the historicity of their heritage (though they are still circumscribed by their race) and can instead be defined by the mass-produced commodities with which they surround themselves. Phrases such as 'I'm making gravy', 'Who's better than me?', and 'Who are you ... if you're not them?', in their defensive externality, reveal the fragility and disintegration of ethnic forms of identity created through λόγος, commodity and consumption.

In contrast to the local, bespoke commodities and λόγος of the Italian Bronx, the suburbs of Middle America 'were deliberately planned to maximize consumption of mass-produced goods' as '[f]amilies moved into a culture of consumption and became dependent on cars' for almost every aspect of their day to day lives.[4] Commercial television provided the dominant medium through which this consumption was established and sustained, broadcasting a procession of images which 'used the model house as the setting' for their depiction of '[m]oms in high heels and dresses' who 'heated frozen dinners in commercials that seemed like extensions of family-orientated, prime-time programming' (Hayden, 2003, p. 148). As Dolores Hayden proceeds to note, commercial television 'reached all households', even those who did have the opportunity to live within such a privileged setting, 'and because of this, many groups excluded from the sitcom suburbs of the 1950s, and from the public subsidies supporting them, still saw the tract house as an emblem of belonging and upward mobility' (Hayden, 2003, p. 149). As a result of such mass-marketed, cultural investment, even though 'American suburbs come in every type, shape, and size; rich and poor, industrial and residential, new and old', a paradigmatic image of the sitcom American suburb came to predominate; a Middle American 'stereotype' which, as Jackson proceeds to note, has a basis in fact (Jackson, 1985, p. 4).

Such a representation can be observed in a section from 'Better Things for Better Living Through Chemistry', set on October 8, 1957, which explores the complex and conflicted relationship between Erica Deming and her son Eric. Within this space, individuals such as Erica view the suburb as 'a landscape of the imagination where Americans situate ambitions for upward mobility and economic security, ideals about freedom and private property, and longings for social harmony and spiritual uplift', achieved

---

4   Dolores Hayden, *Building Suburbia: Green Fields and Urban Growth 1820–2000* (New York: Vintage, 2003), p. 128; p. 147. Further references are given after quotations in the text.

through the heteronormative 'ideology of female domesticity', a form of 'gender-stereotyped "family values"' (Hayden, 2003, p. 6). Erica can be seen to embody this 'ideology of female domesticity', and her enunciation is formed and sustained through investment in mass-marketed products and the motility of their names:

> Sometimes she called it her Jell-O chicken mousse and sometimes she called it her chicken moose Jell-O. This was one of a thousand convenient things about Jell-O. The word went anywhere, front or back or in the middle. It was a push-button word, the way so many things were push-button now, the way the whole world opened behind the button that you push. (DeLillo, *Underworld*, p. 517)

Rather than being fixed, mass-marketed product names are instead motile, able to enter a sentence at a variety of positions and alter vocal rhythm, expressing particular manifestations of the speaker's desires whilst still remaining part of a shared, unifying lexicon. This allowed the commodity to become a more malleable site for the expression of urges, compared to more traditional, ethnic lexicons of consumption. Middle American products were thus eminently repositionable, able to express a huge variety of emotions and longings, explaining the appeal of mass-marketing and its domination over earlier forms of consumption.

This eminent suitability as a means of expressing desire, however, creates an inevitable destabilization in the very Middle American enunciation which it facilitates. As Sidra Stich notes, in the 1950s there arose an inherent 'value conflict between the old Protestant ethic of self-reliance, thrift, and hard work, and the new organizational ethic that fostered belongingness, consumption and leisure' (Stich, 1987, p. 10). Such conflict was particularly apparent in regards to the role and place of desire within the suburban nuclear family unit. As Lauren Berlant and Michael Warner note in their formative essay 'Sex in Public' within US society there is a valorized, 'heteronormative',[5] 'national heterosexuality' which forms the principal 'mechanism by which a core national culture can be imagined as

---

5   Lauren Berlant and Michael Warner, 'Sex in Public', *Critical Enquiry*, 24:2 (1998), pp. 547–66, p. 543. Further references are given after quotations in the text.

a sanitized space of sentimental feeling and immaculate behavior, a space of pure citizenship' untainted by forms of desire which would destabilize the Middle American enunciation (Berlant and Warner, 1998, p. 549). Within this cognitive space a 'familial model of society' functions 'as a mediator and metaphor of national existence in the United States', achieved through the 'nostalgic family-values covenant of contemporary American politics' (Berlant and Warner, 1998, pp. 549–50). As they note, such 'developments, though distinct, are linked in the way they organize a hegemonic national public around sex', were deployed 'in order to protect the zone of heterosexual privacy, the institutions of economic privilege and social reproduction informing its practices and organizing its ideal world' (Berlant and Warner, 1998, p. 550).

In order to mediate this problematic presence of desire, and to ensure its confinement to the heteronormative sphere of the Middle American couple, it is necessary to displace and police, rather than deny, sexual urges. As *Underworld* demonstrates, consumption provides the principal strategy in this process of containment, sublimating *jouissance* into the desire for mass-produced, mass-marketed commodities. Such sublimation can be observed in advertising executive Charles Wainwright's highly gendered fantasy of the perfect advert for Minute Maid orange juice; an example of how David Bell's dream of the universal third person singular is signified, through consumption, into a collective, Middle American enunciation of self:

> You have to go for appetite appeal, for the visual hit, because this is a beautiful and enticing beverage and women's eyeballs reach high levels of excitation when they see bright orange cans in the freezer, gleaming with rime ice. You have to show the pulp. You show the juice splashing in the glass. You show the froth on a perky housewife's upper lip, like the hint of a blowjob before breakfast ... you can suggest, you can make inferences, you can promise the consumer the experience of citrusy bits of real pulp – a glass of juice, a goblet brimming with particulate matter, like wondrous orange smog. You show it. You photograph it lovingly and microscopically. If the can or package can be orgasmically visual, so can the product inside. (DeLillo, *Underworld*, pp. 532–3)

While the degree of sublimation is gendered, what unites heteronormative reactions to the advert is that some form of mediation is undertaken. For the female viewer it is a sublimated arousal which occurs at an unconscious level due to the 'bright orange' of the products packaging, whose appearance is as 'beautiful and enticing' as the beverage itself, causing 'women's eyeballs [to] reach high levels of excitation'. When addressing the attractiveness of the product to the male consumer, it is 'the froth on a perky housewife's upper lip, like the hint of a blowjob before breakfast' which appeals, a more overt form of sexual fulfilment, but one which still remains 'suggest[ed]', the product of 'inferences'. In each case it is not semen, but orange juice – a metaphor – which is consumed as a 'goblet brimming with particulate matter'. The key word in Charles' fantasy, in terms of both male and female desire, is 'like', indicative of a simile – that in place of semen is orange juice, in place of oral sex is a brightly coloured product, full of pulp, sustaining the hygienic space of Middle America.

In the consumption which defines Erica's language of Self, such sublimation can be observed in her attempt to signify her enunciation within the 'promised land where the middle class could realise the American dream – buying a new single-family house and a capacious new car and leading a well-rounded family life in a relaxed, wholesome nonurban environment' (Stich, 1987, p. 58). Of these various products with which she is invested, it is Jell-O which is the most central. As the narrator observes, '[d]oing things with Jell-O' which 'was just about the best way to improve her mood, which was oddly gloomy today'. Rather than gloominess, everything surrounding Erica is normally 'brand-new', vivid and bright, reflected in the colour of the Jell-O meals which she can mould and shape according to her desires. This brightness is echoed by the 'openness' of her surroundings, 'a sense of seeing everything there is to see at a single glance, with nothing shrouded or walled or protected from the glare.' With nothing concealed there is seemingly no threat, nothing that could be hiding beyond or beneath the products which constitute her environment: the 'breezeway', the 'two-tone Kelvinator' and the 'Jello-O'; all desirable, yet all seemingly free of any unsublimated sexual content (DeLillo, *Underworld*, pp. 514–16).

By the 1950s, however, sex itself was commoditized, and as *Underworld* depicts, tensions which were latent between Protestant and consumerist ideologies become explicit, disrupting the delicate balance of consumption, sublimation and desire. As Stich notes, with the advent of '*Playboy* sexuality became a major American business and an acknowledged part of American culture and the American dream – at least the male version of the dream' (Stich, 1987, p. 31). 'The centrefold was [accordingly] presented as a commodity object' (Stich, 1987, p. 31), as can be observed in Eric's objectification of Jayne Mansfield:

> The breasts were real, the face was put together out of a thousand thermoplastic things. And in the evolving scan of his eros, it was the masking waxes, liners, glosses and creams that became the soft moist mechanisms of release. (DeLillo, *Underworld*, p. 515)

As with Erica, it is the product which appeals, what is created, constructed and simulacral. Their activities – Eric's masturbation and Erica's preparation of Jell-O – are linked by the artificiality of the medium in which they are engaged, yet divided by their differing conceptions of the importance of sublimation and heteronormativity in the Middle American enunciation.[6]

This connection in their respective activities increases as Eric sexualizes the products which constituted Erica's enunciation of Self. While Jello-O represents the ultimate expression of Erica's sublimated *jouissance*, Eric finds its hyperreality to be a vehicle for a transgressive sexual expression:

> She remembered coming home one day about six months ago and finding Eric with his head in a bowl of her antipasto salad. He said he was trying to eat it from the inside out to test a scientific theory of his. The explanation was so crazy and unconvincing that it was weirdly believable. But she didn't believe it. She didn't know what to believe. Was this a form of sexual curiosity? Was he pretending the Jell-O was a sort of lickable female body part? Was he engaged in an act of unnatural oral stimulation? He had jellified gunk all over his mouth and tongue. (DeLillo, *Underworld*, pp. 520–1)[7]

---

6   Both are also seemingly modifiable by the user, creating a sense of power over the object which is used.
7   There is also an obvious Oedipal dimension to this image since it is the mother who has constructed this substance and used it as a medium for her enunciation of Self. Eric accordingly performs an act of metaphorical cunnilingus upon the corpus of his mother's enunciation.

'Capital burns off the nuance in a culture'

For Erica, unlike her son, the sexual dimension of their consumption has to remain sublimated so that their 'well-rounded family life' can keep its 'wholesome' aspect (Stich, 1987, p. 58). Eric's overt sexualization thus undermines their suburban language of Self, reshaping its balanced enunciation into a hyperreal space upon which desire can irrupt without constraint or control. As Berlant and Warner note, when forbidden 'pleasure is called sexuality, the spillage of eroticism into everyday social life seems transgressive in a way that provokes normal aversion, a hygenic recoil' (Berlant and Warner, 1998, p. 560) in Middle American adherents. Such aversion can be observed in Eric, who, when faced with the corruption of her values, turns once more to her signifying products, 'put[ting] on gloves just to talk to him' (DeLillo, *Underworld*, p. 521):

> Erica loved gloves. The gloves were indestructible, basically, made of the same kind of materials used in countertops and TV tubes, in the electrical insulation in the basement and the vulcanized tires on the car. (DeLillo, *Underworld*, pp. 519–20)

Through symbolic immersion Erica tries to become one with her products, excluding her son behind layers of constructed material, and defending her enunciation through commodities which embodying the delicate balance of her consumption, sublimation and desire.

Even Erica's gloves, however, are not immune to her son's reinscription, as the narrator observes:

> One of her kitchen gloves was missing – she had many pairs – and she wanted to believe Eric had borrowed it for one of his chemistry assignments. But she was afraid to ask. And she didn't think she looked forward to getting it back. (DeLillo, *Underworld*, p. 519)

Significantly, however, the young Eric does not embrace an unfettered hyperreal in a manner similar to Wendy in *Americana*. Through his use of Jello-O, rubberoid gloves and a condom, to mediate his access to *jouissance*, Eric also uses products to prevent an unconstrained irruption of desire within the hyperreal commodity of the composite Jayne Mansfield. Rather than destroying the Middle American enunciation of Self, Eric, at this point in his development, simply wishes to redraw its boundaries into a form more to his liking.[8] Eric's transformation of the Middle American enunciation thus remains a form of the dream of the third person singular – the suburban version of the American dream – which uses commodities to mediate access to *jouissance*, but one which does not require sexual sublimation. His masturbation through the condom is thus described as 'rubbery dumb and disaffecting' since a product is used to form a barrier between the raw, destructive potentiality of his desire, and the alterity and wounding engendered by the commoditized Other. Just as Erica's gloves function as an emotional prophylactic, so too does Eric's condom – the difference being merely a question of the degree of sublimation.

While the young Eric merely wishes to re-adjust their collective, public enunciation, once its supporting value system is compromised such delicate balance becomes unsustainable. This inevitability was noted by J. Edgar Hoover, who observed that unsublimated sexual expression was innately destabilizing, since '[o]nce you yield to random sexual urges, you want to see everything come loose', a dismantling of heteronormativity (DeLillo, *Underworld*, p. 564).[9] Such an effect can be observed in the aftermath of Eric's sexual act and his wish to invest his masturbation with some emotional content. As the narrator observes, Eric 'wouldn't just walk out the door when it was over', but would instead 'talk to her breasts' and '[b]e tender and lovey', confiding in 'them what his longings were, his hopes and dreams' (DeLillo, *Underworld*, p. 515). After the consummation of his onanistic act, however, Eric chooses not to do so. Despite the supposedly insulating quality of the condom, he still feels the backlash of his longings and the damage it causes to his enunciation of Self:

---

8   Like David Bell, Eric is also obsessed with the idea of film as a medium which could contain the hyperreal, rendering it intelligible and controllable, yet still providing a vessel for the expression of desire as part of an enunciation of Self. It is for this reason that, for Eric, film is a commodity, contained amongst a world of other products such as missile systems, fibre glass curtains and text books.
9   The issues of politics, power and terror raised by this statement will be explored in chapters 7 and 8.

> He took a long look at Jayne Mansfield's picture before he slipped it into the world atlas on his desk. He realized that Jayne's breasts were not as real-looking as he'd thought in his emotionally vulnerable state, dick in hand. (DeLillo, *Underworld*, p. 517)

As Hoover recognized, it is precisely the unloosing of this sexual impulse which results in the eventual fragmentation of the Middle American language of Self – if not in Eric, then in others of his generation who are not as privileged and do not have as much invested in its prevailing social order. In place of the heteronormative stability of the Middle American language of Self, only its patina remains and for individuals such as Eric and Erica, consumption instead leaves them 'lonely' inside their lives (DeLillo, *Underworld*, p. 170).

While *Underworld* shows the transition from small, predominantly ethnic communities to a wider, national enunciation of Self – and the subsequent destabilization of this third person singular as a means of resisting hyperreality – the novel also charts the beginning of a third stage in the evolution of the commodity. In this final phase, rather than providing a means of mediating the hyperreal, the commodity instead becomes divorced from its own materiality, transformed into simulacral capital. As Klara Sax observes:

> Money has no limits. I don't understand money anymore. Money is undone. (DeLillo, *Underworld*, p. 76)

The cause of this transition is the effect of hyperreality, and the four stages of its evolution which Baudrillard noted. While the relation between a commodity and its object may begin as the 'reflection of a profound reality' it evolves into the subsequent '*absence* of a profound reality' – as exemplified by a substance such as Jell-O (Baudrillard, 2006, p. 6). In its final stage, however, the commodity 'has no relation to any reality whatsoever; it is its own pure simulacrum' (Baudrillard, 2006, p. 6) and, within *Underworld*, it is accordingly capital which is divorced from any representational relationship to a material object.

It is in DeLillo's later novel, *Cosmopolis*, however, that such depiction reaches its apogee. The ultimate commodity has become money itself;

infinitely desirable and infinitely exchangeable due to its simulacral nature. As Baudrillard notes, 'it was capital' which 'throughout its history' has 'first fed on the destructuration of every referential, of every human objective, that shattered every ideal distinction between true and false, good and evil, in order to establish a radical law of equivalence and exchange, the iron law of its power'. It was thus capital which facilitated the transition from provincial markets to the dream of the universal third person singular, yet, as Baudrillard proceeds to observe, it was also capital which transformed itself into its own commodity, to be infinitely transferred and reabsorbed until eventually 'it does nothing but multiply the *signs* and accelerate the play of simulation' which reveal and underpin its own existence. It is in attempting to resist this development, that, for Baudrillard, 'every society' is 'continuing to produce, and to overproduce' in a desperate attempt to restore the reality of the commodity and capital which 'escapes it' (Baudrillard, 2006, pp. 22–3).

Just as Klara discusses her loss of certainty in the reality of money, so too does *Cosmopolis* describe a similar evolution from product to capital. As Eric Packer's art expert, Didi Fancher, notes, the relation between commodity and capital has altered:

> 'Money for paintings. Money for anything. I had to learn how to understand money,' she said. 'I grew up comfortably. Took me a while to think about money and actually look at it. I began to look at it. Look closely at bills and coins. I learned how it felt to make money and spend it. It felt intensely satisfying. It helped me be a person. But I don't know what money is anymore.'[10]

Didi's concerns regarding capital's infeasibility as a vessel for the language of Self are also echoed by Kinski, Eric's chief of theory, who notes that 'money had taken a turn' and that '[a]ll wealth has become wealth for its own sake' (DeLillo, *Cosmopolis*, p. 77). Arguing that '[m]oney has lost its narrative quality', Kinski's theory implies that rather than underpinning its possessor's language of Self, money is instead merely 'talking to itself',

---

10 Don DeLillo, *Cosmopolis* (London: Picador, 2003), p. 29. Further references are given after quotations in the text.

hyperreal and divorced of the connection between sign and object, capital and commodity (DeLillo, *Cosmopolis*, p. 77).

While such hyperreality of capital may be a source of concern for Klara, Didi, and perhaps for Kinski – causing a corresponding disruption to their enunciations of Self – for Eric Packer it is something to embrace.[11] It is older forms of relation between object and commodification which Eric perceives as alien.[12] Rather than trying to seek reassurance in these once concrete relations, Eric instead finds commodities such as the diamonds of the Hasidic merchants 'a form of money so obsolete' that he 'didn't know how to think about it' (DeLillo, *Cosmopolis*, p. 64). What is seemingly so alien to him is the tangibility of such a product, its concrete relationship between object and commodification, appearing to Eric to be redolent of 'everything he'd left behind or never encountered, cut and polished, intensely three-dimensional' (DeLillo, *Cosmopolis*, p. 64). He expresses a similar sentiment in regards to any form of street life connected with the exchange of concrete commodities such as 'the shtetl' with its 'hagglers and talebearers', 'scrapmongers' and 'dealers in stray talk' (DeLillo, *Cosmopolis*, p. 65). Significantly, both examples have a strong ethnic dimension, hinting, like *Underworld*'s depiction of the Italian-American Bronx communities, at earlier forms of commodification being rooted in both immigration and a concern with the real. It is for this reason that Eric considered that '[t]he street was an offense to the truth of the future' since it clings to conceptions of reality, and perhaps ethnicity, which, for Eric, no longer have validity (DeLillo, *Cosmopolis*, p. 65).

Rather than traditional commodities, Eric instead delights in the hyperreality of capital. As Kinski observes:

---

11 Kinski, in her embrace of theory, seems to be more ambivalent than the others mentioned above in her assessment of the hyperreality of capital.
12 This is further illustrated by Eric's exploration of the etymology of terms used to describe commodities, such as automated teller, which highlights their anachronistic nature and the extent to which the relationship between object and commodification has altered.

The concept of property is changing by the day, by the hour. The enormous expenditures that people make for land and houses and boats and planes. This has nothing to do with traditional self-assurances, okay. Property is no longer about power, personality and command. It's not about vulgar display or tasteful display. Because it no longer has weight or shape. The only thing that matters is the price you pay. Yourself, Eric, think. What did you buy for your one hundred and four million dollars? Not dozens of rooms, incomparable views, private elevators. Not the rotating bedroom and computerized bed. Not the swimming pool or the shark. Was it air rights? The regulating sensors and software? Not the mirrors that tell you how you feel when you look at yourself in the morning. You paid the money for the number itself. One hundred and four million. This is what you bought. And it's worth it. The number justifies itself. (DeLillo, *Cosmopolis*, pp. 77–8)

Capital has thus become an end in itself and *Cosmopolis* accordingly depicts the final, total shattering of the financial relation between object, commodity and consumption.

Eric thus embodies a new conception of the language of Self which is supposedly adapted to the demands of the hyperreality of capital through an updating of the Greek concept of '*Chrimatistikós*', 'the art of money-making' (DeLillo, *Cosmopolis*, pp. 77–8).[13] Such ability is embodied in Eric's contrasting relationship with hyperreal financial information and

13 In his essay '"An Unsettling, Alternative Self": Benno Levin, Emmanuel Levinas, and Don DeLillo's *Cosmopolis*', Aaron Chandler provides an interesting elucidation of the concept of *Chrismatistikós* through a highlighting of two related Aristotelian terms '*oikinomia*, or the science of household management' and '*chrematistike*, a technique solely concerned with the infinite acquisition of wealth' [Aaron Chandler, '"An Unsettling, Alternative Self": Benno Levin, Emmanuel Levinas, and Don DeLillo's *Cosmopolis*', *Critique*, 50:3 (2009), pp. 241–60, p. 246]. While such intertexts are beyond the scope of this inquiry, Chandler's work provides a helpful reading of the novel. In placing such a distinction within a larger dialectic, however, composed of Heideggerian versus Levinasian ontology, Chandler fails to adequately build upon this nuance. By attempting to make Heidegger and Levinas (of *Totality and Infinity*) into diametric opposites, Chandler distorts Heidegger's thought, failing to pay attention to the distinction between authentic (*eigentlich*) and inauthentic (*uneigentlich*) being-towards-death (*Sein sum Tode*) and stating, erroneously, that Heidegger 'implies that a somehow complete being finds itself tossed into a contingent world', marginalizing the importance of care (*Sorge*), concern (*besorgen*) and Being-towards-death in the

'Capital burns off the nuance in a culture' 139

he instinctively 'understood how much it meant to him, the roll and flip of data on a screen' (DeLillo, *Cosmopolis*, p. 24):

> [Eric] studied the figural diagrams that brought organic patterns into play, birdwing and chambered shell. It was shallow thinking to maintain that numbers and charts were the cold compression of unruly human energies, every sort of yearning and midnight sweat reduced to lucid units in the financial markets. In fact data itself was soulful and glowing, a dynamic aspect of the life process. This was the eloquence of alphabets and numeric systems, now fully realized in electronic form, in the zero-oneness of the world, the digital imperative that defined every breath of the planet's living billions. Here was the heave of the biosphere. Our bodies and oceans were here, knowable and whole. (DeLillo, *Cosmopolis*, p. 24)

Abandoning the supposedly 'shallow thinking' of a Wittgensteinian conception of the λόγος for 'soulful and glowing' data as an end in itself – the world converted to the 'electronic form' of 'zero-oneness' – Eric creates a *Chrimatistikós* suitable for a hyperreal context. There is no mourning for the seeming security of previous hermeneutical connections of language and representation as, for Eric, the hyperreal is seemingly composed of supposedly 'deeper' truths and patterns which accompany the subjectively human.

As Eric is all too quick to note, however, such pattern and cohesion in the near endless proliferation of the hyperreal requires a degree of competence and insight to apprehend, separating his success from the bemusement of the Other. It is this which allows him to create an idiosyncratic enunciation of Self which rejects the Middle American *das Man* and is rooted within supposedly logical relations from which he can derive stability and support. As the narrator observes, Eric 'knew there was something no one had detected, a pattern latent in nature itself, a leap of pictorial language that went beyond the standard models of technical analysis and out-predicted even the arcane charting of his own followers in the field' (DeLillo, *Cosmopolis*, p. 63). It is for this reason that Eric embraced this new form of *Chrimatistikós*, causing people 'to visit his website back in the days when he was forecasting stocks, when forecasting was pure power',

---

formation and shaping of subjectivity [Aaron Chandler, '"An Unsettling, Alternative Self": Benno Levin, Emmanuel Levinas, and Don DeLillo's *Cosmopolis*', p. 244].

enabling him to build up his fund (DeLillo, *Cosmopolis*, pp. 75–6). As a result of such mastery, when Eric 'tout[ed] a technology stock or bless[ed] an entire sector' his actions 'automatically cause[d] doublings in share price and the shifting of worldviews' as 'history became monotonous and slobbering,' 'yielding' to Eric's 'search for something purer, for techniques of charting that predicted the movements of money itself', the ultimate harnessing of the hyperreal (DeLillo, *Cosmopolis*, pp. 75–6). What granted Eric such success was that he had 'found beauty and precision here, hidden rhythms in the fluctuations of a given currency', a seeming Heideggerian *aletheia* within the hyperreal (DeLillo, *Cosmopolis*, pp. 75–6).

While Eric's success has been built upon a proficiency in *Chrimatistikós*, the novel chooses not to concentrate upon this period of ascendancy. *Cosmopolis* instead charts the catastrophic decline of Packer Capital arising from the massive gamble by its founder upon the movement of the yen. Even from within the corporate structure of his own fund, the seeming monomania of Eric's decision meets with resistance. As Michael Chin notes, '[w]hat is happening doesn't chart' and rather than trusting in Eric's competence, Michael now believes that they 'are speculating into the void' (DeLillo, *Cosmopolis*, p. 21). In response to such criticism, Eric continues to cling to his belief that on some 'deep' level there is always a pattern within hyperreal data, rendered intelligible through his competency at *Chrimatistikós*, which can provide the foundation of his language of Self. Believing that '[t]here had to be a way to explain the yen', any failure to do so would jeopardize the seeming invincibility of his *Chrimatistikós* and with it the viability of his idiosyncratic enunciation (DeLillo, *Cosmopolis*, p. 63). Eric accordingly rejects Chin's characterization that rather than a 'deep', analytical form of *Chrimatistikós*, Eric's gift is instead something quasi-mystical; that of a 'seer' who is the beneficiary of unpredictable flashes of understanding and moments of grace (DeLillo, *Cosmopolis*, p. 46). If Eric were to accept such a proposition it would mean that his previous achievements were irrespective of his effort, ability or knowledge; merely provided to him by some higher agency. A seer is thus dependent and continually vulnerable to a sudden withdrawal of grace, whereas a practitioner of *Chrimatistikós* is self-reliant and equipped with skills with which to maintain the stability of an idiosyncratic enunciation.

Rather than accepting the vagaries of the yen, Eric asserts that there must be 'an order at some deep level', a 'pattern that wants to be seen' (DeLillo, *Cosmopolis*, p. 86). The unknowability of the hyperreal is such, however, that Eric is finally forced to concede that 'it's been elusive in this instance' (DeLillo, *Cosmopolis*, p. 86). His 'experts have struggled and just about given up', just as Eric has 'been working on it, sleeping on it, not sleeping on it' (DeLillo, *Cosmopolis*, p. 86). Unlike his employees, however, Eric has staked his competence at *Chrimatistikós*, and therefore the basis of his enunciation, upon its ultimate knowability, a commodity far more valuable to him than fiscal resources. Eric is thus compelled to delve further, striving to 'search a little harder', to '[t]hink outside the limits' and prove the existence of a 'common surface, an affinity between market movements and the natural world' (DeLillo, *Cosmopolis*, p. 86). It is a tenet of Eric's faith, and therefore of his enunciation of Self, that despite capital's divorce from objects or commodities, it does not merely become an infinitely proliferating simulacrum. Rather than trusting to 'standard models' which propose that currency does not follow 'real pattern[s]' or 'predictable components', Eric instead attempts to impose himself upon its hyperreality, compelling it to accord with his language of Self (DeLillo, *Cosmopolis*, p. 46).

As the novel progresses, however, Eric is finally forced to surrender his belief that the hyperreal contains a deeper logic, order and 'essence'. Reflecting upon the supposed truth buried in the data, Eric observes that 'I'm beginning to doubt I'll ever find it', an emotion to which he had previously considered himself to be immune (DeLillo, *Cosmopolis*, p. 86). Losing the stability of his enunciation, Eric is forced into reconsidering both his Self and his relation to the hyperreal, evoking an irruption of unfettered *jouissance* in a similar manner to that which occurred in the decline of ethnic forms of consumption and the Middle American language of Self. As the narrator observes, 'the yen showed renewed strength' and its 'effect' upon Eric 'was sexual, cunnilingual in particular, and he let his head fall back and opened his mouth to the sky and rain' (DeLillo, *Cosmopolis*, p. 106).

With the collapse of his enunciation, Eric feels a momentary sense of relief, a sexual embrace of the unmediated hyperreal which links him to DeLillo's other male protagonists who experience *jouissance* in similar moments of collapse. As the narrator observed, '[t]he yen spree was releasing Eric from the influence of his neocortex', leaving him 'even freer than usual, attuned to the registers of his lower brain and gaining distance from the need to take inspired action, make original judgments, maintain independent principles and convictions, all the reasons why people are fucked up and birds and rats are not'. Eric's former indifference to the effects of his actions upon Others is transformed into an active delight in the widespread destruction which his pursuit of the yen has caused. As the narrator observes, Eric's 'actions regarding the yen were causing storms of disorder' as '[h]e was so leveraged, his firm's portfolio large and sprawling, linked crucially to the affairs of so many key institutions, all reciprocally vulnerable, that the whole system was in danger.' Rather than guilt or compassion, Eric's reaction to the chaos which he has created is to feel 'strong, proud, stupid and superior', yet 'also bored and a little dismissive' (DeLillo, *Cosmopolis*, pp. 115–16).

Such *jouissance* in the destruction of his enunciation and its effect upon Others cannot be sustained – as the latter emotions would indicate – and it is significant that the action of the novel spans only a single day. While Eric's various advisers suggest that he 'can ease off and take a loss and come back stronger', such admonitions fail to appreciate what is truly at stake. Jerry Varsava touched upon this issue in his essay 'The "Saturated Self": Don DeLillo on the Problem of Rogue Capitalism', in which he proposed that Eric's refusal to back down is part of his quest for an 'oversized failure', the product of his 'megalomaniac's paradox' in which the 'epical of whatever stripe – whether gains and victory or losses and defeat – is the megalomaniac's narcotic.'[14] While such a theory captures the *jouissance* Eric obtains from his decision – and which his employees fail to appreciate – it fails to account for the language of Self and the demands of Eric's enunciation: it is not simply wealth, pride, or megolomania which is at stake, but instead the very possibility of Eric's subjectivity which is wagered on the Yen. As Kinski observes, '[t]o pull back now would not be

---

14 Jerry Varsava, 'The "Saturated Self": Don DeLillo on the Problem of Rogue Capitalism', *Contemporary Literature*, 46:1 (2005), pp. 78–107, p. 102.

authentic', merely 'a quotation from other people's lives', rendering him into the 'paraphrase of a sensible text', an individual lost within the publicness of *das Man* (DeLillo, *Cosmopolis*, p. 85).

Such a retreat would thus be an acknowledgement that the hyperreal is in fact 'all random phenomena' to which fund managers such as Eric merely 'apply mathematics and other disciplines' in a desperate attempt at containment. It would mean that 'in the end you're dealing with a system that's out of control', with a '[h]ysteria at high speeds, day to day, minute to minute' within which, as Kinski proposes, '[w]e create our own frenzy, our own mass convulsions, driven by thinking machines that we have no final authority over.' Eric cannot admit to such a failure, and in the tradition of Glen and Bill, he chooses death over the inevitable collapse of his certainty of Self. Even at the novel's denouement, Eric cannot escape the simulacral and as he dies, his image is sampled by the camera in his watch, uploaded to the internet and rendered hyperreal in its near infinite, unreferential proliferation, another commodity for a viewing public to consume (DeLillo, *Cosmopolis*, p. 85).

As the above analysis has shown, consumption seems to initially offer a stable vessel for a fulfilling enunciation of Self, a means of evading the uncertainty of the representational power of the λόγος and the perils of unfettered *jouissance* in the hyperreal. Ultimately, however, commodities prove as susceptible to destabilization as denotation and image. Charting the changing nature of the modes of consumption from local, ethnic conceptions rooted in concrete relations between Self and commodity, to the universal third person singular of the Middle American enunciation, to the final dominance of the hyperreal, and the attempt at its mastery through *Chrimatistikós*, DeLillo's novels have shown that while founding the public, *das Man* enunciation of Middle America, the inevitable progression to capital leads to pervasive instability. Just as with the λόγος and image, commodities prove insufficient in the quest for a stable medium within which to enunciate both a public and private Self. As the next chapter will show, however, commodification and consumption pose a further problem in the search for a stable individual and collective Self in the form of its antithesis, waste.

CHAPTER 6

'[T]he banned materials of civilization'[1]: Waste, *Sinthomo*sexuality and Middle America

As discussed above, the transition from the predominance of material commodities to that of formless capital altered the relationship between subject, consumption and the language of Self. While such an evolution undermines the use of commodities in signifying the Middle American enunciation of Self, this chapter will explore how consumption itself sows the seeds for its own destabilization. This principally occurs through the presence of waste, the unavoidable by-product of consumption, which endangers the values which the latter endeavours to signify. As with the hyperreal, waste facilitates the irruption of unconstrained *jouissance*, altering the consumption and signification of the Middle American enunciation of Self. Principally using the theoretical perspective of Lee Edelman's *No Future: Queer Theory and the Death Drive*, this chapter argues that in both cases it is waste which provides the catalyst for such transition and the facilitation of an unrestrainable *jouissance*.

Using a Lacanian model of subjectivity,[2] Edelman argues that the socially mediating effect of the Symbolic leaves the individual 'always inhabit[ing] the order of the Other, the order of a social and linguistic reality articulated from somewhere else'[3]; a *das Man* conscious which

---

[1] Don DeLillo, *Underworld*, p. 286.
[2] As with most Lacian theorists, Lee Edelman attributes specific emphases to the shared psychoanalytical terminology used in his work. While such minutiae are beyond the scope of this inquiry, Edelman addresses this issue in the second chapter of his monograph.
[3] Lee Edelman, *No Future: Queer Theory and the Death Drive* (London: Duke University Press, 2004), pp. 7–8. Further references are given after quotations in the text.

limits and restricts authentic idiosyncrasy. For Edelman, such subjectivity is created through the utilization of '[t]he signifier, an alienating and meaningless token of our Symbolic constitution as subjects' in which the Self exists solely within the realm of the Imaginary (Edelman, 2004, pp. 7–8). For adherents of the Middle American enunciation such signifiers were predominantly derived from the commodification of the objects with which they are surrounded: the bright new products of Erica and Rich's suburban home. Within a Lacanian reading, such praxis is problematic since the 'signifier only bestows a sort of *promissory* identity, one with which we can never succeed in fully coinciding because we, as subjects of the signifier, can only be signifiers ourselves, can only ever aspire to catch up to whatever it is we might signify by closing the gap that divides us and, paradoxically, makes us subjects *through that act of division alone*' (Edelman, 2004, pp. 7–8). A perspective echoed by Gloria Anzaldúa who suggests that identity is accordingly a 'process' which flows 'between' and 'over' all 'aspects of a person', yet one with which they can never wholly coincide.[4] This inability to unify the Imaginary and the Symbolic, to create a Self which is whole, 'necessitates' the 'various strategies designed to structure the subject in the space of meaning where Symbolic and Imaginary overlap' (Edelman, 2004, pp. 7–8), and, in regards to this monograph, the most relevant of these strategies is that of reproductive futurity.

Edelman argues that it is such investment which provides a defence mechanism that strives towards 'externalising and configuring' the Imaginary into the realm of the Symbolic (Edelman, 2004, p. 9). Reproductive futurity thus functions as a 'narrativity of desire', preventing the disarticulating effect of 'overdeterminations of libidinal positions and inconsistencies of psychic defenses' (Edelman, 2004, p. 9) which arise from divergent sexualities that are not centred upon the family home and its supporting commodities. As would be expected from a Lacanian conception, the force which 'disarticulates' this 'narrativity of desire' is that of 'the drives',

---

4   Gloria Anzaldúa, 'To(o) queer the writer: loca, escrita y chicana', in Betsy Warland (ed.), *InVersions: Writing by Dykes, Queers and Lesbians* (Vancouver: Press Gang, 1991), pp. 249–63, pp. 252–3.

most predominantly the death drive (Edelman, 2004, p. 9). It is for this reason, Edelman argues, that 'the whole register of sexuality' evolves as a 'displacement' of these 'energies' (Edelman, 2004, pp. 22–3), the cornerstone of Middle American sublimation. For those within such an enunciation, it appears, as Darieck Scott notes, as if 'the only available option' were one which involved 'subordinating one characteristic to another, as if identity cannot be expressed except as an undisturbed center around which satellite qualifiers revolve.'[5] Sexuality[6] thus functions as the means by which this subordination can occur, achieved through reproductive futurity and safely ensconced within the bourgeois nuclear couple which orders the social structure of the Deming's section and that of the Middle American enunciation as a whole. Such urges still remain, however, and the Symbolic can never wholly deny their irruption; the *'embodying* [of] the remainder of the Real internal to the symbolic order' (Edelman, 2004, p. 25). The divergent drives which are experienced by the Demings consequently remain 'intractable, unassimilable to the logic of interpretation or the demands of meaning-production' (Edelman, 2004, p. 9), termed by Edelman as *jouissance*, 'a movement beyond the pleasure principle, beyond the distinctions of pleasure and pain, a violent passage beyond the bounds of identity, meaning, and law' (Edelman, 2004, p. 25).

Such a destabilizing effect of *jouissance* and the death drive can be observed in Eric's masturbatory practice.[7] In addition to its signification

---

5   Darieck Scott, 'Jungle Fever?: Black Gay Identity Politics, White Dick, and the Utopian Bedroom', *GLQ: A Journal of Lesbian and Gay Studies*, 1 (1994), pp. 299–321, p. 301.
6   For the purposes of this book, sexuality will be defined within a Foucauldian context as a social phenomenon produced by the accretion of certain sanctioned and prohibited practices, deployed in order to compel and maintain a particular public enunciation. Sexuality thus differentiates itself from a *jouissance* which is ephemeral and uncodified.
7   While beyond the scope of this inquiry, Eric shares a number of commonalities with the actor Montgomery Clift, active during the same period, who, whilst publicly appearing to be normative, concealed a number of characteristics shared by Eric such as unconventional desires, his penchant for eating other people's food with his fingers, idiosyncratic verbal tics and a sadistic sense of humour.

as a commodity, the condom he uses can also be seen as a purpose-built receptacle designed to contain an unwanted substance – mediating the transition of product to by-product and finally to waste product. Eric's semen, associated in reproductive futurity with fertility and propagation, becomes the unwanted waste of an activity centred purely upon pleasure, divorced from any concern with reproduction or the heteronormative Middle American couple. Eric's masturbation is thus a means of accessing *jouissance*, mediated by a commodity which separates him from the materiality of his semen and the irruption of the Real. It is for this reason that the condom is described as 'rubbery dumb and disaffecting' (DeLillo, *Underworld*, p. 515), a statement both of sensory deprivation compared to unmediated sexual sensation, but also an awareness that the commodity exists as a form of emotional prophylaxis between Self and desire; attempting to preserve the Imaginary form of the Middle American enunciation. This role of the commodity conforms with other, less overtly sexual praxis depicted within the section which, likewise, stress artificiality. Just as Eric uses a condom as a medium of containment, so too does his mother, Erica, deploy her gloves as an emotional defence which she has to put on 'just to talk to him'; the preventative force of which is rooted in their 'indestructible' nature, 'protect[ing] her from scalding water and the touch of food scraps' (DeLillo, *Underworld*, pp. 519–21). As with Eric and his semen, it is not just detritus – the particulates of their excessive consumption – whose materiality Erica attempts to inure herself against, but also an emotional dimension which she strives to escape, rooted in an attempt to deny alterity and the damage which Eric is causing to their shared enunciation.

Paradoxically, however, Eric simultaneously wishes for protection from, and access to, the very same alterity which his mother denies. Rather than striving for total separation from Jayne, the young Eric instead uses commodification to mediate his engagement with the Other, ensuring that his language of Self remains principally one of isolation, a process which transforms the object of his desire into a commodity whose consumption causes their transformation into waste. Equally, however, total separation is rejected since it would eliminate the *jouissance* which could be obtained in a mediated, though reduced, form. Wishing for his sexual practice to be invested with an emotional component, Eric instead creates a parody of

'[T]he banned materials of civilization'

the 'oneness' of the heteronormative Middle American couple, even as he attempts to shield himself from any accompanying possibility of wounding.

Such ambiguity can therefore be seen as the defining quality of the subject's relationship to the Other, and to waste, captured in Eric's imagining of what form the aftermath of his consumption will take:

> [...] he wouldn't just walk out the door when it was over. He would talk to her breasts. Be tender and lovey. Tell them what his longings were, his hopes and dreams. (DeLillo, *Underworld*, p. 515)

While he tries to imagine a genuine, emotional communing with his sexual object, within the scenario he envisages she does not tell him her own longings, hopes or dreams; a reciprocity which would encourage unmediated connection. Equally, he also does not imagine communicating his mental Being to Jayne in a Benjaminian manner. Instead, it is to 'her breasts' that he 'would talk', displacing the emotional element of his sexual practice onto a commodified element of her image. The problematically emotional relation to the simulacra of Jayne Mansfield can be seen as an example of the ambiguous effect of the drives within the subject. While they may help in 'congealing identity around the fantasy of satisfaction or fulfilment by means of that object', as *jouissance* they also 'dissolv[e] such fetishistic investments, undoing the consistency of a social reality that relies on Imaginary identifications, on the structures of Symbolic law, and on the paternal metaphor of the name' (Edelman, 2004, p. 25). It is precisely this ambiguity which Eric encounters as he endeavours to invest his masturbation with emotional content.

This highlights the role played by consumption in ensuring an enunciation rooted in partial connection, conforming to the publicness of the Middle American *das Man*. It is not a holistic Jayne Mansfield, or even her hyperreal image, which provides the stimulus for Eric's masturbation, but instead the shattering of Jayne into component parts[8] each of which can be used or ignored at will and all of which can be separated – at least pro-

---

8 A phenomenon further accentuated by the circumstances surrounding her death which included decapitation.

visionally – from the alterity of the whole. Such a transition in the status of the Other can be seen in the nature of Eric's arousal:

> The breasts were real, the face was put together out of a thousand thermoplastic things. And in the evolving scan of his eros, it was the masking waxes, liners, glosses and creams that became the soft moist mechanisms of release. (DeLillo, *Underworld*, p. 515)

Jayne has accordingly become merely a collective noun for a group of arousing elements, and crucially, as discussed above, it is the hyperreal which proves to be the most effective 'release', the furthest removed from the alterity of a holistic Other and the order of the Symbolic. Equally, however, the object of desire still forms the other, heteronormative fascia of the reproductive, Middle American couple, providing the raw material upon which such commodification operates: the same fantasy of 'oneness' (Edelman, 2004, p. 86), but one whose emotional balance has shifted, providing the subject with a seemingly heteronormative *jouissance* which is still free of connection and dependence. While accessing a transgressive pleasure, the heteronormative fantasy of Eric's praxis continues to function as what Teresa de Lauretis terms the 'psychic mechanism that structures subjectivity by reworking or translating social representations into subjective representations and self-representations,'[9] seemingly sustaining the Middle American enunciation of Self.

While fragmentation may partially defend the Self against alterity, it only serves to more easily facilitate the transition of the sexual object into waste, allowing the emergence of non-normative desires. Once Eric has consumed the polyvalent surfaces of the composite Jayne, the continued presence of her image becomes a source of distaste, indicative of the very waste product which he strives to avoid. Jayne becomes analogous to the troubling materiality of the dirt and food scraps with which Erica interacts

---

9   Teresa de Lauretis, 'Popular culture, public and private fantasies: femininity and fetishism in David Cronenberg's *M. Butterfly*', *Signs: Journal of Women in Culture and Society*, 24:2 (1999), pp. 303–33, p. 307.

whilst wearing 'rubberoid' gloves – just as Eric wears the condom, a rubber in American slang:

> He took a long look at Jayne Mansfield's picture before he slipped it into the world atlas on his desk. He realized that Jayne's breasts were not as real-looking as he'd thought in his emotionally vulnerable state, dick in hand. (DeLillo, *Underworld*, p. 517)

Eric's sexual consumption is thus characterized as a state of emotional susceptibility, and while alterity may have been largely denied by fragmentation and the presence of a mediating commodity, such defences only serve to make Jayne's transition to the ineluctability of waste more disturbing in Eric's 'vulnerable state'. His masturbatory practice, augmented and defended by the deployment of a prophylactic commodity, can be seen as a means of accessing *jouissance* whilst still attempting to protect the stability of the Imaginary Self: a striving for pleasure which, in its fascination with, and arousal in, the thermoplastic and the nuclear, hints at 'mechanisms of release' beyond the heteronormative figure of Jayne. The wounding which occurs following Eric's masturbation is indicative of the extent to which this incipient, alternate, non-heteronormative *jouissance* creates a conflict within the subject between transgressive desires and the need to contain such longings within the bounds of Middle American reproductive futurity. Rather than the heteronormativity central to the Middle American symbolic order, it is instead towards unsublimated – though not unmediated – *jouissance* that Eric is drawn, leading away from the land of lawns towards an obscured realm of unregulated, complex desires.

Constructed through, and undermined by his urges, Eric's praxis is indicative of the extent to which the Self is forced to struggle to maintain subjectivity, to contain itself within the public enunciation of *das Man*, avoiding an encounter with the Lacanian conception of *jouissance* as a 'truth' which 'chafes against "normalization"' (Edelman, 2004, p. 6). Such disruption refuses to find 'its value' in any 'good susceptible to generalization', instead presenting a 'radical challenge to the very value of the social itself' (Edelman, 2004, p. 6). In order to avoid confrontation with the Lacanian truth of *jouissance*, the mythical 'Child' at the heart of reproductive futurity comes 'to serve as the repository of variously sentimentalized cultural identifications', 'embody[ing] for us the telos of the social order and com[ing] to be seen as the one for whom that order is held in perpetual trust' (Edelman, 2004, pp. 10–11).

Erica and Rich have accordingly signified their son as the figural child who functions as 'the prop' of a 'secular theology', underpinning their 'social reality' (Edelman, 2004, p. 12). As the 'Oneness' of his parent's union, Eric's supposed future as the progenitor of subsequent generations stretches before him, providing the Middle American enunciation with its supporting futurity rooted in a heteronormative historicity (*Historizität*). Such continuity is contingent upon Eric's behaviour since reproductive futurity 'imagin[es] each moment as pregnant with the Child of our Imaginary identifications, as pregnant, that is, with a meaning whose presence would fill up the hole in the Symbolic' (Edelman, 2004, pp. 15–16), ensuring the survival and stability of the Middle American enunciation.

The tension created by this potential investment can be observed in Erica's concern regarding her son's sexual practice. Reflecting upon Eric's 'crazy and unconvincing' explanation for his 'unnatural' act of 'oral stimulation' undertaken upon her Jell-O antipasto salad, Erica is left with the feeling that she 'didn't know what to believe' (DeLillo, *Underworld*, pp. 520–1). Similarly, when she thought about the glove he had borrowed 'she was afraid to ask' to what use it had been put and 'didn't think' that 'she looked forward to getting it back' (DeLillo, *Underworld*, p. 519). As Foucault observed, those surrounding the onanist are 'left with the suspicion that all children were guilty' and that 'their conduct' needed to be 'prescribed and their pedagogy recodified' in order to limit their transgression:[10] what Foucault classed as the 'series composed of perversion-heredity-degenerescence' against which the bourgeois attempted to counter and defend itself (Foucault, 1998, p. 118). Since every moment for Erica is 'pregnant' with the possibility of the gap of the symbolic being filled, shoring the Middle

---

10   Michel Foucault, *The Will To Knowledge: The History of Sexuality Volume 1*, Robert Hurley (trans.) (London: Penguin, 1998), p. 42. Further references are given after quotations in the text.

'[T]he banned materials of civilization' 153

American enunciation of Self, Eric's 'sexual curiosity' jeopardizes not only his own enunciation but also those of his parents (DeLillo, *Underworld*, pp. 520–1). As Judith Butler observes, it is for this reason that 'identity categories tend to be instruments of regulatory regimes',[11] since it is through the constraining force of a socially sanctioned identity that divergent praxis can be restrained, preserving the stability of a collective enunciation for the majority of its adherents.

Rather than embracing such reproductive futurity, however, Eric rejects his role as the figural Child, becoming what Edelman terms a 'queer' presence (Edelman, 2004, p. 4). In accessing a *jouissance* free of reproductive futurity, Eric's encounter with the death drive 'embod[ies] the order's traumatic encounter with its own inescapable failure' (Edelman, 2004, pp. 25–6). As Eric's troubling presence within the Deming household attests, any 'sacralization of the Child thus necessitates the sacrifice of the queer', preserving the Self and its collective enunciation from destroying the 'suture' of Middle American subjectivity and revealing the illusion of its futurity (Edelman, 2004, p. 28; p. 24). It is this which, for Butler, provides the impetus to embrace such 'cultural fictions', the illusory nature of which is 'obscured by the credibility of those productions' and whose maintenance is ensured by 'the punishments that attend not agreeing to believe in them' (Butler, 1990, p. 140). Such a cultural imperative thus attempts to 'compel' subjects to identify themselves 'with what's to come by way of haven or defense against the ego's certain end' (Edelman, 2004, p. 34), what this monograph terms as a public, inauthentic form of being-towards-the-end (*Sein sum Ende*) which characterizes the third person singular.

As Edelman observes, and Eric's praxis attests, this 'sacralization of the Child' as a 'constant movement toward realization cannot be divorced, however, from a will to undo what is thereby instituted, to begin again ex nihilo' (Edelman, 2004, pp. 9–10): the desire to shed the constrictive burden of the heteronormative, Middle American enunciation. For the majority of its adherents it is therefore a constant battle to control urges

---

11 Judith Butler, *Gender Trouble: Feminism and the Subversion of Identity* (London: Routledge, 1990), pp. 13–14. Further references are given after quotations in the text.

and subsume them within the political sphere of reproductive futurity and the 'Oneness' of the heterosexual couple; to resist the lure of *jouissance* and the death drive. The particular form which this struggle takes for each individual is referred to, by Edelman, as the '*sinthome*', defined as 'the singularity of the subject's existence', consisting of the 'particular way each subject manages to knot together the orders of the Symbolic, the Imaginary, and the Real' (Edelman, 2004, p. 35), revealing the 'site of a jouissance around and against which the subject takes shape and in which it finds its consistency' (Edelman, 2004, pp. 38–9). It is the close connection of the *sinthome* to the death drive which provides the basis for Edelman's theorizing of '*sinthomo*sexuality' as 'an unregenerate, and unregenerating, sexuality whose singular insistence on jouissance' is a result of its 'rejecting every constraint imposed by sentimental futurism' (Edelman, 2004, pp. 47–8). As a nascent *sinthomo*sexual, Eric's onanism is a denial of 'the reification that turns the sexed subject into a monolith, a petrified identity' (Edelman, 2004, pp. 73–4) that constitutes a public enunciation of Self. Eric's masturbation is a refusal to surrender his quest for *jouissance* – of his wish to wring pleasure from the polyvalency of Jayne's hyperreal surfaces whatever the societal cost.

Rejecting this social imperative to conformity, and embracing *sinthomo*sexuality, individuals such as Eric deny reproductive futurity's compulsion to abandon the queer for the sake of the survival of the heteronormative Middle American enunciation. Such a sexuality thus 'endanger[s] the fantasy of survival by endangering the survival of love's fantasy, insisting instead on the machine-like working of the partial, dehumanizing drives and offering a constant access to their surplus of jouissance' (Edelman, 2004, pp. 73–4). Since 'the Child of the heteroreproductive Couple stands in, at least fantasmatically, for the redemption' of the Self, 'the *sinthomo*sexual, who affirms' subjectivity's 'loss, maintaining it as the empty space, the vacuole, at the heart of the Symbolic' is therefore responsible for 'effectively destroying that Child and, with it, the reality it means to sustain' (Edelman, 2004, pp. 114–15). The *sinthomo*sexual endangers both the Self and the social, raising the question of '[w]hat future could one build' when 'communal relations, collective identities, the very realm of the social itself'

'*[T]he banned materials of civilization*'

(Edelman, 2004, pp. 67–8) are all rejected by the *sinthomo*sexual, a 'child-aversive, future-negating force' (Edelman, 2004, pp. 113–14)?

It is precisely this aversion to futurity which appeals to Eric in his *sinthomo*sexuality and which conditions his masturbation. Rather than the destructive force of the death drive encouraging Eric to abandon his divergent sexuality, it instead becomes part of the mechanisms of arousal. While the condom may provide Eric with protection from the materiality of his own body's waste, he also 'liked' using it 'because it had a sleek metallic shimmer, like his favourite weapons system, the Honest John, a surface-to-surface missile with a warhead that carried yields of up to forty kilotons' (DeLillo, *Underworld*, pp. 514–15). Eric's masturbation can therefore be seen to have two dimensions, the first a consuming of the commoditized Other and the transition of their materiality into waste, and, secondly, a connection with a fantasy of global destruction and death. Eric's masturbation accordingly hinges upon two seemingly contradictory erotic forms: the 'soft moist mechanisms of release' of Jayne's hyperreal image and the 'sleek metallic shimmer' of the Honest John weapon system with its 40 kilotonne Nuclear payload, nearly twice that of the Nagasaki device and three times the destructive power of the Hiroshima bomb. For Eric, these images of disaster are as arousing as the pin-up, and are inextricably linked with his form of sexual practice, that which, as a *sinthomo*sexual, embraces the *jouissance* of the death drive in all of its forms.

Surrendering to urges unmediated by commodities and free of the heteronormative patina provided by a pin-up image – to 'a radical coming without reserve that expends itself improvidently, holding nothing in trust for tomorrow' (Edelman, 2004, p. 132) – we re-encounter Eric 'in his early thirties' and discover that he has become 'one of the bombheads' at a military nuclear research centre in New Mexico. Rather than the heteronormative world of suburban living, with everything open to view, Eric has instead chosen to reside in the desert of 'Jornada del Muerto', rich in the history of the Manhattan project (DeLillo, *Underworld*, pp. 403–4). In place of the new, heteronormative Suburban homes of his childhood with the sense of nothing hidden from view, Eric has instead chosen 'the underground operation in the Pocket, where weapons were conceived and designed' in a place governed by and conditioned upon secrecy; exemplified by its existence, or lack thereof, as a 'white place' on the map, reflected in its 'interdunal flats' which 'were map-white, on the page and in living fact' (DeLillo, *Underworld*, p. 404). In entering this space, Eric obtains access to the *jouissance* he imagined as a masturbating child in a butterfly chair, hidden in his room behind fibreglass curtains; a physical access to death on a massive scale. As Alan Sinfield observed, 'while we may like to think of fantasy as free-ranging, in fact it often shows astonishing fixity',[12] as exemplified by the continuity of Eric's *sinthomo*sexuality and its *jouissance* derived from nuclear material.

Just as he did in the Deming's household, Eric thrives upon what is hidden, upon the pleasure of handling something which is potentially life-threatening,[13] yet which is still contained within a product designed for such a purpose. As the narrator observes, 'Eric worked in a lab area that Matt was not cleared to enter', handling 'radioactive materials inside a sealed glove box', an echo of the rubberoid pair worn by Erica which Eric borrowed and overtly sexualized (DeLillo, *Underworld*, p. 403). Just as with the condom, Eric handles the site of his *jouissance* through a plethora of fetishized products which become a part of the mechanisms of arousal, the 'protective gloves' and 'overgloves attached to his sleeves', the 'layers of treated clothing equipped with a number of film badges and rad-detectors' (DeLillo, *Underworld*, p. 403). It is these which allow him to work 'with bomb components – the neutron initiator, the detonators, the subcritical pieces, the visceral heat inside the warhead', providing access to his *jouissance* (DeLillo, *Underworld*, p. 403).

While the intervention of a material commodity may remain constant in the practice of his older and younger Selves, what has altered is that Eric no longer engages with the death drive within the realm of fantasy. Aroused by the thought of nuclear material, of its destructive power and the structures and order contained within its explosive force, Eric has chosen a career

---

12   Alan Sinfield, *On Sexuality and Power: Between Men – Between Women* (New York: Columbia University Press, 2004), p. 1.
13   The materiality of Eric's semen was 'life'-threatening to his parents' enunciation of Self.

which allows him physical access to the means of such destruction, engaging with its materiality. Rather than the heteronormativity of the suburbs, Eric has abandoned reproductive futurity for the material embodiment of the death drive which could never be contained or encountered within such a suburban realm. Such is the extent to which Eric embraces this *sintho-mo*sexuality, that even within the closed, specialist world of The Pocket, Eric's sexual enjoyment of his work distinguishes him from his colleagues. As the narrator observed, the 'bombheads loved their work but weren't necessarily pro-bomb, walking around with megadeath hard-ons' (DeLillo, *Underworld*, p. 404). They were instead 'detail freaks' who 'were awed by the inner music of bomb technology' and 'carried an afterglow of sixties incandescence, a readiness to give themselves compulsively to something' (DeLillo, *Underworld*, p. 404). For these other bombheads, the attraction of the secret, parochial nature of The Pocket is that it is 'one of those nice tight societies that replaces the world', a 'self-enclosed and self-referring' space in which the technicians could communicate in 'a language' which was 'inaccessible to others' (DeLillo, *Underworld*, p. 412). Such exclusion grants its participants a supportive context in which they could give themselves wholly to the shaping of a new, collective enunciation of Self, free from the demands of Middle American heteronormative reproductive futurity and its commitment to spouses and children.

Even in the context of this specialist enunciation Eric still differs from the other bombheads as it is not the 'afterglow of sixties incandescence' which shapes his engagement with the post-Manhattan nuclear project, but instead the 'placid nineteen-fifties' in which '[e]verybody dressed and spoke the same way' and '[i]t was all kitchens and cars and TV sets' (DeLillo, *Underworld*, p. 410): the hegemony and heteronormativity of the Middle American enunciation of Self. Unlike the majority of individuals such as Erica who subscribed to this enunciation, however, Eric possesses a visceral awareness that this placidity was merely the surface appearance of the various roiling power structures responsible for its maintenance. As he observes, '[m]eanwhile way out here they were putting troops in trenches for nuclear war games' with '[f]ireballs roaring right above them' (DeLillo, *Underworld*, p. 410).[14]

Considering such a prospect, of fire and 'megadeath', Eric, unlike his co-workers, literally gets a hard-on, transgressing the pure logic and order of the other bombheads' investment in their work and instead embracing a more elaborate form of his nascent *sinthomo*sexuality. What is of particular interest in terms of his evolution to such a category is that his later state is merely the flowering of his earlier anti-normative traits which he had hidden beneath a patina of heteronormative desire. The verbal mannerisms which 'used to throw a pall' over his family also remain and as the narrator observes 'Eric [still] had a fake stutter he liked to use to texture the conversation', the social purpose and meaning of which 'wasn't clear', beyond the *jouissance* he obtained from such usage (DeLillo, *Underworld*, p. 417). This fake stutter is also matched by Eric's conversational style which is predominantly depicted as focusing upon 'spread[ing] astounding rumors' whose veracity, for Eric, is a subject of indifference (DeLillo, *Underworld*, p. 403). What is instead perceived as important, and the reason why he chooses to disseminate such stories, is '[f]or the tone', 'the edge', the 'bite' and the 'existential burn' (DeLillo, *Underworld*, p. 406).

Present in all of Eric's behaviours, such antisocial tendencies can also be observed in his eating habits. As the narrator notes, he 'tended to eat with his hands' (DeLillo, *Underworld*, p. 403) in an almost bestial manner, taking 'a strand of spaghetti in his fingers' before he 'slow-lowered it down his throat with a certain amount of snakely constriction' (DeLillo, *Underworld*, p. 410). Such eating habits mirror Eric's behaviour within the family home, the sexually-charged consumption of the antipasto salad from 'the inside out'. So great is Eric's disregard for social conventions that he even 'stuck a finger in Matty's creamed spinach and hooked a shreddy morsel toward his mouth' (DeLillo, *Underworld*, p. 410).[15] Similarly, Eric's expression

---

14 This issue of the power structures beneath 1950s consumerism will receive further treatment in Chapter 7.
15 Eric is also depicted examining a *Playboy* centrefold echoing his earlier objectification of Jayne Mansfield.

of pleasure takes the form of a 'shadow smile' which 'appeared at the far end of the sprawled body' and 'came and went, like some inner dialogue he was conducting that ran parallel to the spoken lines, a thing of elusive drift', a symbol of his focus upon his own *jouissance* and his indifference to the Symbolic order of the social (DeLillo, *Underworld*, p. 417). Within The Pocket, separated from any last vestige of reproductive futurity, Eric has wholly embraced his transgression of heteronormativity, finding an environment where the deviance of his *sinthomo*sexuality is tolerated and where he can actively engage with the objects of his *jouissance*. Thus, the very factors which cause Matt Shay to abandon The Pocket for the reproductive futurity of marriage and family are precisely what draws and sustains Eric's involvement in such a rarefied occupation.

While Eric's *sinthomo*sexuality is an extreme divergence from the heteronormative order of the Middle American enunciation of Self, the breadth and range of *Underworld*'s depiction illustrates the extent to which such urges are pervasive, albeit in a more repressed form, constituting the alternate fascia of Middle American consumption. Even Eric's father, Rick, a seemingly archetypical Middle American patriarch, can be observed to struggle against the pull of the death drive, fighting the urge to escape the signification of the social order and begin again 'ex nihilo'. Spending the majority of the Demming section alone in 'the breezeway', Rich is preoccupied with 'simonizing' his 'two-tone Ford Fairlane convertible, brand-new, like the houses and the trees, with whitewall tires and stripes of jetstreak chrome that fairly crackled when the car was in motion' (DeLillo, *Underworld*, p. 515). The fact that 'running a shammy over the chromework' was something that 'he could do forever' would seem to be closer to Erica's investment in the bright colours and strontium whites of the household and its consumer goods, rather than an analogue of Eric's masturbatory practice (DeLillo, *Underworld*, p. 516). As the section demonstrates, however, there is a crucial gendering in their investment of the commodities with which they are surrounded. By engaging with their motor vehicle, Rick 'could look at himself in a strip of chrome, warp-eyed and hydrocephalic, and feel some of the power of the automobile, the horsepower, the decibel rumble of dual exhausts, the pedal tension of Ford-O-Matic drive' (DeLillo, *Underworld*, p. 516). Unlike Erica, who is drawn to commodities which seemingly embody openness and a lack of secrecy,[16] for Rick such seeming visibility merely functions as a camouflage beneath which he embraces the power, and, most significantly, the 'tension' and 'drive' of the automobile. Viewing himself in its surfaces, Rick's image is 'hydrocephalic', a predominantly congenital brain condition which, in its accumulation of fluid, compresses the higher reasoning centres of the brain, leaving the urges and desires unrestrained.[17]

Crucially, however, such a distension is only visible to the Self, and from the perspective of the Other the pressure and threat of the drives remains invisible, hidden within the sublimation of masculine forms of Middle American consumption. While Erica may delight in the supposed wholesomeness of their commodities, matching her 'swirly blue skirt and buttercup blouse' to 'the colors of their Fairlane', she is unaware that there is a 'sneaky thing about this car' which appeals to her husband Rick. As the narrator observes, he 'drove it sensibly to the dentist and occasionally carpooled with the Andersons and took Eric to the science fair but beneath the routine family applications was the crouched power of the machine, top down, eating up the landscape.' (DeLillo, *Underworld*, pp. 516).

The car is thus the embodiment of the unsymbolizable remainder of the Real beneath the Symbolic; the urge towards an unsublimated consumption without restraint and a delight in the waste which it produces, echoing the younger Nick's longing for an automobile. In matching her outfit with the vehicle, Erica comes to symbolize the body from which Rick wishes to wring his *jouissance*, irrespective of her wishes and values; a desire which he has sublimated into the car whose raw power and 'drive' instead violates the landscape opened up by the phallic thrust of the highway. While corresponding to Eric's eating of the antipasto salad from 'the inside out' in 'an act of unnatural oral stimulation' – namely the penetration, consumption and stimulation of the commodities from which Erica has

---

16   Erica's emotional investment in the rubberoid gloves reveal the illusory superficiality of such an outlook, contingent as it is upon hiding and preventing the contact with waste which is an inevitable product of consumption.
17   As discussed above, a similar reference to hydrocephalia can be observed in Bill Gray's description of the distorting quality of his final, unsuccessful novel.

constructed her enunciation and invested her Self – Rick's desires remain socially acceptable due to the degree of their sublimation. Though both Rick and Eric manifest an urge to consume and seize *jouissance* from Erica's body, regardless of her volition, what continues to separate father and son is the manner in which such desires are expressed. While both conceal their urges out of fear of social disapproval, Rick displaces his within a commodity and practice which is not noticeably sexual beyond the Self. Erica can thus engage and integrate such a vessel into her own enunciation, without conflict or revulsion, unaware of what it represents for her husband and that she has been relegated to the same status as a commoditized Jayne. In doing so, Rick can continue to appear as the perfect embodiment of the suburban husband and *paterfamilias* of a bourgeois, nuclear family, seemingly untouched by sexual urges beyond those ascribed to the 'One-ness' of the heteronormative couple and its reproductive futurity. In spite of such appearances, however, the urges remain, hidden beneath the patina of heteronormativity: a waste product produced by consumption and the commoditization of the Other. Whether or not such tendencies are acted upon and converted into *sinthomo*sexuality, they still remain, their ubiquity highlighting the provisional nature of the heteronormative, Middle American enunciation.

In the scope of its depiction, *Underworld* thus provides a detailed exploration of the transition, within the Middle American enunciation of Self, of the unavoidable conversion of commodity into waste. As the above analysis has demonstrated, by portraying Eric at two points in his life – as a 'masturbating child' and a *sinthomo*sexual adult – the novel achieves a complex depiction of the interaction of waste, heteronormativity and the Middle American enunciation of Self. By so doing, it can be seen that the power structures which support such a collective, public enunciation, rest upon issues of sublimation, and the transferring of omnipresent urges and drives into a form of consumption which supports the social, and which defers waste into an 'underworld' excluded from contact. The novel is thus able to show that resistance to the effect of waste is contingent upon the exclusion of its materiality, and, even more crucially, the continued sublimation of a gendered, heteronormative sexual urge. While, as I have demonstrated, individuals such as Rick are content to remain within the bounds of heteronormative, reproductive futurity, sublimating their sexual urges within ostensibly non-sexual commodities, for nascent *sinthomo*sexuals such as Eric, restraint proves unpalatable. Confronted with the opportunity for a transgressive *jouissance*, the restrictions necessary for the maintenance of the Middle American enunciation and the pre-eminence of reproductive futurity are not followed.

Once hyperreality allows the fragmentation of the Other into component parts, aided by the deployment of purpose-designed commodities, the final obstacle to the realization of *jouissance* can be avoided. As the rise and proliferation of pornography demonstrates, Eric comes to be increasingly representative of individuals within the Middle American enunciation of Self as the values of Eisenhower-era Middle America collapse beneath their own contradictions, jeopardizing the vitality of a heteronormative '"class" body' (Foucault, 1998, p. 124). Whilst Eric later finds a sanctioned, socially 'useful' outlet for his *sinthomo*sexuality, for the majority of DeLillo's transgressive characters, such an opportunity is comparatively rare. The bulk of *sinthomo*sexuals instead remain trapped within the sphere of Middle American hegemony as a destabilizing and troubling presence, even as they provide a justification for an increasing rigidity in the maintenance of such heteronormative, suburban values. The means by which such individuals either find, or are denied, access to such opportunities for *sinthomo*sexual expression will be addressed in the next pair of chapters which explore power and terror.

CHAPTER 7

'[To] maintain a force in the world that comes into people's sleep'[1]: Power, Alterity and the Formation of Hegemony

As the previous two chapters have shown, public, collective enunciations of Self compete to sustain their dominance. While the Middle American enunciation became hegemonic through the pervasiveness of the marketed dream of the universal third person singular – rooted in a particular form of λόγος, image and consumption – its stability is contested and its parameters required policing. Issues of power and control accordingly acquire a prominent position in any understanding of this public language and the manner in which it is defended. Using a lattice-like conception, it will be argued that, as with any language, issues of power and control inform practices of signification, maintenance and deployment. Due to the range and scope of its portrayal, *Underworld* contains DeLillo's most nuanced and complex depictions of such networks of power and will accordingly form the focus of this chapter, providing a variety of perspectives which reveal the interconnections between individual and collective enunciations.

Such a nuanced conception of power can be observed in the depiction of J. Edgar Hoover and the idiosyncrasy of his enunciation of Self. First encountered in *Underworld*'s opening section which charts the final game of the 1951 pennant race, and which captures both senses of the shot heard around the world – the winning home run and the news of the Russian testing of a nuclear device – Hoover is shown to be central to geopolitical events which would provide, for Americans at least, the first prospect of nuclear annihilation. The Russian test marked the emergence

[1] Don DeLillo, *Underworld*, p. 76.

of the 'nuclear' age, the 'spectacular slope of a system of deterrence that has insinuated itself from *the inside* into all the cracks of daily life', ensuring that even '[t]he most insignificant of our behaviors' are ultimately 'regulated' and 'neutralized' by 'indifferent, equivalent signs' which underpin the mutually assured destruction of Cold War hegemony (Baudrillard, 2006, p. 32).[2] Whilst the news of the Russian test hints at the possibility of massive destruction, it also, in inaugurating the 'spectacular slope' of an unprecedented 'system of deterrence', conversely reinforces the social cohesion of the Middle American enunciation of Self, marking the formation of a stable Cold War binary. As Hoover observes, with the evolution of this nuclear Damocles' sword the spectators at the game 'have never had anything in common so much as this, that they are sitting in the furrow of destruction' (DeLillo, *Underworld*, p. 28). Looking 'at the faces around him, open and hopeful', Hoover wishes 'to feel a compatriot's nearness and affinity' with 'these people formed by language and climate and popular songs and breakfast foods and the jokes they tell and the cars they drive': the unity of a heteronormative Middle American enunciation. It is thus with people such as Erica that Hoover 'tries to feel a belonging, an opening of his old stop-cocked soul' (DeLillo, *Underworld*, p. 28).

Instead of conforming to the 'open' and 'hopeful' values of such a public enunciation, however, Hoover is concerned with issues of power and control, perceived as a force to be mastered or contained: a means by which the Self can shape individual and collective enunciations. His primary concern, as an agent of American hegemony, is to 'prevent the Soviets from putting their own sweet spin on the event', ensuring that the establishment is perceived by the American public as having 'maintained

---

[2] For Baudrillard, contemporary Western hegemony is the product of both nuclear deterrent and the hyperreality of capital, the latter of which 'was the first to play at deterrence, abstraction, disconnection, [and] deterritorialization' [Jean Baudrillard, 2006, p. 22]. Such a phenomenon was noted by the third person narrator of *Underworld*, who observes that: '[c]apital burns off the nuance in a culture. Foreign investment, global markets, corporate acquisitions, the flow of information through transnational media, the attenuating influence of money that's electronic' [Don DeLillo, *Underworld*, p. 785].

control of the news if not of the bomb' (DeLillo, *Underworld*, p. 28). Like Eric, Hoover abandons the Middle American land of lawns and baseball crowds to embrace this 'bitter condition [that] he has never been able to name', but which arises 'when he encounters a threat from outside, from the moral wane' perceived by him as being 'everywhere in effect' (DeLillo, *Underworld*, p. 28). Rather than the shared values of Middle America, of a collective enunciation of Self rooted in the dream of the universal third person singular, Hoover instead shapes an idiosyncratic language of self from this 'bitter condition', which, in its rejection of Middle American, heteronormative reproductive futurity, constitutes a *sinthomo*sexuality comparable to Eric's existence within the pocket (DeLillo, *Underworld*, p. 28). Hoover's idiosyncratic enunciation thus finds 'balance' and 'restoring force' through an engagement with manifestations of power which he realizes 'depends on the strength of the enemy' for its vigour and force, forming an interconnection, rather than simply a tool to be wielded (DeLillo, *Underworld*, p. 28).

Just as with Eric, it is against a wider social enunciation that Edgar's language of Self can be understood and upon which its sustainability depends. As a protester at The Black and White Ball held during the Vietnam era observes, 'the business executives, the fashion photographers, the government officials, the industrialists, the writers, the bankers, the academics, the pig-faced aristocrats in exile' all share a commonality of enunciation, such that 'we can know the soul of one by the bitter wrinkled body of the other and then know all by the soul of the one' since 'they're all part of the same motherfucking thing' (DeLillo, *Underworld*, p. 575). This 'thing' is '[t]he state, the nation, the corporation, the power structure, the system, the establishment' which forms a particular public enunciation; a hegemonic complement of the dream of the universal third person and the Middle American language which this book will characterize as the Military-industrial Complex[3] to which Eisenhower referred. The latter thus both

---

3   Dwight D. Eisenhower, *Dwight D. Eisenhower: 1960–61: Containing the Public Messages, Speeches, and Statements of the President, January 1, 1960, to January 20, 1961* (Ann Arbor, MI: University of Michigan, 2005), pp. 1035–40. The above term

profits from and defends the stability of the former, more widely available, public language of Self, and without which Hoover's own idiosyncratic enunciation could not exist (DeLillo, *Underworld*, p. 575).

Such a privileged, public language of Self accordingly arises as the product of the delicate balance of forces maintained and structured by the balance of power and opposition. It is within such a context that Hoover's 'bitter condition' forms as the product of the conflict between 'the battered century of world wars and massive violence' and the permanent 'undervoice that spoke through the cannon fire and ack-ack and that sometimes grew strong enough to merge with the battle sounds' (DeLillo, *Underworld*, p. 563). Rather than the Russians, it is against these further oppositions of culture and counter-culture, revolution and conformity, that Hoover forges his own idiosyncratic and 'bitter' enunciation, becoming part of the 'struggle between the state and secret groups of insurgents, state-born, wild-eyed – the anarchists, terrorists, assassins and revolutionaries who tried to bring about apocalyptic change' (DeLillo, *Underworld*, p. 563). In adopting such a role, however, Hoover creates a distance[4] between himself and both the Military-industrial Complex and the Middle American enunciation whose hegemony he protects, and who, as the Ball scene demonstrates, strive to forget the 'undervoice' and live in a world from which the latter is excluded.

As with Eric, Hoover's idiosyncratic enunciation centres upon nuclear weapons and he works to ensure that '[t]he state controlled the means of apocalypse', embracing the power to utterly destroy those in opposition, just as he, in turn, helps control the state's access to such weaponry (DeLillo, *Underworld*, p. 563).[5] It is only in so doing, for Hoover, that the state can fulfil its 'passionate task' and 'hold on' irrespective of opposition, providing his own private enunciation with both a purpose and supporting network;

---

has been selected to highlight its shared genesis with the suburban enunciation of Middle America, which also rose to prominence during the Eisenhower era.

4   Hoover is not initially invited to The Black and White Ball, symbolizing the extent to which such individuals do not consider him to share the 'class body' of their enunciation. He is only subsequently permitted entrance due to the unsettling fear which his idiosyncratic enunciation invokes.

5   A fascination for nuclear weapons which Hoover also shares with Eric.

a lattice-like network of power (DeLillo, *Underworld*, p. 563). Edgar is thus instrumental in encouraging the state to undertake a 'stiffening [of] its grip', 'preserving its claim to the most destructive power available' and ensuring that it becomes 'identified totally with the state', permitting Hoover to maintain his own stable, lifelong enunciation in a manner which eludes David Bell, Glen Selvy, Bill Gray, Nick Shay and the majority of DeLillo's other male characters who have been discussed (DeLillo, *Underworld*, p. 563).[6] The key difference from such earlier examples is that Hoover, like Eric Deming, shaped his enunciation to conform with the elaborate, lattice-like structure of power surrounding the Middle American language of Self, which helps to sustain and support the idiosyncrasy of his enunciation in a way in which the other characters, with the exception of Eric, are unable to achieve.

It is the state's acquisition of nuclear weapons and the need, through secrecy and concealment, to maintain this hegemony which provides Hoover's enunciation of Self with a sense of purpose, allowing his divergent presence to be socially sanctioned.[7] As the narrator observes, '[t]here is the secret of the bomb and there are the secrets that the bomb inspires' and while there are 'things even the Director cannot guess' surrounding such a deployment, this lack of knowledge is only 'because these plots are only now evolving' (DeLillo, *Underworld*, p. 51). For Hoover 'every atmospheric blast, every glimpse we get of the bared force of nature' becomes the source, 'he reckons [for] a hundred plots [to] go underground, to spawn and skein' (DeLillo, *Underworld*, p. 51). They accordingly become things with which Hoover's enunciation can engage and attempt to master and signify, allowing him to believe he is 'a man whose own sequestered heart holds every festering secret in the Western world', justifying his continued toleration within a wider social context (DeLillo, *Underworld*, p. 51). Hoover thus occupies a liminal, policing position between two public enunciations of

---

6   Eric is an exception, finding a comparable niche to Hoover through an analogous engagement with state manifestations of power.

7   A secrecy which, in the hands of individuals such as Hoover, paradoxically protects the seeming openness – of nothing hidden from view – which characterizes the Middle American enunciation of Self, revealing its *uneigentlich, das Man* quality.

Self: that of Middle America and that of the Military-industrial Complex criticized and railed against by the protester present at The Black and White Ball. Just as the microbes[8] with which Hoover is obsessed, he becomes a symbiotic parasite within the social body of Middle American and the Military-industrial Complex; idiosyncratic and separate, yet unsubjected to an immune response.

In order to maintain this position, and remain safe within the corpus of his host, Hoover uses 'the dossier' as 'an essential device' with which to shape 'the endless estuarial mingling of paranoia and control'. Since 'Edgar had many enemies-for-life' the only 'way to deal with such people was to compile massive dossiers' in an attempt to construct 'a deeper form of truth, transcending facts and actuality', altering the networks of power and control to suit his liking.[9] Through the construction of such files, '[p]hotographs, surveillance reports, detailed allegations, linked names, transcribed tapes – wiretaps, bugs, break-ins' can be combined with 'unfounded rumor' until the amalgam becomes 'promiscuously true', a form of 'truth without authority and therefore incontestable': a hyperreal

8   The FBI director is obsessed with microbes and their invidious potential. As the narrator observes, Hoover believed that if 'you knew anything about modern war, you knew that weapons utilizing pathogenic bacteria could be every bit as destructive as megaton bombs' [DeLillo, *Underworld*, p. 557]. For Edgar, this was '[w]orse, in a way, because the sense of infiltration was itself a form of death' which, unlike nuclear material, was not as susceptible to the director's manipulation and control [DeLillo, *Underworld*, p. 557]. The extent to which this prospect effects him is shown by the extensive precautions which he insists are undertaken. These include changing the light bulbs, pads and pens in each hotel room in which the director stayed, the construction in his home of 'a toilet that was raised on a platform, to isolate him from floorbound forms of life' and the development of a 'white room manned by white-clad technicians, preferably white themselves, who would work in an environment completely free of contaminants, dust, bacteria and so on, with big white lights shining down, where Edgar himself might like to spend time when he was feeling vulnerable to the forces around him' [DeLillo, *Underworld*, p. 560]. This fear and need is rooted in the potential which such micro-organisms hold for unmediated connection with the Other; a shared, unseen life which connects everyone, irrespective of enunciation, affiliation or colour.
9   This correlates to Eric's dissemination of groundless rumours discussed above.

narrative which attempts to control a hyperreal threat, mirroring the function of capital and nuclear deterrence. The dossier thus provides a site from which to try and construct synthetic networks, ensuring '[f]actoids seeped out of the file and crept across the horizon, consuming bodies and minds' and becoming 'the essence of Edgar's revenge', microbial and insidious. Through this vengeance, Hoover is able to defend himself and both US public enunciations against the alterity of the Other – both foreign, but more importantly domestic – preventing any immune reaction from his host which could potentially damage the delicacy of his own enunciation. In pursuit of this aim, Hoover 'rearrang[es] the lives of his enemies, their conversations, their relationships, [and] their very memories', making them 'answerable to the details of his creation': the ultimate embodiment of a power which can regulate public and private enunciations through a seeming mastery of the hyperreal (DeLillo, *Underworld*, p. 559).

While Edgar may have found a means of socially sanctioning his desire for domination, power and control – ensuring that his particular sadistic *sinthomo*sexuality remains unconstrained – his need for dominance over the Other is shown to arise out of complex personal urges. Assailed, like Eric, by non-normative desires, it is paradoxically Hoover who, in the deployment of the dossiers which underpin his enunciation, is at the forefront of sustaining such social disapproval. As he observes, the destruction which such desires can cause 'begins in the inmost person' and '[o]nce you yield to random sexual urges, you want to see everything come loose', thereby 'mistak[ing] your own looseness for some political concept' (DeLillo, *Underworld*, p. 564). Any such disruption of social cohesion consequently results in an altering of the networks of power that form the context upon which Hoover's enunciation depends, jeopardizing its sustainability.

Such is the force of non-normative desire that these 'thoughts had to remain unspoken, even unfinished in one's own mind'. For Hoover, this is 'the point of his relationship with Clyde' Tolson, a connection predicated upon 'keep[ing] the subject unspoken' and 'the feelings unfelt, the momentary urges unacted-upon'. Rather than *jouissance* through the consummation of homosexual desire, 'Edgar thought there was something noble in a constant companionship that does not fall to baser claims.' In keeping Tolson close, housed in an adjoining room, Hoover allows himself 'a glimpse, a passing glance, a spyhole peek at Junior as he busied himself dressing or undressing or taking a bath': a momentary access to *jouissance*, but one which remains unconsummated and is consequently unthreatening. Such an 'arrangement' allows 'the moment' to 'seem wholly accidental, should the subject realize he was being watched, and an accident not just from his perspective but to Edgar's own mind as well', freeing the director from a sense of guilt concomitant with this partial hint of *jouissance* and the irruption of the death drive (DeLillo, *Underworld*, p. 564).

While Hoover chooses not to eliminate all trace of non-normative desire, he implacably resists full consummation, remaining within the sheltering realm of fantasy. As the narrator observes, 'Edgar's own power had always been double-skinned' not just 'the power of his office' but 'also the power that his self-repression gave him' (DeLillo, *Underworld*, p. 573). It is precisely the juxtaposition of these forms of control which provides the 'stern measures' Hoover undertakes 'as Director' with 'an odd legitimacy' due to 'the rigor of his insistent celibacy' (DeLillo, *Underworld*, p. 573). Having 'earned' his 'monocratic power' through 'the days and nights of his self-denial, the rejection of unacceptable impulses', Hoover can justify the fact that '[e]very official secret in the Bureau had its blood-birth in Edgar's own soul' (DeLillo, *Underworld*, p. 573). Yoking together power and resistance to non-normative desires, Hoover and Tolson can prevent themselves from becoming what the narrator terms, 'a couple of old queens doddering on', transforming them instead into 'men of sovereign authority', who, at least in Hoover's case, 'did not intend to yield control anytime on this earth' (DeLillo, *Underworld*, p. 578).

What shapes Hoover's enunciation into its social and political form is thus the fact that his resistance to desire arises from the sadistic dominance and control which he obtains over the suffering of Others, just as such control is initially granted by the suppression of his own urges in a masochistic game of temptation and denial which, while providing *jouissance*, still remains rooted in isolation. As the narrator observes, it is out of the '[c]onflict' between the 'nature of his desire and the unremitting attempts he made to expose homosexuals in the government', the 'secret of his desire and the refusal to yield', that Hoover moulds his enunciation, maintaining the 'traditional background' of 'early American righteousness' upon which it rests and providing himself with a reason to resist homosexual congress and its unrestrained alterity: mirroring the resistance of Middle American hegemony to the Other, both foreign and domestic, upon whose enmity it depends. It is accordingly the 'continuation of the Kennedy years' which is Hoover's true opposition and he deploys the tools he has accrued against any undermining of the conservative social context caused by the appearance of 'a certain fluid movement' within 'which sex, drugs and dirty words began to unstratify the culture', destabilizing the previously 'well-founded categories' and causing them 'to seem irrelevant' – the same threat which is undermining both the hegemony of the Military-industrial Complex present at The Black and White Ball and the heteronormative, Middle American enunciation of Self with which it is interlaced (DeLillo, *Underworld*, pp. 571–3).

As the complexity of this relationship between power and Hoover's idiosyncratic enunciation of Self has demonstrated, the former manifests as a more complex, devolved, and lattice-like construction, correlating to a Foucauldian theory that power does not take the form of 'a group of institutions and mechanisms that ensure the subservience of the citizens of a given state', or a 'subjugation which, in contrast to violence, has the form of the rule'. Equally, Foucault does not argue for 'a general system of domination exerted by one group over another, a system whose effects, through successive derivations, pervade the entire social body'. Manifestations of power are instead perceived as 'only the terminal forms power takes' and 'force relations' should rather be theorized as a 'multiplicity', which, 'through ceaseless struggles and confrontations', result in power being neither 'an institution', nor a 'structure', nor 'a certain strength we are endowed with' but instead 'the name that one attributes to a complex strategical situation in a particular society.' Power is thus 'not something that is acquired, seized, or shared, something that one holds on to or allows to slip away', but instead an accretion 'exercised from innumerable points, in the interplay of nonegalitarian and mobile relations'. Rather than a force which acts from 'a position of exteriority with respect to other types of relationships (economic processes, knowledge relationships, sexual relationships)' power is instead 'the basis for [the] wide-ranging effects of cleavage that run through the social body as a whole' and with which Hoover's enunciation attempts to shape, contain and master (Foucault, 1998, pp. 92–4).

The '[m]ajor dominations' of the Military-industrial Complex present at The Black and White Ball can accordingly be viewed as 'the hegemonic effects that are sustained by all these confrontations' between various social groups, families and interpersonal relations – the most predominant and pervasive of which is the Middle American enunciation of Self – rather than 'the choice or decision of an individual subject', or 'the caste which governs,' or 'the groups which control the state apparatus,' or 'those who make the most important economic decisions'. Foucault's theory of power accordingly explains how multiple enunciations of Self, all vying for stability and control, can create large, public forms such as the Middle American enunciation of Self, which, in its dream of the universal third person singular, constructs for its adherents a simultaneous collective and particular enunciation of Self, interrelated through the lattice-like matrix which supports and structures such articulation. It is this which allows for idiosyncratic, *sinthomo*sexuals such as Eric and Hoover to simultaneously destabilize forms of public enunciation such as the Middle American language of Self, yet also underpin the very forms which their desires transgress. This seemingly paradoxical duality allows subjects to find a means of accessing a *jouissance* which is both particular, and unassimilable, yet simultaneously socially constructed, contained and integrated in a 'useful' and 'productive' manner: a parasite tolerated by its host for the benefits which it brings (Foucault, 1998, pp. 94–5).

While *Underworld* provides intricate depictions of extreme figures such as Eric and Hoover, the novel also focuses upon adherents to the Middle American enunciation, revealing, through the lattice-like nature of power structures, everyday individual complicity within public enunciations of Self and the hegemonies which they engender. This can be observed in the figure of Brian Glassic, who, as Marvin notes, 'need[s] the leaders of both sides to keep the cold war going' as it is 'the one constant thing' which is 'honest' and 'dependable', ensuring the survival and shelter of his personal enunciation within a wider, social matrix of lines of power and suasion. It is once this global 'tension and rivalry come[s] to an end' that Brian's 'worst nightmares begin' as 'the power and intimidation of the state' start to 'seep out' of his 'personal bloodstream'. Brian is thus not portrayed as the essentially passive recipient of macro forms of power, but instead the active participant in the establishment and maintenance of American – and in particular Middle American – hegemony. What Brian is losing with the breakdown of the Cold War is precisely that dominance, and in the post war period he will cease to 'be the main ... [p]oint of reference' in this network of power, at least from his own perspective. Instead, 'other forces will come rushing in, demanding and challenging', destabilizing not just the overarching forms of power of those supposedly running the Cold War, but also the networks of privileges and hegemony which sustains Brian's place in the world and his sense of entitlement that allows him 'to stay on top' (DeLillo, *Underworld*, p. 170).

For people like Brian – white, comfortable, heteronormative and Middle American[10] – the Cold War is ambiguous. Though it brings the possibility of nuclear annihilation and an accompanying *angst*, it is also maintains hegemony and justifies consumption. As Stich notes, government campaigns like '"Buy, Buy, Buy, It's Your Patriotic Duty," and "Think Prosperity – Have Prosperity,"' meant that '[m]oney was no longer simply a desirable or necessary medium of exchange, but an end in itself and a cornerstone of American life' (Stich, 1987, p. 39). The consumption of Middle Americans such as Brian was thus a principal means of strengthening the state, just as the state's power in turn supports such individual enunciations. As Molly Wallace observes, since 'the American economy was inextricably caught up with the question of national identity', opposed to 'an enemy defined primarily by its differing economic system', a 'celebration of the American economy was [thus] virtually mandatory' for individuals such as Brian.[11] The consumerism of Middle America therefore underpins its

---

10   As Ian Barnard observes, 'race and sexuality are not two separate axes of identity that cross and overlay in particular subject positions, but rather, ways to circumscribe systems of meaning and understanding that formatively and inherently define each other' [Ian Barnard, 'Queer race', *Social Semiotics*, 9:2 (1999), pp. 199–212, p. 200], echoing Hoover's concern with the race of his lab technicians.

11   Molly Wallace, '"Venerated emblems": DeLillo's *Underworld* and the history-commodity' *Critique*, 42:4 (2001), pp. 367–84, p. 368.

public enunciation of Self through the dream of the universal third person singular, in turn supporting each individual's particular form of this public language, just as, on a national level, it created an affluent state capable of building advanced weapons systems. Creating munitions to defend the right of its citizens to consume further, the state in turn gains increased wealth to produce more advanced weaponry, supporting ever more elaborate private consumption – a self-propagating circularity that, for individuals such as Brian, gave consumption a direct connection to hegemony and the Middle American enunciation of Self: a Foucauldian lattice-like network of power.

With the incipient collapse of the stabilizing binary of the Cold War, individuals such as Brian are left to 'feel sorry for' themselves, believing they are 'missing something' though they 'don't know what'. Without the support and integration of the Cold War, they no longer 'have the same dimensions as the observable universe', conferred by the dominance of the Middle American enunciation of Self and the importance of individual consumption within such a language. Without such valorization of commodities, Brian becomes 'a lost speck' who 'look[s] at old cars and recall[s] a purpose, a destination', condemned, in the post-war, to a directionless existence of collapsing hegemony and a destabilizing public enunciation, leaving such individuals 'lonely inside' their lives. The manifestation of the Middle American enunciation of Self has thus altered from the security of hegemony, into a perpetual state of flux in which 'the whole point' for the Self 'is to die prepared, die legal, with all the papers signed' so that the material from which an individual's enunciation is constructed can be liquidated without consequence and 'convert[ed] to cash' – into the hyperreality of capital rather than the materiality of commodity (DeLillo, *Underworld*, p. 170).

This contrasts with the thesis of Boxall's monograph which drew upon Fukuyama's theory of the end of history, arguing that the post-Cold War constituted a form of 'American completion' (Boxall, 2006, p. 192) in which the 'constraints against which DeLillo's narrators have struggled' have seemingly 'been lifted' (Boxall, 2006, p. 167). While Boxall acknowledged a contrapuntal 'movement towards the distant, alienated third person', opposing 'the interpellating power of the patriarchal American voice' (Boxall, 2006, p. 192), his analysis fails to adequately account for the experience of Brian

'*[To] maintain a force in the world that comes into people's sleep*' 175

Glassic, or indeed, for that of Nick Shay. Far from completion, the supposed end of history instead brings loneliness and isolation, concomitant with the decadence of the Middle American language of Self.

While J. Edgar Hoover and Brian Glassic provide cross-sections through the lattice-like power structures of the Middle American enunciation and that of the Military-industrial Complex, it is Klara Sax's art project 'Long Tall Sally' which functions as the novel's most holistic exploration of the manifestation of power in the Cold War. Charting the evolution of Klara's art – from the early canvases that were treated as a hobby by her husband, Bronzini; to the found art she subsequently produced from waste; and, finally, to the massive project 'Long Tall Sally' – *Underworld* depicts the networks of power underpinning the Middle American enunciation of Self and its Cold War context. Unlike Brian, however, Klara's investment in the Middle American enunciation and the categories which are founded upon it is not that of an adherent. Rather than a Middle American, Klara is variously shown as a member of the ethnic, local community of the Italian Bronx into which she married (a heteronormative union she subsequently abandons), a peripheral presence in the Bohemian artists' community of New York, and, through a further marriage, a spectre on the perimeter of the Military-industrial Complex.[12] Throughout the novel Klara consistently eludes integration into public enunciations of Self, remaining on the edge of whatever community she is passing through: a transitory unassimilated presence. Unlike Eric or Hoover, Klara does not make any lasting attempt to find a place within the social order where her own, idiosyncratic enunciation as an artist of found material can attain a stable and 'productive' niche which escapes being blurred by the publicness of *das Man*.

Instead, through the Heideggerian dimension of her art, Klara resists any social integration and her liminal status allows her to create work which engages with her personal, social and historical context: her historicity (*Historizität*).[13] Viewing a picture of herself at The Black and White

---

12   Due to the novel's predominantly reverse-chronological portrayal, Klara's shifting enunciation is not depicted in linear terms.
13   This process has a commonality with the Heideggerian art which Lauren produces.

Ball '[s]urrounded by famous people and powerful people, men in the administration who were running the war', Klara cannot recognize her own form. Looking at the photograph, Klara 'thought, I don't know who that person is' or even '[w]hy is she there exactly', leading her to wonder '[w]hat it is about this picture that makes it so hard for me to remember myself?' Confronted with such alienation, Klara's instinct is to try and reconnect with the particularity of her enunciation, that of art, separating herself from the blurring of her social context. Viewing the picture, Klara instinctively wanted 'to paint it over, paint the photograph orange and blue and burgundy and paint the tuxedos and long dresses and paint the grand ballroom of the Plaza Hotel', removing the monochromatic patina of the binary public enunciation of the Cold War Military-industrial Complex, replacing it with a polychromatic embodiment of particularity and difference. Such an initial 'graffiti instinct', however, is insufficient for the recovery of her idiosyncratic Self. Looking at the photograph Klara cannot separate herself from the 'famous people and powerful people' who comprise 'the administration' in 'the dark days of Vietnam'. Obscured by a public enunciation within which she has resisted participating, even when gazing at the photograph more than twenty years later Klara still feels 'completely sort of out-of-body looking at this scene', leaving her unable to 'understand that the woman at the edge of the frame' was her (DeLillo, *Underworld*, pp. 77–9).

It is only once Klara begins to actively explore the past through the Heideggarian medium of her art, that, as with Lauren, she gains access to *aletheia* (truth), enabling her to understand what it was that distorted her own enunciation during the Vietnam era. As a practitioner of found art, Klara chooses to engage with a material symbol of this Vietnam-era, Cold War hegemony in the form of a mothballed fleet of B-52 strategic bombers in a disused desert airbase in New Mexico. In keeping with her resistance to the publicness of *das Man*, Klara selected this particular medium due to a personal connection between the B-52s and an experience she had whilst lying at anchor on her husband's yacht off the coast of Maine; thereby combining the personal, social and historical in a Heideggerian concept of historicity.

Looking up, Klara catches sight of strange glimmers in the night sky which she 'decided' was 'the refracted light from an object way up there,' the 'circular form it takes' (DeLillo, *Underworld*, p. 75). While this could conceivably be the result of a wide variety of objects or processes, Klara decides that it was 'B52s' which they were 'seeing' because that was what Klara 'wanted to believe' (DeLillo, *Underworld*, p. 75). Through engaging with the strategic bombers as what Heidegger terms as equipment (*Zeug*),[14] Klara is able to explore the reasons why she 'wanted to believe' that they were B-52s in the night sky. Transforming disparate strategic bombers into a cohesive found art project through 'putting our puny hands to great weapons systems', Klara comes to realize her complex feelings regarding American Cold War hegemony and the shaping force which it has had upon her own Vietnam-era enunciation (DeLillo, *Underworld*, p. 77). As Klara observes, '[w]ar scared me all right but those lights, I have to tell you those lights were a complex sensation' (DeLillo, *Underworld*, p. 75).

When Klara views that 'refracted light' whilst 'rocking lightly at anchor in some deserted cove' on the Maine coast, aboard a powerful image of individual freedom and empowerment, a part of her wishes to abandon this isolation for the enveloping force of American hegemony embodied in the bombers 'on permanent alert, ever present you know, sweeping the Soviet borders'. Her belief that she is never beyond the reach of her government and that it is this which is the 'exercising' of 'a meaningful power', a 'force' which is maintained 'in the world that comes into people's sleep', accordingly acquires an ambiguous dimension. While the individual subjected to such power faces the permanent threat of nuclear annihilation indicated by the bomber's presence, and an according dilution of the singularity of the individual's own enunciation, Klara still feels 'a sense of awe, a child's sleepy feeling of mystery and danger and beauty', indicative of a degree of complicity and comfort which she feels, however unwillingly, with US hegemony. It is precisely this ambiguity which Klara's project explores, not merely the particularity of her own enunciation within the period, or the

---

14   c.f. Martin Heidegger, *Being and Time*, p. 98.

lattice-like quality of power relations within American Cold War hegemony, but instead the interrelation of the two (DeLillo, *Underworld*, pp. 75–6).

While her project partially arises out of 'a sort of survival instinct', it also functions as what Heidegger characterizes as an endeavour to structure truth's clearing through an attempt to 'discover tradition, preserve it, and study it explicitly', thereby learning what it 'transmits' and how it is 'transmitted' (Heidegger, 2000, p. 41). By engaging with the B-52 bombers Klara can attempt to understand the historicity of the period they embody[15] which is a 'determining characteristic' (Heidegger, 2000, p. 42) of both Dasein's individual and collective past, and is therefore responsible for the blurring she experiences of her own enunciation of Self:

> Its own past – and this always means the past of its 'generation' – is not something which *follows along after* Dasein, but something which already goes ahead of it. (Heidegger, 2000, p. 41)

Both Klara's past and that of her generation are thus shown by 'Long Tall Sally' to be rooted in the confluence of hegemonic power structures, individual complicity and the interactions of public and private enunciations of Self, which both construct, and are supported by, weapon systems such as the B-52 strategic bomber. In this 'putting' of 'puny hands to great weapons systems' Klara attempts to explore the materiality of the weapon systems that 'came out of the factories and assembly halls as near alike as possible, millions of components stamped out, repeated endlessly' – and in so doing, to understand the power structures underpinning such mechanization and hegemony – whilst also trying 'to unrepeat, to find an element of felt life' which constitutes individual existence within such a collective, hegemonic enunciation (DeLillo, *Underworld*, p. 77).

---

15 And still embody. While the B-2 Spirit Bomber was intended as a replacement for the B-52 – due to its stealth technology which negated superior enemy air power – the collapse of the Cold War made such an advanced weapons system seem unnecessary. The B-52 thus remained the main strategic and conventional bomber of the US air force.

'[To] maintain a force in the world that comes into people's sleep' 179

    For Klara, the B-52s accordingly constitute equipment, the raw material for her found art. Rather than trying to understand an object through abstract analysis, for Heidegger the achievement of meaningful 'phenomenological access to the entities which we encounter, consists rather in thrusting aside our interpretative tendencies', which he proposes 'conceal not only the phenomenon', but the 'entities themselves *as* encountered of their own accord *in* our concern with them' (Heidegger, 2000, p. 96). While Klara has 'walked and stooped and crawled from the cockpit to the tail gun armament' and seen the B-52s 'in every kind of light', she does so thinking 'about the weapons they carried and the men who accompanied the weapons', using her interpretative tendencies and accordingly getting further away from the strategic bombers essence as equipment (DeLillo, *Underworld*, p. 76).

    The inherent paradox of the B-52s, for individuals such as Klara, is that to know them equipmentally in the sense they were intended would be to experience them as a means of bringing about mass destruction and the end of her very existence. Such an understanding would take Klara further away from the historicity with which she is trying to engage, since as she notes 'the bombs were not released' (DeLillo, *Underworld*, p. 76).[16] For Klara, rather than as equipment, the B-52 is instead 'met as something unusable, not properly adapted for the use ... decided upon' and accordingly it 'becomes conspicuous' (Heidegger, 2000, p. 102). By climbing over the B-52's and using them as materials for her art, however, she comes to view the planes with a differing concern which transforms them into a new form of equipment. Klara accordingly takes something which in its original form was unusable to her, conspicuous, and reforms it through her concern into an artwork which explores the fundamental historicity of both her enunciation and that of her social context.

    Refashioning the strategic bombers into such objects, Klara repaints the planes in '[s]weeps of color, bands and spatters, airy washes, the force

---

16 While B-52s were used extensively in Vietnam, this was in a conventional role. Except by accident, the B-52 never deployed its nuclear payload. The *Enola Gay* and *Bock's Car* were B-29 Superfortresses, possessed of a differing historicity.

of saturated light', making 'the whole thing oddly personal, a sense of one painter's hand moved by impulse and afterthought as much as by epic design', capturing the haphazard nature of power. While it contains a unified vision, the product of a single hand, it is not simply a work of the triumph and recovery of an individual enunciation extricated from the blurring of the collective Self. The colours with which Klara emblazoned the B-52s were 'in conflict with each other, to be read emotionally', a competing mass of 'skin pigments and industrial grays' capturing the tension between the individual and the publicness of the Military-industrial Complex and the Middle American enunciation whose security it ensured. It is precisely this mixture of the mechanical and the organic, of waste and alienation, conformity and collapse, embodied in the 'rampant red appearing repeatedly through the piece – the red of something released, a burst sac, all blood-pus thickness and runny underyellow', which the Heideggerian dimension of Klara's artwork succeeds in capturing (DeLillo, *Underworld*, p. 83).

Through her art, Klara thus comes to understand how the grounded fleet of B-52s, symbolizing the height of technological advancement when '[p]ower meant something thirty, forty years ago', are now emblematic of the collapse of that very binary which 'held the world together' (DeLillo, *Underworld*, p. 76). As she observes, where once '[y]ou could measure hope and you could measure destruction' now 'things that were anchored to the balance of power and the balance of terror seem to be undone, unstuck', destabilizing the enunciations from which they were constituted (DeLillo, *Underworld*, p. 76). While Klara wishes to be glad that the Cold War conditions are gone, as with Brian, her artwork reveals the ambiguity which she feels:[17]

> 'I don't want to disarm the world,' she said. 'Or I do want to disarm the world but I want it to be done warily and realistically and in the full knowledge of what we're giving up. We gave up the yacht. That's the first thing we gave up. [...]' (DeLillo, *Underworld*, p. 76)

---

17 The irony of her tone is a form of defence, distancing herself from the emotional force of this ambiguity whilst simultaneously revealing its presence.

Just as Klara and her husband surrendered their commodity, so too did both Klara and her generation give up the security which hegemony brings, and with it the social justification for conspicuous individual consumption. Reflecting upon the B-52s, Klara observes that '[v]iolence is undone, violence is easier now, it's uprooted, out of control, it has no measure anymore, it has no level of values', just as the consumption, underpinning the Middle American enunciation no longer serves an affirmative, social purpose (DeLillo, *Underworld*, p. 76).

As J. Edgar Hoover, Brian Glassic and in particular Klara Sax and her artwork 'Long Tall Sally' demonstrate, power is a complex process which constitutes a Foucauldian, lattice-like network of conflicts and interpersonal relations that evolve and form competing enunciations. While power seemingly stabilizes and maintains hegemonic forms of American enunciation, its lattice-like quality means that it is not simply a force to be grasped and wielded. It is instead produced by the accretion of significations and practices and any shift in these deployments accordingly results in a transformation of the balance of power and the stability of the enunciations which it underpins. Through the portrayal of Brian and the Heideggerian aspect of Klara's art, *Underworld* is able to show the problematically interconnected relationship between the collapse of the Cold War and the Middle American enunciation of Self. On an individual level, the novel also reveals the shifting tensions between the individual and collective language which are manifest in Brian's and Klara's enunciation of Self. It is in the depiction of J. Edgar Hoover, however, that the complexity of this interaction reaches its apogee, demonstrating how networks of power and the enunciation of Self enjoy a reciprocal relationship, providing a haven for those who reject heteronormativity. The final chapter, '[T]he balance of power and the balance of terror', will explore the interaction of power and the language of Self for those *sinthomo*sexuals who fall on the wrong side of US hegemony and are unable to acquire such parasitical niches within the social body of their host.

CHAPTER 8

'[T]he balance of power and the balance of terror'[1]: Terrorism and the *uneigentlich* Publicness of *das Man*

For *Sinthomo*sexuals who find their enunciations excluded from, and unsupported by, US hegemony, such non-normative urges leave the Self alone with the burden of maintaining an unsupported enunciation. Since the dominant Middle American enunciation is antithetical to their unsublimated desires – provided that they are not concealed or put to 'productive' use – such individuals are forced to find or create alternative networks within which to integrate their language of Self. One of the principal forms which such alternative contexts can take within DeLillo's fiction is that of the terrorist plot and cell. Such depiction has ranged from anti-capitalist networks in DeLillo's early novels, as well as *Underworld* and *Cosmopolis*, to the JFK conspirators in *Libra*, and finally the Islamicist terrorists in *Mao II* and *Falling Man*. It will be shown that in DeLillo's fiction the adherents to all forms of terror share a comparable enunciation, irrespective of divergent ideology. Furthermore, it will also be demonstrated that this enunciation correlates to that of Eric and Hoover, comprising a sadistic and controlling non-normativity: all that differs is whether or not such an individual is fortunate enough to find an existing social context in which their transgressive desires are at least tolerated, if not sanctioned. Finally, through analysis of the portrayal of The Texas Highway Killer, it will be shown that even the label of terrorism merely denotes a particular fault-line along which such non-normative urges can manifest, making an alternate enunciation simpler to maintain. Rather than sociopolitical context, it is

1   Don DeLillo, *Underworld*, p. 76.

instead *sinthomo*sexual desire which underpins terrorism and encourages violent opposition to Symbolic, public enunciations.

For Jean Baudrillard, 11 September 2001 marked a 'fundamental change' in the nature of terrorism.[2] While he considers previous attacks to have failed to breach hegemony's 'integrative power' which 'largely succeeded in absorbing and resolving any crisis, any negativity', the collapse of the towers means that 'the terrorists have ceased to commit suicide for no return' and are instead 'bringing their own deaths to bear in an effective, offensive manner'. Through 'an intuitive strategic insight' on their part they have been able to 'sense' and exploit 'the immense fragility' of a Western 'system which has arrived at its quasi-perfection', and, 'by that very token, can be ignited by the slightest spark.' For Baudrillard, terrorism in the 9/11 model is thus 'not the descendant of a traditional history of anarchy, nihilism and fanaticism', but instead a new phenomenon which is 'contemporaneous with globalization' (Baudrillard, 'The Spirit of Terrorism', pp. 15–16).

The principal strategy which such terrorists use to exploit this fragility is the transformation of massive destruction into spectacle, allowing them to 'have succeeded in turning their deaths into an absolute weapon against a system that operates on the basis of the exclusion of death, a system whose ideal is an ideal of zero deaths' (Baudrillard, 'The Spirit of Terrorism', p. 16). While Baudrillard's assertion of 'zero death' as the desired form of the US hegemonic system cannot withstand even cursory inspection,[3] more conventional loss of life can be integrated within prevailing patterns of

---

2   Jean Baudrillard, 'The Spirit of Terrorism' in *The Spirit of Terrorism and Other Essays*, Chris Turner (trans.) (London: Verso, 2003), pp. 1–34, pp. 15–16. Further references are given after quotations in the text.
3   The United States enforces the death penalty at the federal level, within the US military and in thirty-six states as of the time of writing; its news reports are fixated upon the spectacle of natural disasters and, in times of war, upon the death of enemy combatants achieved through the medium of superior technology; and its art has a preoccupation with violent death as exemplified by Andy Warhol's electric chair and car crashes series (an artist of particular relevance to DeLillo, as can be observed in *Mao II*), US film and television output of crime shows, action programmes, horror films, a fascination with portraying torture and the commercial dominance of crime fiction and true crime accounts within the publishing industry.

commoditization and is thus muted by US hegemony: in essence replicating what Heidegger characterized as the *uneigentlich*, 'everyday manner' characteristic of *das Man*'s understanding of mortality, in which 'death is "known" as a mishap which is constantly occurring – as a "case of death"' and consequently is talked of 'in a "fugitive" manner' that seems to say '"One of these days one will die too, in the end; but right now it has nothing to do with us"' (Heidegger, 2000, pp. 296–7). Through mass destruction as spectacle, however, 'the non-equivalence of the four thousand deaths inflected at a stroke' is such that even if Baudrillard's conception of a US 'zero-death system' is rejected, the event still transcends successful commodification or neutering, and, in this respect, the terrorists succeeded in turning 'death into a counterstrike weapon' (Baudrillard, 'The Spirit of Terrorism', p. 16).[4]

While such analysis would seemingly encourage the schema of a dialectical struggle, Baudrillard is keen to observe that post-9/11 terrorism was not a manifestation of 'a clash of civilizations or religions' (Baudrillard, 'The Spirit of Terrorism', p. 11). The alteration instead 'reaches far beyond Islam and America, on which efforts are being made to focus the conflict in order to create the delusion of a visible confrontation and solution based on force' (Baudrillard, 'The Spirit of Terrorism', p. 11). Proposing that 'Islam was merely the moving front along which the antagonism crystallized', Baudrillard argues that an 'asymmetric terror' has arisen which 'leaves global omnipotence entirely disarmed' and a hegemonic power now '[a]t odds with itself' (Baudrillard, 'The Spirit of Terrorism', p. 15). Confronted with such opposition, the only response of power is to 'plunge further into its own logic of relations of force', an attempt to compel the enemy to 'attack the system' in the manner of 'the (revolutionary) imagination the system itself forces upon you – the system which survives only by constantly drawing those attacking it into fighting on the ground of reality, which is always its own' (Baudrillard, 'The Spirit of Terrorism', pp. 15–17). For Baudrillard,

---

[4] While a number of films, books and television series have attempted to address the 9/11 attacks they thus far have failed to exhaust the alterity of the source material which resists mimesis and its eventual transition to a simulacrum.

terrorist attacks such as those upon the Twin Towers '[d]efy the system' by 'giving it a gift to which it cannot respond except by its own death and its own collapse' (Baudrillard, 'The Spirit of Terrorism', p. 17), striking down 'the nerve-centre of the system'[5] and putting 'the finishing touches to the orgy of power, liberation, flows and calculation which the Twin Towers embodied'; the 'extreme form of efficiency and hegemony' which they represent (Baudrillard, 'Hypotheses on Terrorism', pp. 15–16).

This seeming alteration in the nature of terrorist praxis can be observed in *Falling Man*, which, as with *Mao II*, also attempts to explore the enunciation of foreign-born adherents of terrorist organizations. Concentrating upon Hammad, *Falling Man* depicts those trapped on the other side of the boundary of American hegemony. Denied access to its privileges, such individuals are left with a 'feeling of lost history', of being 'too long in isolation' and 'crowded out by other cultures, other futures, the all-enfolding will of capital markets and foreign policies' (DeLillo, *Falling Man*, p. 80). It is precisely these exclusionary forces of capital and realpolitik which facilitate the hegemony and 'world domination' of the enunciation of the 'people jogging in the park' and the 'old men who sit in beach chairs', allowing them, from Hammad's perspective, to 'control our world' (DeLillo, *Falling Man*, p. 173).

Denied access to power and a socially proscribed framework to support his divergent enunciation, Hammad instead embraces terror as a 'counter-strike weapon' against the restricting hegemony of US public enunciations. Membership within a plot and its facilitating fraternity allows Hammad to '[f]orget' and '[b]e unmindful of the thing called the world', separating himself from any public enunciation and embracing his divergent *sinthomo*sexuality, which, as with Eric and Hoover, revels in the suffering and death of Others (DeLillo, *Falling Man*, p. 238). By so doing, he and the other conspirators dismiss alterity and assume that 'there are no others', that they 'exist only to the degree that they fill the role we have designed

---

[5] Jean Baudrillard, 'Hypotheses on Terrorism' in *The Spirit of Terrorism and Other Essays*, Chris Turner (trans.) (London: Verso, 2003), pp. 49–84, pp. 58–9. Further references are given after quotations in the text.

for them', fulfilling 'their function' and preventing an enunciation forming which is rooted in connection: an attitude which ironically parallels that of Middle Americans towards the foreign Other which they themselves embody (DeLillo, *Falling Man*, p. 176). The conspirators are accordingly able to believe that those 'who will die have no claim to their lives outside the useful fact of their dying', beyond the strictures of history and terror which the hijackers have devised (DeLillo, *Falling Man*, p. 176). Through constructing a plot and executing a terrorist attack, US 'power' can be rendered 'helpless' in the face of concerted opposition, analogous to the transition which Baudrillard proposed had occurred in the 9/11 attacks (DeLillo, *Falling Man*, p. 81).[6] As the narrator observes, the 'more power' the state possesses 'the more helpless' it seems in the face of defeat at the hands of such a small, though determined cadre: a transformation correlating to Baudrillard's theory of a symbolic destruction which turns the perfection of the US system against itself, igniting it with the spark of two collapsing towers (DeLillo, *Falling Man*, p. 81).

Freed through plot from the burden of unwanted alterity and of any immersion within a conventional, globalized enunciation, individuals such as Hammad are able to use terror as a way of establishing a new fraternity to support their own language of Self, free of the publicness of *das Man*. As the narrator observes, '[t]hey felt things together, he and his brothers', the 'magnetic effect of plot' which 'drew them together more tightly than ever'. Such an immersion 'closed the world to the slenderest line of sight, where everything converges to a point' and everything beyond what they desire to think or feel is excluded, freeing them from alterity and US power. Through its 'claim of danger and isolation' the 'plot shapes every breath' its conspirators take, ensuring '[t]here is no word they can speak' which 'does not come back to this', their symbolic resistance to the prevailing, globalized enunciation (DeLillo, *Falling Man*, pp. 174–6).

---

6   Such helplessness was also experienced by Hammad during the Iraq/Iran war when he witnessed 'ten thousand boys enacting the glory of self-sacrifice to divert Iraqi troops and equipment from the real army massing behind front lines': such a strategy resulted, from Hammad's perspective, in 'these children defeating us in the manner of their dying.' [Don DeLillo, *Falling Man*, p. 78].

More insidious than this refinement of terror into a counterstrike weapon, however, is Baudrillard's theory that a complicity exists between US citizens and the 9/11 conspirators. Proposing that anti-US 'antagonism' is not just 'everywhere' but also 'in every one of us' (Baudrillard, 'The Spirit of Terrorism', p. 15), Baudrillard argues that there is an '(unwittingly) terroristic imagination which dwells' within the Self in response to the 'unbearable power' of US hegemony (Baudrillard, 'The Spirit of Terrorism', pp. 4–5). Such 'imagination' manifests itself as 'the prodigious jubilation at seeing this global superpower destroyed', a force which, as the title of the last chapter implied, has entered people's sleep, resulting in them having 'dreamt of this event, that everyone without exception has dreamt of it' (Baudrillard, 'The Spirit of Terrorism', pp. 4–5). While it is US hegemony which sustains the space and integrity necessary for such individuals' enunciations, it is simultaneously a force which oppresses the very people it sustains; an ambiguity captured in Klara's artwork. For Baudrillard, 'no one can [thus] avoid dreaming of the destruction of any power that has become hegemonic to this degree', despite the 'unacceptab[ility] to the Western moral conscience' of such imaginings (Baudrillard, 'The Spirit of Terrorism', p. 5). It is this that creates the proliferation of writing, discourse and reportage surrounding the collapse of The Twin Towers, the abundance of which captures the extreme 'emotive violence' that accompanies the subject's 'deep-seated complicity' (Baudrillard, 'The Spirit of Terrorism', pp. 5–6). An intense 'effort' is consequently required to try and 'dispel' such a 'resonance', an attempt which fails to reduce the event to 'a pure accident, a purely arbitrary act, the murderous phantasmagoria of a few fanatics' (Baudrillard, 'The Spirit of Terrorism', pp. 5–6).

Lacking a model comparable to the language of Self, however, Baudrillard's theory fails to fully conceptualize the complexity of what occurs within US enunciations in response both to the intrusion of this alterity and the urge within the Self to revel in hegemony's destruction. The desire to transform 9/11 into a conflict between Islam and the West is thus not something solely enacted in order to return events to the province of the real, governed by issues of force and superiority within which the US dominates. As *Falling Man* demonstrates, such a transformation also occurs as a means of defending and redefining the margins of the Middle

American enunciation from the spectres of alterity and complicity, re-establishing who is, and who is not, contained within its auspices.

Such nuance in the domestic response to 9/11 can thus be observed in the interaction between Nina, her partner Martin and her daughter Lianne. For the former, the key task in the aftermath of the terrorist attacks is to place events within the materialist, geo-political context characteristic of the US public enunciation; a means of returning the terrorist actions to questions of force which remain safely within the bounds of US hegemony and which ignores the alterity of divergent, terrorist enunciations. For Nina, desperate to re-immerse herself within her previous, insulating perspective – an evasion characteristic of *das Man* – she must assert the importance of power, stressing that there 'are no goals' which the terrorists 'can hope to achieve', neither 'liberating a people' nor 'casting out a dictator'; a perspective that conforms to the revolutionary imagination which Baudrillard characterized as defined by the real. By characterizing the terrorists' enunciation as merely 'sheer panic' in the face of US hegemony, she attempts to dismiss their actions as the purposeless killing of 'the innocent' which does not signify a divergent language and its accompanying, destabilizing alterity. As her dismissive translation of أكبر الله ('God is great') attests, killing is an occurrence which for Mina must remain within the Baudrillardian real, reducing the terrorist attacks to a manifestation of the cultural struggle between Islam and the West. 9/11 is thus perceived as the result of the terrorists' 'own history' and 'mentality' defined against US hegemony; the 'closed world' in which they live and from which they 'haven't advanced because they haven't wanted to or tried to': a characterization which prevents terror from being viewed as the corollary to the global power and control that accompanimies Middle American dominance. Such a clear distinction between 'us' and 'them', Islam and the West, sophisticated and unsophisticated, allows Nina to attempt to alleviate the culpability of her own enunciation, freeing her from any sense of complicity with the terrorists' actions. Asserting that it is 'not the history of Western interference that pulls down these societies,' but instead their own indolence and refusal to conform to US values, Nina is able to deny Western complicity, thus obscuring the particularity of the terrorists' enunciation and its accompanying alterity (DeLillo, *Falling Man*, pp. 46–7).

A comparable concern with re-stabilizing and reinforcing boundaries can also be observed regarding the cultural and racial context of post-9/11 US enunciations. Unaccustomed 'to the sight of police and state troopers in tight clusters' or 'guardsmen with dogs' on the streets of New York, Lianne cannot reconcile this phenomenon with the previous composition of her US enunciation, and she feels they belong to '[o]ther places, she thought, other worlds, dusty terminals, major intersections' (DeLillo, *Falling Man*, p. 32): part of an alternate racial and geographical context. Within her domestic sphere an altered cultural context can also be observed in Lianne's reaction to the presence of art forms with an Islamic focus. Gazing upon a postcard depicting the cover illustration of Shelley's *Revolt of Islam*, Lianne 'understood in the first taut seconds that the card had been sent a week or two earlier', prior to the 9/11 attack (DeLillo, *Falling Man*, p. 8). In intruding upon her enunciation the object causes a profound wounding as it now possesses a signification which it previously lacked, highlighting the extent to which her social context has been altered by the actions of a divergent enunciation. This sense of an Eastern threat to US enunciations is further compounded by the playing of Islamic music within Lianne's apartment building, a comparable auditory contamination of foreign alterity which causes her to feel an instinctive resentment towards her neighbour. As the narrator observes, 'a certain kind of music' can represent 'a certain form of political and religious statement' by virtue of its context, a potential for wounding which highlights the fragmentation that has occurred in US hegemony, and which forces Lianne to confront her feelings towards Islam (DeLillo, *Falling Man*, p. 69):

> They're the ones who think alike, talk alike, eat the same food at the same time. She knew this wasn't true. Say the same prayers, word for word, in the same prayer stance, day and night, following the arc of sun and moon. (DeLillo, *Falling Man*, p. 68).

The very structure of her thought – its initial assertion of a derogatory stereotype, a subsequent retreat to a socially conventional pseudo-liberal viewpoint, and, finally, a return to an inescapable and deeply held anger and dismissal of Islamic culture – reveals the deep-seated unease and damage which has occurred as the result of the alterity of the Other. In order to recover the security she has lost, the hermetic seal of her public enunciation, Lianne wishes to complain about 'the noise' of the music rather than its cultural context, to 'adopt a posture of suave calm' when she complains to her neighbour, one which does not 'allude to the underlying theme', and which instead uses 'the language of aggrieved tenancy', thus remaining within the discourse of capital, of the Baudrillardian real which characterizes public US enunciations (DeLillo, *Falling Man*, p. 69).

Even within her own home, away from the 'noise' of her neighbour and the heightened security conditions of public spaces, Lianne is still forced to confront alterity in the behaviour of her child and his friends. In the wake of the attack, the children have turned secretive and insular, conspiring with each other and concealing their actions from their parents. When their silence is finally broken, it is revealed that they have devised a secret name, Bill Lawton – a corruption of Bin Laden. The 'whole point' of their creation, as her son observes, 'snapping the words clearly and defiantly', is the 'things' which this figure confides 'about the planes' to them alone as a result of their act of naming. These confidences, and the creation of a mystery figure, become a means of re-inscribing chaotic and unpredictable events within a new, divergent enunciation which the children have generated for themselves, an action which symbolizes the damage done to the desirability of more conventional, American languages of Self. In order to maintain and develop this enunciation the children spend their days waiting for the planes to strike again, as the Bill Lawton figure they have created 'says' that 'they're coming' and that 'this time the towers will fall' – despite their actual collapse – a 'repositioning of events' which caused Lianne to feel an instinctive aversion that 'frightened her in an unaccountable way'. Feeling a 'menace' which she 'couldn't locate', Lianne has an instinctive awareness of the alteration in the balance of power which her children's behaviour represents. Re-imposing the prevailing US enunciation of Self, Lianne and her husband talked to their son and 'tried to make gentle sense', an attempt to reincorporate him within their collective enunciation, to police its boundaries and attempt to remove any visible indication of foreign alterity. Only by eliminating every trace of alterity's effect can their denial be total, reinvigorating and re-establishing their belief in the supremacy of US power (DeLillo, *Falling Man*, p. 102).

While the depiction of Hammad, Nina and Lianne, would seem to accord with Baudrillard's theory of 9/11 as a watershed moment in the history of terror, such a conception is contested within the field of terrorism studies. As Richard English notes, 'however understandable it is that these [9/11] atrocities should prompt reflection about whether there had emerged another 'new' terrorism (this time jihadist, and embodied in the activities of al-Qaeda), there was actually much terrorist continuity between the pre- and post-9/11 terrorist worlds.'[7] And within *Falling Man* itself such a perspective is supported by Martin, Nina's partner. Rather than viewing the 9/11 attacks as the product of religion or the clash of civilizations, Martin instead ascribes opposing motivations to the terrorists in question, blurring the division between the collective Self of the third person singular and that of the foreign Other. While conceding Nina's point that the terrorists may be driven by panic, he emphasizes the connection which exists between US hegemony and the existence of terror. As he observes, 'they think the world is a disease' and 'this society' – the public, US enunciation of Self – is a contagion 'that's spreading'. While Nina refuses to perceive any point to the killings, no possibility for achievement within the perspective of the real, Martin is able to see a symbolic dimension, arguing that the terrorists are striking 'a blow to this country's dominance' by 'show[ing] how a great power can be vulnerable'. Acknowledging that they 'use the language of religion', Martin still argues that this is not principally 'what drives them'. Instead, he believes that their actions are motivated by 'matters of history', 'politics and economics', the very factors which constitute the US enunciation and upon which its hegemony rests. While America may have these factors on its 'side' – the 'capital, the labor, the technology, the armies, the agencies, the cities, the laws, the police and the prisons' – the terrorists are able to juxtapose, on the 'other side', the symbolic opposition of 'a few men willing to die' and the spectacle which they create. While such a deployment may be unable to obtain significant advantage in the realm of the real, it can still have a profound effect in symbolic terms, highlighting the

---

7   Richard English, *Terrorism: How to Respond* (Oxford: Oxford University Press, 2009), p. 15. Further references are given after quotations in the text.

'[T]he balance of power and the balance of terror' 193

complicity which Martin acknowledges and which individuals such Nina deny (DeLillo, *Falling Man*, pp. 46–7).

Such a perspective can also be observed in the post-9/11 concern with Martin's historicity (*Historizität*). Whereas the ambiguity of his background was a 'secret' which Lianne 'respected' prior to the collapse of The Twin Towers, with the destabilization which has occurred to the Middle American language of Self she now struggles to reconcile her Self to Martin's past (DeLillo, *Falling Man*, p. 195). In order to do so, Lianne attempts to differentiate between Islamic and Western terrorists, characterizing Martin as 'one of ours, which meant godless, Western, white', as opposed to the supposed Islamic fundamentalism of Hammad and his terrorist cell (DeLillo, *Falling Man*, p. 195), echoing her mother's assertion and rejecting the idea of a continuity in the underlying nature of terrorism. While such anti-Islamic prejudice is incompatible with the patina of liberal values which characterize Lianne's public enunciation, leaving her 'chilled' and 'shamed', it is still necessary for her to be able to draw a categorical difference between Martin and the 9/11 terrorists, allowing him to remain within the boundary of the Middle American enunciation (DeLillo, *Falling Man*, p. 195). It is only through the logical aporia of such prejudice that Lianne is able, once again, to have 'yielded to his mystery', viewing his historicity with a certain tolerance which she could not extend towards the 9/11 attackers (DeLillo, *Falling Man*, p. 195). As she notes, rather than being part of a Jihadist cell, Martin was instead a secular 'member of a collective in the late nineteen sixties' named 'Kommune One' who opposed 'the German state, the fascist state', before later heading to Italy and the milieu of 'the Red Brigades' (DeLillo, *Falling Man*, p. 146). Since he is western and white, Lianne is able to convince herself that '[w]hatever it was he'd done' was 'not outside the lines of response' for a member of the prevailing Middle American enunciation of Self (DeLillo, *Falling Man*, p. 195).[8] Her differentiation, however, deliberately ignores the fact that Martin's motivation for his terrorist actions was a belief that the prevailing,

---

8   A similar after-effect can be observed in portrayals of the IRA and the Real IRA, post 9/11, as the prevailing US perspective upon their actions became a site of contestation.

Western, hegemonic order represented a social sickness, a contagion which needed to be cleansed; an enunciation he shares with both other western, 'godless', white terrorists, and with the 9/11 hijackers. In doing so Lianne has to deny what English terms as the 'heterogeneity' of terror (English, 2009, p. 22). As he observes, such diversity 'is true in terms of the identity or character of the practitioner (non-state, anti-state, pro-state, state) and of the victim, and also of the associated ideological justification or political goal: terrorism can be of the left or the right, religiously inflected or utterly secular, revolutionary or favouring the consolidation of the *status quo*' (English, 2009, p. 22).

Such 'heterogeneity' of terror is further emphasized in DeLillo's earlier fiction, providing further support for the growing conception in terror studies that rather than ideology, it is instead methodology which provides the most epistemological certainty for describing and exploring the workings of terror. As English observes, 'terrorism might best be considered as a method' (English, 2009, p. 23) which

> involves heterogeneous violence used or threatened with a political aim; it can involve a variety of acts, of targets, and of actors; it possesses an important psychological dimension, producing terror or fear among a directly threatened group and also a wider implied audience in the hope of maximizing political communication and achievement; it embodies the exerting and implementing of power, and the attempted redressing of power relations; it represents a subspecies of warfare, and as such it can form part of a wider campaign of violent and non-violent attempts at political leverage. (English, 2009, p. 24)

In a detailed attempt at creating a usable schema of what constitutes terrorism, based upon method, not ideology, Louise Richardson outlines 'seven crucial characteristics': that 'a terrorist act is politically inspired'; it 'involve[s] violence or the threat of violence'; that 'terrorism is not to defeat the enemy but to send a message'; in which 'the act and the victim usually have symbolic significance'; that 'terrorism is the act of substate groups, not states'; the 'victim of the violence and the audience the terrorists are trying to reach are not the same'; and that the 'final and most important

'[T]he balance of power and the balance of terror' 195

defining characteristic of terrorism is the deliberate targeting of civilians.'[9] In light of such methodological attempts at definition DeLillo's earlier fiction reveals that far from the collapse of the twin towers representing a new form of terror, similar pre-9/11 strategies can be observed on the part of both terrorists and Middle America.

Win Everett's existence can be viewed as a rejection of the 'ordinary mysteries' (DeLillo, *Libra*, p. 76) and the 'happiness' which arises as a 'sum of small awarenesses' attained from a conventional, public language of Self 'lived minute by minute' (DeLillo, *Libra*, p. 135). Instead, his own enunciation revolves around the keeping of secrets and the devising of plots: the most prominent of which is the assassination of President Kennedy, undertaken with his confederates Parmenter and T.J. Mackey. Win is thus emblematic of the same tendency as Hammad, namely the desire to reject the public enunciation of Middle America, and in its place devise a partially collective form of the language of Self: one achieved through secrecy, terror and the possession of knowledge known only to a few cognoscenti. Such a conception echoes that of John Horgan who argued that '[m]ost terrorist movements are relatively small, (semi-)clandestine collectives'.[10]

For the majority of Win's life, as for that of Parmenter and T-J, this need for a divergent, *sinthomo*sexual language of Self was fulfilled by membership within the CIA, likewise a small and relatively clandestine collective. Like J. Edgar Hoover's position in the FBI, the CIA provides Win and his co-conspirators with a social framework which shelters their alternate, non-normative enunciations. By providing 'a society' which was 'a better-working version of the larger world, where things have an almost dreamy sense of connection to each other' and where 'the plan was tighter', men such as Win were able to believe that 'history was in their care' (DeLillo, *Libra*, pp. 126–7). The 'idea' of being recruited to the CIA thus 'seemed immediately right', providing 'a possible answer to the restlessness'

---

9   Louise Richardson, *What Terrorists Want: Understanding the Enemy Containing the Threat* (New York, Random House, 2006), p. 1. Further references are given after quotations in the text.
10 John Horgan, *The Psychology of Terrorism* (London: Routledge, 2005), p. 1. Further references are given after quotations in the text.

he had 'felt working through his system,' a 'sense' that he 'needed to risk something important,' to 'challenge' his 'moral complacencies' before he could 'see' himself 'complete', free of the blurring of *das Man* (DeLillo, *Libra*, p. 146): a comparable feeling to that of Hammad and the other 9/11 conspirators. Through Win's employment for 'twenty-some-odd years' within the agency he was able to live 'in a special society that pretty much satisfied the most serious things' within his 'nature', allowing him access to '[s]ecrets to trade and keep' and preventing him from having to live limited to the 'ordinary mysteries' that delight his wife, Mary Francis (DeLillo, *Libra*, p. 63).

Once access to such a society is denied, however, as Bannister observes, '[p]eople like us' are confronted with a 'dilemma we have to face', '[s]erious men deprived of an outlet' for whom '[e]veryday lawful pursuits don't meet' such 'special requirements' (DeLillo, *Libra*, p. 63). As Win observes of his descent from the facilitating enunciation of the CIA into the *normal* Middle American life of a small town college professor, it 'was all part of the long fall, the general sense that he was dying' which accompanies the feeling of bleeding into the conventional, normative US public enunciation (DeLillo, *Libra*, p. 79). Denied an outlet, such individuals felt a deep-seated 'rage' not only 'toward the administration', but also 'partly a reaction to public life itself' (DeLillo, *Libra*, p. 62), the pain of being a 'zero in the system' (DeLillo, *Libra*, p. 151): a comparable emotion to that felt by Martin and Hammad. So intense is this 'hatred' that it had 'a size to it, a physical force' which becomes 'the thing that kept' such individuals 'going after career disappointments, bad health, a forced retirement' and the pain of living diminished within a conventional language of Self (DeLillo, *Libra*, p. 62). While individuals such as Marguerite, Parmenter's wife, 'cannot survive in the world' without their 'American way of life' – their heteronormative public enunciation – for Win, Mackey and Parmenter such an existence, in its denial of a space for their *Sinthomo*sexual rage, proves to be intolerable (DeLillo, *Libra*, p. 200). As Agent Bateman observes, 'there's nothing in the world that's harder to do than live a straightforward life', to conform and contain the Self within the undesired publicness of *das Man* (DeLillo, *Libra*, p. 309). In order to escape this social constraint, the pain of normality and the denial of access to power, it is to an alternate, partially-public enunciation, that such individuals turn. 'Stalking a victim' or constructing a plot thus becomes a means 'of organizing one's loneliness, making a network out of it, a fabric of connections' through which '[d]esperate men give their solitude a purpose and a destiny', whilst simultaneously evading the social limitations placed upon them (DeLillo, *Libra*, p. 147).

While Win, Parmenter and Mackay had all experienced the facilitating enunciation of the CIA and subsequently lost this connection to grace, such membership was never possible for Lee Harvey Oswald. While he 'wanted to carry himself with a clear sense of role', to find 'the only end to isolation' by reaching 'the point where he was no longer separated from the true struggles that went on around him' – what the novel terms as 'history', a characterization which *Falling Man* would later echo – any socially-sanctioned opportunity for such a transition is denied (DeLillo, *Libra*, p. 248). As with the other conspirators, it is instead a terrorist plot which provides the means of entering this historical moment and abandoning a powerless Self. Oswald would seem to be a paradigmatic case of what Richardson believes creates a terrorist, the 'lethal cocktail that combines a disaffected individual, an enabling community, and a legitimizing ideology' (Richardson, 2006, p. xxii). While such individuals attempt to rationalize their behaviour as the product of an historical imperative – the amalgam of 'forces in the air that compel men to act' and whose aggregate 'men sense at the same point' (DeLillo, *Libra*, p. 68; p. 143) – such an appeal to ideology merely functions as an excuse for the expression of underlying *sinthomo*sexual motivations discussed above; a commonality shared by both pre- and post-9/11 terrorism. Though the summer preceding Kennedy's assassination was seen by such individuals as 'building towards a vision, a history' in which they were 'being swept up, swept along', such a claim cannot obscure the fact that their prime motivation was that they were merely 'done with being a pitiful individual, done with [the] isolation' caused by having to cope with *sinthomo*sexual urges in the absence of a supporting fraternity (DeLillo, *Libra*, p. 322).

While the conspirators of both 9/11 and the assassination of JFK share a comparable enunciation – disputing Baudrillard's theory of a categorical difference in terrorism following the collapse of The Twin Towers – the depiction of The Texas Highway Killer in *Underworld* further questions the way which the boundaries of what constitutes terrorism are defined and policed. Though Richardson, English and Horgan are all united in seeing the political dimension of terrorism as one of its defining characteristics – as Horgan notes 'from a psychological perspective, an important characteristic even in the simplest analyses distinguishing terrorism from other kinds of crime involving murder, or violence committed for some personal reasons (as for example, sexually motivated murder, or rape), is the *political* dimension to the terrorist's behaviour' (Horgan, 2005, p. 1) – *Underworld* shows the problematic nature of such a distinction and the importance of appreciating the role of the language of Self and of *sinthomo*sexuality. For those Middle American adherents watching the video of one of the Texas highway killings, the 'starkness' and 'seared realness' of the tape causes the 'things' surrounding the viewer to reveal their 'rehearsed', 'layered and cosmetic look' (DeLillo, *Underworld*, p. 157). Highlighting the extent to which the Middle American enunciation is merely 'the layers of cosmetic perception' which hide the 'realness beneath', the video forces such individuals to confront what 'lies at the scraped bottom of all the layers' they 'have added' to the bareness of their own existence, mirroring Lianne's reaction in the aftermath of the 9/11 attacks (DeLillo, *Underworld*, pp. 157–8). Such a phenomenon is exacerbated by the circumstances surrounding the tape's production which contrasts the 'jostled sort of noneventness that marks the family product', its heteronormativity, with the random slaying of a passing motorist (DeLillo, *Underworld*, p. 157). Transformed from 'just another video homicide' by the figural child who filmed it, the 'chance quality of the encounter' thus 'speaks' to the Middle American adherent 'directly, saying terrible things about forces beyond your control, lines of intersection that cut through history and logic and every reasonable layer of human expectation' (DeLillo, *Underworld*, p. 157). Destabilizing the supposed certainties of the real upon which such a public enunciation depends, it poses a series of questions that the Middle American language of Self is unable to answer, replicating the after-effects of terrorism (DeLillo, *Underworld*, p. 158):

'[T]he balance of power and the balance of terror'

> Why? What are you telling her? Are you making a little statement? Like I'm going to ruin your day out of ordinary spite. Or a big statement? Like this is the risk of existing. Either way you're rubbing her face in this tape and you don't know why. (DeLillo, *Underworld*, p. 159)

For Middle Americans such as Matt Shay, the more they 'watch the tape, the deader and colder and more relentless it becomes', 'suck[ing] the air right out of your chest', yet compelling the viewer to 'watch it every time', and, in so doing, creating a relationship between consumer and instigator, mirroring the media aftermath of the assassinations of Kennedy, Oswald and the collapse of The Twin Towers (DeLillo, *Underworld*, p. 160).

As with *Libra* and *Falling Man*, *Underworld* also presents the instigator's perspective, revealing the common *sinthomo*sexual motivations underpinning the enunciations of those who violently resist the *das Man* publicness of Middle American hegemony and, in so doing, problematizes what is and is not a political killing. For Richard, The Texas Highway Killer, the reasons for his actions are shown to be analogous to those of individuals who are typically designated as terrorists. The prime cause of his actions is the oppressive nature of the conventional Middle American enunciation and the socio-economic system upon which it rests; an echo of the complaints of Hammad, Martin and Win. Working in a supermarket, Richard is forced to interact with customers who 'said unbelievable things' to him, indifferent to the travails he suffers as a result of his domestic situation and the stresses which it places upon him (DeLillo, *Underworld*, p. 267). Compelled to work within an economic system which ensured that 'he had to talk in the open space where anyone could hear' (DeLillo, *Underworld*, p. 272), irrespective of his wish for a mediated publicness, his personal enunciation is thus denied by economically enforced connection. While he has previously been allowed 'a booth' which had a 'talk hole to talk through' – a commodity allowing an element of the mediation to which he aspires – 'they' (*Man*) had 'put him back at the checkout', without reason or warning, in spite of his desires (DeLillo, *Underworld*, p. 272). Economically conscripted by 'having two sick parents at home, or one sick and one bad-tempered', Richard is forced to acquiesce to the demands of the public sphere, deforming his desired language in order to conform to what is expected of him within a Middle American enunciation (DeLillo, *Underworld*, p. 267). Viewed within such a context the question thus arises of whether the dominance of the heteronormative Middle American enunciation of Self, and its policing of the *sinthomo*sexual, is itself a political struggle, and the resistance of the minority such as Richard a form of terror.

As the narrator observes of the news coverage of the victims, Richard 'came alive in them', 'lived in their histories, in the photographs in the newspaper, he survived in the memories of the family, lived with the victims, lived on, merged, twinned, quadrupled, continued into double figures' in a manner comparable to that of Hammad and the other hijackers (DeLillo, *Underworld*, p. 271). This alternate enunciation, and the skills required to ensure its maintenance – such as having 'taught himself to shoot with the left hand' – are thus 'how he had to take his feelings outside himself so's to escape his isolation' (DeLillo, *Underworld*, p. 266). In a similar, paradoxical manner to the other terrorist conspirators in *Libra* and *Falling Man*, 'Richard had to take everything outside, share it with others, become part of the history of others, because this was the only way to escape, to get out from under the pissant details of who he was', yet, simultaneously, to do so by creating a mediated connection which provides agency and rejects unfettered connection (DeLillo, *Underworld*, p. 266).

Just as with more conventional forms of terrorism, Richard's alternate enunciation becomes a site of public and private contestation. As he observes, 'I feel like my situation has been twisted in with the profiles of a hundred other individuals in the crime computer', reducing particularity to an undifferentiated publicness: Dasein to *das Man* (DeLillo, *Underworld*, p. 216). Attempting to co-opt Richard's production – as Lianne and Nina strive to do with the 9/11 attacks – the prevailing social order dismisses the cause and motivation of his actions as apolitical; variously the product of 'head trauma', adoption and abuse (DeLillo, *Underworld*, p. 267): representative of a wish to deny the alterity of his acts and to reintegrate his behaviour within the bounds of the Middle American enunciation and its paradoxical, Baudrillardian conception of the real, determined by issues of force and predictability; the very phenomena which the 'starkness' and 'seared realness' of the tape denigrates as merely cosmetic impositions (DeLillo, *Underworld*, p. 157).

Richard's subsequent, quixotic engagement with the media is an attempt to regain control of his enunciation in a manner analogous to terrorist proclamations: to sustain a mediated privateness which he strives to reclaim through the unfettered publicness of a hyperreal mediascape. The paradoxical nature of such an attempt can be observed in his 'request' that he 'would only talk to Sue Ann Corcoran, one-on-one' (DeLillo, *Underworld*, p. 217); a mediated privateness undermined by the live broadcast of such a conversation to an unknown number of viewers; the antithesis of partial connection and a parody of a heteronormative union. Replicating the earlier 'talk hole' of his booth, Richard 'made the call and turned on the TV, or vice versa, without the sound, his hand wound in a doubled hanky, and he never felt so easy talking to someone on the phone or face-to-face or man to woman as he felt that day talking to Sue Ann' (DeLillo, *Underworld*, p. 270). As he 'watched her over there and talked to her over here' Richard is able to fragment the Other in the manner of David Bell and Eric Deming, ensuring that he 'saw her lips move silent in one part of the room while her words fell soft and warm on the coils of his secret ear', shaping the Self he endeavours to create through technological mediation (DeLillo, *Underworld*, p. 270):

> He talked to her on the phone and made eye contact with the TV. This was the waking of the knowledge that he was real. This alien-eyed woman with raving hair sending emanations that astonished his heart. He spoke more confidently as time went on. He was coming into himself, shy but also unashamed, a little vain, even, and honest and clever, evasive when he needed to be, standing there in a stranger's house near a lamp without a shade and she listened and asked questions, watching him from the screen ten feet away. She had so much radiance she could make him real. (DeLillo, *Underworld*, p. 270)

Fragmented into component parts, Sue Ann Corcoran is stripped of her alterity and ceases to pose the threat which the supermarket customers represent.[11] Rather than bruising him by saying 'unbelievable things' (DeLillo, *Underworld*, p. 267), the fragmented Sue Ann, as a collection of images,

---

11   For the viewer of the interview a similar fragmentation of Sue Ann occurs, rendering her a polyvalent collection of surfaces analogous to the hyperreal, commoditized

possesses a televisual 'radiance' which can instead be used by Richard as a medium upon which to reconstruct his desired enunciation (DeLillo, *Underworld*, p. 270). As a result, he felt that he was 'coming into himself' and making 'him[self] real' (DeLillo, *Underworld*, p. 270).

While his conversation with Sue Ann seemingly allows him to re-appropriate his idiosyncratic Self, such articulation proves to be temporary. The hyperreal nature of the medium and the culture which it helps engender results in the switchboard being subsequently swamped with callers claiming to be The Texas Highway Killer, leaving Richard unable to re-establish his self-mediated connection with the fragmented Sue Ann. Just as the viewer of the tape is struck by its 'seared realness', destabilizing their own enunciation and revealing the complicity of their consumption, so too is Richard impacted by the image which he unwittingly helped create (DeLillo, *Underworld*, p. 157). As the narrator observes, every time he 'watched the tape he thought he was going to turn up in his own living room, detached from who he was, peering squint-eyed over the wheel of his compact car' (DeLillo, *Underworld*, p. 270). The very hyperreality of the medium which lets him fragment Sue Ann and engage in an enunciation-affirming discourse, is the same phenomenon which lets the taped image dominate his own recollection of the event, colonizing the particularity of his memories: just as it facilitated the emergence of the Middle American enunciation whose hegemony he violently rejects.[12] Damaged by the prevalence of these media images and his inability to establish himself as the authentic Texas Highway Killer, the certainty which Richard gained through his conversation with Sue Ann and the agency of his serial killing is gradually diluted. Instead, without such an insulating language of Self, all of his 'little failures' slowly eat 'away at his confidence' and in his final depiction within the novel he is shown heading out in his compact

Jayne. A similarly voyeuristic pleasure is obtained watching her converse, knowing that she is forced to passively receive both Richard's voice and the gaze of the camera.

12   A similar destabilizing effect can be observed in Richard's reaction to the existence of a copycat killer, again revealing the blurring which occurs between his own memories and public accounts of his actions, dissolving the certainty of the 'original' with the increasing prevalence of its simulacrum.

car with his father's gun in search of another victim, striving to reassert his enunciation through the destruction of an Other, further entering media history (DeLillo, *Underworld*, p. 263). In so doing, however, Richard will again become a product to be consumed and exhausted; like the spectacle of the Twin Towers or the shooting of John F. Kennedy, though in the process of so doing, he will blur the hermeneutic certainty of what does and does not constitute a political and non-political act.

Viewed within such a context, 9/11 terrorism, as portrayed in *Falling Man*, can thus be seen to correlate with the portrayal of earlier forms of the phenomenon advanced in DeLillo's previous novels, contesting Baudrillard's assertion that the collapse of The Twin Towers marked a distinct watershed in the historicity (*Historizität*) of terror. As a comparison of *Falling Man* and *Libra* demonstrates, the urge towards terrorism originates from the same cause in both Islamic and non-Islamic practitioners: that of the pressure of societal conformity to a perceived *uneigentlich*, public enunciation, opposed by the insistence of non-normative, *sinthomo*sexual desires. From the perspective of those within the boundaries of the dominant US enunciation of Self a comparable similarity can likewise be observed between the effects of 9/11 and those of earlier attacks. The struggle of Nina and Lianne to create a clear distinction between 'godless, Western, white' domestic terrorists and a supposed Islamic fundamentalism can therefore be understood as another in a series of attempts to sustain the hegemony and stability of an inauthentic public enunciation against concerted opposition; an endeavour to reject the alterity of the Other and deny hegemonic complicity.

As the actions of The Texas Highway Killer demonstrate, however, ideology and politics merely act as a faultline, facilitating the emergence of an alternate enunciation rooted in partial publicness and *sinthomo*sexuality. For individuals such as Martin, Hammad, Win, Louis, T-J, Oswald and Richard, terror can thus be seen as the cultural signification of urges which are denied social sanction. Whether or not such resistance is subsequently contained within the prevailing public enunciation of Self is therefore not a product of the aims or motivations of the terrorists themselves, but instead a function of social interpretation, rooted in the competing complexities of public and private enunciations of Self. In either case, it is the urges themselves which are the driving force behind the formation of this concerted resistance and the cause of the social destabilization which occurs. As the portrayal of Lianne, Nina and Matt Shay demonstrates, such emergence reveals the inauthentic nature of the Middle American enunciation and the chaotic randomness which it attempts to deny.

CONCLUSION

To '[e]xplore America in the screaming night'[1]: The Language of Self as the Foundation of Future DeLillo Criticism

As Martin Heidegger observed in *Sein und Zeit* phenomenal ontology begins with the following observation, quoted from Plato's *Sophistes*:

> ... δῆλον γάρ ὡς ὑμέν ταντ (τί ποτε βούλεσθε σημαίνειν ὁπόταν ὄν Φθέγγησθε) πάλαι γιγνώσκετε, ἡμεῖς δέ πρό τον μεν ᾠόμεθα, νύν δ' ἠπορήκαμεν ...
> 'For manifestly you have long been aware of what you mean when you use the expression "*being*". We, however, who used to think we understood it, have now become perplexed.' (Heidegger, 2000, p. 19)

Proposing that Dasein has 'proximally and for the most part' lost its primordial understanding of Being, Heidegger uses the above quotation as the starting point of an historically contingent theory of subjectivity (Heidegger, 2000, p. 43). While the individual may have known what it meant *to be* in a particular moment, shaped by a specific historicity (*Historizität*), once that context alters, so too does the form into which its Being is shaped. Preoccupied with etymology, Heidegger's project emphasizes the interrelation of Being (*Sein*) – a noun – and to be (*Zu-sein*) – a verb – conveying the sense in which existence is an action that the subject undertakes, governed by issues of tense and case: linguistic embodiments of temporality and the influence of the Other; a particular instance in a language of Self which changes with time and is shaped by an intersubjective context.

Correlating with such an ontological vision, DeLillo's novels offer a series of ontical depictions of Dasein's subjectivity, demonstrating

---

[1] Don DeLillo, *Americana*, p. 10.

the range and variety with which such enunciations manifest. While Heidegger's theory is concerned with an abstract form of *das Man* (the 'they'), DeLillo's work, by contrast, charts the foundation and evolution of specific US public enunciations, rooted in twentieth- and twenty-first-century American historicity. Striving to address such complexity on both an individual and collective level, this book used a tripartite structure of 'Dasein', 'Phenomenology' and 'Das Man' to engage, respectively, with the individual, phenomeno-linguistic, and socio-environmental context, of the language of Self.

Divided into two chapters, '"[L]ife narrowed down to unfinished rooms"[2]: Isolation and the Language of Self' and '"[Y]our link to the fate of mankind"[3]: Connection and the Language of Self', the first section, 'Dasein', explored Dasein's vacillation between the desire to deny alterity and the opposing wish to embrace the Other. Assailed by urges, wounded by connection, drawn to alterity and haunted by the certainty of its own death, the subject in DeLillo's work negotiates, consciously or not, a particular enunciation: an ontical expression of this ubiquitous ontological dilemma. Shaping Self along a continuum which varies between the desire for total isolation, a mediated publicness and the absolute surrender to alterity, the first section reveals the multiplicity of enunciations present in DeLillo's fiction.

The second section, 'Phenomenology', explored the role of the λόγος and image – addressed in chapters three and four respectively, entitled '"With a word they could begin to grid the world"[4]: Denotation and the Language of Self' and '"[T]o smash my likeness, prism of all my images"[5]: Hyperreality, ἀλήθεια (truth) and the Language of Self' – as the media within which Dasein's subjectivity is enunciated and this ontological dilemma is enacted. Tracing the evolution of the linguistic theory espoused in DeLillo's texts, the third chapter argued that this process culminated in

---

2   Don DeLillo, *Running Dog*, p. 54.
3   Don DeLillo, *Mao II*, p. 78.
4   Don DeLillo, *Libra*, p. 414.
5   Don DeLillo, *Americana*, p. 236.

a phenomenological model of language, which, unlike prior conceptions, offered a sufficiently fluid vessel for an authentic language of Self. Building upon this analysis, the fourth chapter explored how the hyperreal image challenged the epistemological stability of earlier forms of denotation portrayed in DeLillo's novels, and how the inextricability of phenomenon (Φαινόμενον) and λόγος in a phenomenological model of language ensured a more authentic relationship to the simulacra, as evidenced in Lauren's artwork.

'Das Man', the third section, explored the evolution of public enunciations of Self which used λόγος and phenomenon as media upon which to negotiate the collective desire for isolation and connection. The fifth chapter, '"Capital burns off the nuance in a culture"[6]: Consumption, Capital, *Chrimatistikós* and the Middle American Enunication of Self', explored how commodification was used as a form of collective signification to mediate the hyperreal into a controllable, malleable form which was able to support and sustain the Middle American language of Self and its subsidiary enunciations. As the analysis of The Deming section reveals, however, such signification was undermined by the very hyperreality used to create mass-marketed products. This destabilization was accentuated by the inevitable transformation of commodity into waste, explored in the sixth chapter '"[T]he banned materials of civilization"[7]: Waste, *Sinthomo*sexuality and Middle America'. The hyperreal nature of the commodity and the presence of waste ultimately resulted in the shattering of Self and Other into a collective noun which encompassed a polyvalency of surfaces; the mechanism of commodification which underpinned Middle America, but that also provided a medium through which non-normative, *sinthomo*sexual desires could irrupt.

The final binary, power and terror, demonstrates that it is only Middle America's unrelenting quest for hegemony and resistance to divergent alterity, undertaken at both an individual and collective level, which allows such non-normative presences to be contained. '"[To] maintain a force in the

6   Don DeLillo, *Underworld*, p. 776.
7   Ibid., p. 286.

world that comes into people's sleep"[8]: Power, Alterity and the Formation of Hegemony' and '"[T]he balance of power and the balance of terror"[9]: Terrorism and the *uneigentlich* Publicness of *das Man*' thus chart the use, policing and co-option of *sinthomo*sexuals such as J. Edgar Hoover and Eric Deming in aiding the state to control capital markets and nuclear weapons: twin manifestations of complex power networks upon which the stability of the Middle American enunciation depends. As the final chapter argues, *sinthomo*sexuals who were not used by the prevailing order discovered that Middle American hegemony ensured that their enunciations were restricted and forcibly re-inscribed.

While heteronormative individuals such as Erica Deming encounter the Middle American language of Self as a supporting framework which they help evolve and sustain, correlating to the desired form of their own enunciation, for those whose language deviates from such a model an inevitable blurring of Self occurs. Compelled towards an inauthentic, fallen form of Being, such individuals experience social interaction as a predominantly repressive force. Actively selected against, *sinthomo*sexuals are presented with the stark choice of passively suffering social oppression or undertaking violent, divergent opposition. As only a few are fortunate enough to find a niche within the prevailing social order where their non-normativity can obtain approbation, for the remainder, terror, conspiracy and a figural understanding of history provide the only outlet.

A nuanced understanding of terrorism can thus be obtained from DeLillo's work, highlighting Middle American complicity and revealing the inevitable Janus-like quality of power and terror. Through an understanding of the language of Self, such analysis demonstrates the quixotic nature of The War on Terror and the inevitable failure of the attempt, by Middle America, to wholly exclude alterity. No matter to what extent the prevailing enunciation strives to eliminate opposition, the phenomenon will remain, growing stronger the more manifestly coercive forms of power are used against its practitioners.

8   Ibid., p. 76.
9   Ibid., p. 76.

To return once more to Heidegger's concept of Dasein as an entity which 'is ontically distinguished by the fact that, in its very Being, that Being is an issue' (Heidegger, 2000, p. 32), social existence, as this book has argued, forms the principal component of such ontological dilemma. Connection, and what form, if any, it should take, is therefore the foundation of both public and private enunciations and the genesis of the various strategies of subjectivity discussed above. Such is the spectre of its presence that the Self is forced to perpetually signify, resist, support and deform larger social enunciations: ontical manifestations of this ubiquitous ontological problem of Dasein's social Being. Permanently haunted by the Other, subjectivity in DeLillo's fiction is a phenomenon which cannot be adequately understood without an analysis of the social existence of the individual, conceptualized through the language of Self.

It is this aspect of DeLillo's work which can be characterized as its most Heideggerian, since, as the above analysis has demonstrated, an adequate understanding of this issue can only be obtained through an appreciation of the interaction of Self and community against a context of American historicity. Just as *Sein und Zeit* attempts to derive the origin, function and morphology of large-scale social systems through the detailed, nuanced analysis of the minutiae of Dasein's phenomenal ontology, so too does this project attempt to achieve a comparable understanding of DeLillo's representation of society and the individual in twentieth- and twenty-first-century America. It is precisely this inextricability of Self and context, characteristic of a Heideggerian understanding of subjectivity, which has allowed this book to underscore the particularly active nature of this relationship in DeLillo's work, stressing that social context does not arise irrespective of the individual and their actions.

Instead, building upon the shared etymology of Dasein and *das Man*, this project was able to demonstrate that it is through individual historicity – which, as Heidegger notes, is both that of the Self and of its generation – that this social context is first formed, manifested in the dream of the universal third person singular, a particularly American form of 'the neuter' (Heidegger, 2000, p. 164) which parallels the evolution and decline of the Cold War – the period upon which DeLillo chooses to focus. Having achieving a critical understanding which, as with the phenomenal ontology of *Sein und Zeit*, is able to encompass both a personal and public understanding of subjectivity, this book has posited a Heideggerian conception of DeLillo's portrayal of subjectivity through the language of Self: one which shows the inseparability of Self, Other and historicity (*Historizität*) – the unity of which has often been marginalized and left largely uncommented upon in the majority of existing DeLillo criticism.

Due to the focus of this project, which endeavours to engage with these overarching themes – stressing the unity of the trifecta of Self, Other and historicity – each novel has only been explored in terms of its relation to such broader, ubiquitous concerns. There is accordingly scope for subsequent inquiries to build upon this foundation, analysing in additional detail the myriad, ontical forms of individual and collective enunciation particular to each novel. This monograph opens such new, critical ground, providing a nuanced and versatile framework which would allow subsequent analysis to stress the particular ontical form of enunciations within a given work, and to do so in a manner which is able to elucidate the place of such phenomenological significations within the larger ontological project of DeLillo's fiction.

Though marking a conclusion to the work undertaken, this final section, and the book in general, can more accurately be seen as an extensive form of beginning which has strived to establish, through the theorizing of a language of Self, what Heidegger characterized as a clearing of truth (*aletheia*): one rooted in '[l]anguage as the house of being', the 'home' in which 'man dwells'.[10] Once such a clearing is established it is the place of subsequent inquiry to use this starting point to create a more nuanced understanding of this truth; one which, rather than losing the primordiality and ambiguous nature of such inquiry, instead highlights its provisionality and uses this as a strength with which to engage with DeLillo's continued literary production and the shifting nature of American historicity, free of preconception.

---

10   Martin Heidegger, 'Letter on Humanism', in *Basic Writings from Being and Time (1927) to The Task of Thinking (1964)*, David Krell (ed.) (London: Routledge, 1993), pp. 213–66, p. 217.

To '[e]xplore America in the screaming night'

Any work of DeLillo criticism, if it is alive to the nuance and doubt which characterizes the author's own production, should function in a manner analogous to that of David Bell heading out of New York, searching for an understanding of the historicity of 'America in the screaming night' and alive to the problematic nature of any such attempt; secure in the knowledge that any discoveries made will function like Heidegger's clearing: as an ephemeral light which will require subsequent preservation in order to survive and illuminate.

Selected Bibliography

Adorno, T., *The Jargon of Authenticity*, Tarnowski, K., and Will, F. (trans.) (London: Routledge, 2003)
Anon, 'The Cloud of Unknowing', in *The Cloud of Unknowing and Other Works*, Spearing, A. (trans.) (London: Penguin, 2001)
Anzaldúa, G., 'To(o) queer the writer: loca, escrita y chicana', in Warland, B. (ed.) *InVersions: Writing by Dykes, Queers and Lesbians* (Vancouver: Press Gang, 1991), pp. 249–63
Barnard, I., 'Queer race', *Social Semiotics*, 9:2 (1999), pp. 199–212
Barrett, L., '"How the Dead Speak to the Living": Intertextuality and the Postmodern Sublime in *White Noise*', *Journal of Modern Literature*, 25:2 (2002), pp. 97–113
Baudrillard, J., 'Hypotheses on Terrorism' in *The Spirit of Terrorism and Other Essays*, Turner, C. (trans.) (London: Verso, 2003), pp. 49–84
Baudrillard, J., 'The Precession of Simulacra' in *Simulacra and Simulation*, Glaser, S. (trans.) (Ann Arbor: The University of Michigan Press, 2006), pp. 1–42
Baudrillard, J., 'The Spirit of Terrorism' in *The Spirit of Terrorism and Other Essays*, Turner, C. (trans.) (London: Verso, 2003), pp. 1–34
Baudrillard, J., 'The Violence of The Global' in *The Spirit of Terrorism and Other Essays*, Turner, C. (trans.) (London: Verso, 2003), pp. 85–105,
Benjamin, W., 'On Language as Such and on the Language of Man' in Bullock, M., and Jennings, M. (eds) *Selected Writings Volume 1 1913–1926* (London: The Belknap Press of Harvard University Press, 1997), pp. 62–74
Berlant, L, and Warner, M., 'Sex in Public', *Critical Enquiry*, 24:2 (1998), pp. 547–66
Birman, B., 'Reading the Techno-Ethnic Other in Don DeLillo's White Noise' in *The Arizona Quarterly*. 61:2 (2005), pp. 87–103
Bloom, H. (ed.), *Bloom's Modern Critical Views: Don DeLillo* (London: Chelsea House, 2003)
Bonca, C., 'Being, Time, and Death in DeLillo's *The Body Artist*', *Pacific Coast Philology*, 37 (2002), pp. 58–68
Bonca, C., 'Don DeLillo's *White Noise*: The natural language of the species', *College Literature*, 23:2 (1996), pp. 25–45
Boxall, P., *Don DeLillo: The Possibility of Fiction* (London: Routledge, 2006)
Buell, L., *Writing for an Endangered World: Literature, Culture and Environment in the U.S. and Beyond* (Cambridge, Mass.: Harvard University Press, 2001)

Butler, J., *Gender Trouble: Feminism and the Subversion of Identity* (London: Routledge, 1990)
Carmichael, T., 'Lee Harvey Oswald and the Postmodern Subject: History and Intertextuality in Don DeLillo's *Libra, The Names,* and *Mao II*', *Contemporary Literature*, 34:2 (1993), pp. 204–18
Chandler, A., '"An Unsettling, Alternative Self": Benno Levin, Emmanuel Levinas, and Don DeLillo's *Cosmopolis*', *Critique*, 50:3 (2009), pp. 241–60
Cixous, H., 'The Laugh of the Medusa', Keith Cohen and Paula Cohen (trans.), in *Signs*, 1:4 (1976), pp. 875–93
Cowart, D., 'For Whom Bell Tolls: Don DeLillo's *Americana*', *Contemporary Literature* (37:4) (Madison; WI: University of Wisconsin Press, 1996), pp. 602–19
Cowart, D., *Don DeLillo: The Physics of Language* (Athens; GA: University of Georgia Press, 2002)
Deitering, C., 'The Postnatural Novel: Toxic Consciousness in Fiction of the 1980s' in Glotfelty, C., and Fromm, H. (eds) *The Ecocriticism Reader: Landmarks in Literary Ecology* (Athens; GA: University of Georgia Press, 1996), pp. 196–203
DeLillo, D., 'The River Jordan', *Epoch*, 10:2 (1960), pp. 105–20
DeLillo, D., *Americano* (London: Penguin, 2006)
DeLillo, D., *Cosmopolis* (London: Picador, 2003)
DeLillo, D., *End Zone* (London: Penguin, 1986)
DeLillo, D., *Falling Man* (London: Picador, 2007)
DeLillo, D., *Mao II* (London: Penguin, 1992)
DeLillo, D., *Players* (New York: Vintage, 1989)
DeLillo, D., *Running Dog* (London: Picador, 1992)
DeLillo, D., *The Body Artist* (London: Picador, 2001)
Delillo, D., *The Names* (London: Picador, 1987)
DeLillo, D., *Underworld* (New York: Scribner, 1997)
Dewey, J., *Beyond Grief and Nothing: A Reading of Don DeLillo* (Columbia: University of South Carolina Press, 2006)
Duvall, J., *Don DeLillo's Underworld: A Reader's Guide* (London: Continuum, 2002)
Edelman, L., *No Future: Queer Theory and the Death Drive* (London: Duke University Press, 2004)
Eisenhower, D., *Dwight D. Eisenhower: 1960–61: Containing the Public Messages, Speeches, and Statements of the President, January 1, 1960, to January 20, 1961* (Ann Arbor, MI: University of Michigan, 2005)
English, R., *Terrorism: How to Respond* (Oxford: Oxford University Press, 2009)
Foucault, M., *The Will To Knowledge: The History of Sexuality Volume 1*, Hurley, R. (trans.) (London: Penguin, 1998)

Geyh, P., 'Assembling postmodernism: Experience, meaning, and the space in-between', *College Literature*, 30:2 (2003), pp. 1–29

Hantke, S., '"God save us from bourgeois adventure": The figure of the terrorist in contemporary American conspiracy fiction', *Studies in the Novel*, 28:2 (1996), pp. 219–44

Hardack, R., 'Two's a Crowd: Mao II, Coke II, and the Politics of Terrorism in Don DeLillo', *Studies in the Novel*, 36:30 (2004), pp. 374–93

Hayden, D., *Building Suburbia: Green Fields and Urban Growth 1820–2000* (New York: Vintage, 2003)

Heidegger, M., *Being and Time*, Macquarrie, J., and Robinson, E. (trans.) (London: Blackwell, 2000)

Heidegger, M., 'Letter on Humanism', in *Basic Writings from Being and time (1927) to The task of thinking* (1964), Krell, D. (ed.) (London: Routledge, 1993), pp. 213–66

Heidegger, M., 'The Origin of the Work of Art', in *Poetry, Language, Thought*, Hofstadter, A. (trans.) (London: Harper Perennial, 2001), pp. 15–86

Horgan, J., *The Psychology of Terrorism* (London: Routledge, 2005)

Jackson, K.T., *Crabgrass Frontier: The Suburbanization of the United States* (Oxford: Oxford University Press, 1985)

Jameson, F., *Postmodernism, or, The Cultural Logic of Late Capitalism* (London: Verso, 1991)

'Jerusalem Prize for Don DeLillo', *Publishers Weekly*, http://www.publishersweekly.com/pw/print/19990503/31660-jerusalem-prize-for-don-delillo.html [accessed 28 July 2007]

Kavadlo, J., 'Recycling authority: Don DeLillo's waste management', *Critique*, 42:4 (2001), pp. 384–402

Kavadlo, J., *Don DeLillo: Balance at the Edge of Belief* (Frankfurt: Peter Lang, 2004)

Keesey, D., *Don DeLillo* (New York; NY: Twayne, 1993)

Kristeva, K., *Revolution in Poetic Language* (New York, NY: Columbia University Press, 1984)

Lacan, J., 'The Agency of the Letter in the Unconscious or Reason Since Freud', in *Ecrits*, Alan Sheridan (trans.) (London: Routledge, 2005), pp. 111–36

Lacan, J., 'The Function and Field of Speech and Language in Psychoanalysis', in *Ecrits*, Alan Sheridan (trans.) (London: Routledge, 2005), pp. 23–86

Lacan, J., 'The Signification of the Phallus', in *Ecrits*, Alan Sheridan (trans.) (London: Routledge, 2005), pp. 215–22

Laist, R., *Technology and Postmodern Subjectivity in Don DeLillo's Novels* (Frankfurt: Peter Lang, 2010) de Lauretis, T., 'Popular culture, public and private fantasies: femininity and fetishism in David Cronenberg's *M. Butterfly*', *Signs: Journal of Women in Culture and Society*, 24:2 (1999), pp. 303–33

LeClair, T., *In the Loop* (Champaign; IL: University of Illinois Press, 1987)

Levinas, E. *Totality and Infinity*, Linguis, A. (trans.) (Pittsburgh, PA: Duquesne University Press, 1999)

Longmuir, A., 'The Language of History: Don DeLillo's *The Names* and the Iranian Hostage Crisis', *Critique*, 46:2 (2005), pp. 105–23

Mackenzie, L., 'An Ecocritical Approach to Teaching *White Noise*', in Engles, T. and Duvall, J. (eds) *Approaches to Teaching DeLillo's White Noise* (New York; NY: The Modern Language Association of America, 2006)

Maltby, P., 'The Romantic Metaphysics of Don DeLillo', *Contemporary Literature*, 37:2 (1996), pp. 258–77

Martucci, E., *The Environmental Unconscious in the Fiction of Don DeLillo* (London: Routledge, 2007)

Morris, M.J., 'Murdering Words: Language in Action in Don DeLillo's *The Names*' in *Contemporary Literature*, 30:1 (1989), pp. 113–27

McGowan, T., 'The Obsolescence of Mystery and the Accumulation of Waste in Don DeLillo's *Underworld*', *Critique*, 46:2 (2005), pp. 123–46

Mexal, S., 'Spectacularspectacular!: Underworld and the Production of Terror', *Studies in the Novel*, 36:3 (2004), pp. 318–36

Moses, M., 'Lust Removed from Nature' in Lentricchia, F. (ed.) *New Essays on White Noise* (Cambridge: Cambridge University Press, 1991)

Nel, P. 'Don DeLillo's Return to Form: The Modernist Poetics of *The Body Artist*', *Contemporary Literature*, 43:4 (2002), pp. 736–59

Orr, L., *Don DeLillo's White Noise: A Reader's Guide* (London: Continuum, 2003)

Osteen, M., *American Magic and Dread: Don DeLillo's Dialogue with Culture* (Philadelphia; PA: University of Pennsylvania Press, 2000)

Packer, M., '"At the Dead Center of Things" in Don DeLillo's *White Noise*: Mimesis, Violence, and Religious Awe' in *Modern Fiction Studies*, 51:3 (2005), pp. 648–66

Peyser, T., 'Globalization in America: The case of Don DeLillo's *White Noise*', *Clio*, 25:3 (1996), pp. 255–72

Richardson, L., *What Terrorists Want: Understanding the Enemy Containing the Threat* (New York, Random House, 2006)

'Revelation', *The Bible* (Swindon: Bible Society, 1994)

Schuster, M., *Don DeLillo, Jean Baudrillard, and the Consumer Conundrum* (Youngstown; NY: Cambria Press, 2008)

Scott, D., 'Jungle Fever?: Black Gay Identity Politics, White Dick, and the Utopian Bedroom', *GLQ: A Journal of Lesbian and Gay Studies*, 1 (1994), pp. 299–321

Sinfield, A., *On Sexuality and Power: Between Men – Between Women* (New York: Columbia University Press, 2004)
Stich, S., *Made in U.S.A.* (Berkeley: University of California Press, 1987)
Tanner, T., 'Afterthoughts on Don DeLillo's Underworld', *Raritan: a Quarterly Review*, 17:4 (1998), pp. 48–71, p. 49
'The Gospel According to St. John' *The Bible* (Swindon: Bible Society, 1994)
Thomas, G., 'History, Biography, and Narrative in Don DeLillo's *Libra*', *Twentieth Century Literature*, 43:1 (1997), pp. 107–24
Thornton, Z., 'Linguistic disenchantment and architectural solace in DeLillo and Artaud', *Mosaic*, 30:1 (1997): pp. 97–133 <http://gateway.proquest.com/openurl?ctx_ver=Z39.88-2003&xri:pqil:res_ver=0.2&res_id=xri:lion&rft_id=xri:lion:ft:mla:R03128046:0> [accessed 7 May 2010]
Todorov, T., *The Poetics of Prose* (Oxford: Blackwell, 1977)
Varsava, J., 'The "Saturated Self": Don DeLillo on the Problem of Rogue Capitalism', *Contemporary Literature*, 46:1 (2005), pp. 78–107
Wallace, M., '"Venerated emblems": DeLillo's *Underworld* and the history-commodity' *Critique*, 42:4 (2001), pp. 367–84
Wilcox, L., 'Baudrillard, DeLillo's *White Noise*, and the End of Heroic Narrative', *Contemporary Literature*, 32:3 (1991), pp. 346–65
Wilcox, L., 'Don DeLillo's *Underworld* and the Return of the Real', *Contemporary Literature*, 43:1 (2002), pp. 120–37
Wilcox, L., 'Terrorism and Art: Don DeLillo's *Mao II* and Jean Baudrillard's *The Spirit of Terrorism*', *Mosaic*, 39:2 (2006), pp. 89–106
Willman, S., 'Traversing the Fantasies of the JFK Assassination: Conspiracy and Contingency in Don Delillo's *Libra*', *Contemporary Literature*, 39:3 (1998), pp. 405–33
Wittgenstein, L., *Philosophical Investigations*, Anscombe, G. (trans.) (London: Blackwell, 2000)
Wittgenstein, L., 'The Nature of Philosophy', *The Wittgenstein Reader*, Kenny, A. (ed.) (London: Blackwell, 2006), pp. 46–69
Wittgenstein, L., *Tractatus Logico-Philosophicus*, Pears, D., and McGuinness, B. (trans.) (London: Routledge, 2006)

Index

apophasis 33–8
   The Cloud of Unknowing 33–8

Baudrillard, Jean 101–20, 136, 163–4, 184–8
   'The Precession of Simulacra' 101–3, 108–9, 113, 136, 163
   The Spirit of Terrorism and Other Essays 184–8
Benjamin, Walter 85–94, 107–13
Boxall, Peter 9–10, 63–7, 174–5

Cixous, Hélène 82–5
Cowart, David 7–8, 71, 105

DeLillo, Don
   Americana 26–8, 41–9, 80, 103–7
      David Bell 26–8, 41–9, 103–7
      the dream of the third person singular 47–9, 105–7
   The Body Artist 95–8, 115–20
   Cosmopolis 135–43
   End Zone 73–4, 75–85
   Falling Man 98–100, 186–94
   Libra 195–7
   Mao II 14–17, 31–3, 52–60
      Bill Gray 31–3, 52–60
      Karen Janney 14–17
      Scott Martineau 32, 53–60
   The Names 90–4
   Players 74–5, 88–9
   Running Dog 28–30, 49–52
      Glen Selvy 28–30, 49–52
      Moll Robbins 50–1

Underworld 33–8, 60–7, 95, 124–35, 147–81, 197–203
   baseball 36–8
   Brian Glassic 172–5
   Donna 60–3
   Eric Demming 128–35, 147–62
   Erica Demming 128–35, 152–3, 159–62
   J. Edgar Hoover 163–72
   Klara Sax 135, 175–81
   Marian Shay 34–5, 63–7
   Nick Shay 33–8, 60–7, 95
   Rick Demming 159–62
   Texas Highway Killer 197–203
White Noise 109–13

Edelman, Lee 145–7, 149–56
   see also Sinthomosexuality

Foucault, Michel 152, 162, 171–2

Heidegger, Martin 35–6, 42–7, 50, 52, 55, 58–9, 81–2, 84–5, 94–100, 113–15, 118–20, 138, 140, 176–80, 185, 205–11
   Angst 44, 52
   aletheia (truth) 114–15, 119–20, 140, 210
   das Man 46–7, 206
   eigentlich (authentic) 44
   Historizität (historicity) 35–6, 81–2, 176–80, 205, 210
   In-der-Welt-sein (being-in-the-world) 43
   language, *see* λόγος (logos)

Heidegger, Martin *(continued)*
  Mitsein Andere (being-with-others) 43, 84–5
  Sein schuldig (being-guilty) 55
  Sein sum Tode (being-towards-death) 45, 52, 58–9, 115, 185
  Sein zum Ende (being-towards-the-end) 45, 99–100
  Sorge (care) 44, 84–5
  uneigentlich (inauthentic) 58–9, 185
  Zeug (equipment) 177–80

Kavadlo, Jesse 8–9, 38
Kristeva, Julia 78–80, 86–7

Lacan, Jacques 76–7
λόγος (logos) 19, 42–5, 53–4, 71–120, 124–8

Middle America 14–17, 93–4, 123–35, 145–68, 170–5, 180–1, 186–203
  see also suburbanism
Military-Industrial Complex 155–9, 165–81
  see also nuclear weapons
  see also state
modernism 2–13, 106–7
  see also postmodernism

nuclear weapons 64–5, 155–9, 163–81
  see also Military-Industrial Complex

ontology
  see Heidegger, Martin

phenomenology
  see Heidegger, Martin
postmodernism 2–13, 73, 101–7
  see also modernism

products 47–9, 105–12, 123–65, 172–5
  and ethnic identity 124–8, 136–7
  and mass marketing 47–9, 105–12, 126–38, 164–5, 172–5
  see also Middle America
  see also suburbanism
  see also waste

queer theory
  Berlant, Lauren and Warner, Michael 129–33
  Butler, Judith 153
  see also Edelman, Lee
  see also Sinthomosexuality

*Sinthomo*sexuality 145–204
  see also Edelman, Lee
  see also queer theory
state 163–204
  see also Military Industrial Complex
suburbanism 14–17, 34–5, 124–35, 146–62
  Suburban Studies 124, 128–9
  see also Middle America

terrorism 164–7, 186–203
  'Domestic' terrorism 195–203
  'European' terrorism 193–4
  'Islamic' terrorism 186–94

waste 145–62
  see also products
  see also Sinthomosexuality
Wittgenstein, Ludwig 71–6, 78–82, 87–8, 102–7
  Philosophical Investigations 76, 103
  Tractatus Logico-Philosophicus 72–5, 102–3